SWALLOW PRESS

OHIO UNIVERSITY PRESS

ATHENS

CONTENTS

ILLUSTRATIONS

Cougar!

HAROLD P. DANZ

Swallow Press/Ohio University Press, Athens, Ohio 45701
© 1999 by Harold P. Danz
Printed in the United States of America
All rights reserved. Published 1999

Swallow Press/Ohio University Press books are printed on acid-free paper ∞ ™

12 11 10 09 08 07 06 05 04   5 4 3 2

Book design by Chiquita Babb

Cougar photo on cover and frontispiece © Sharon Walleen/AccentAlaska.com

Library of Congress Cataloging-in-Publication Data
Danz, Harold P.
Cougar! / Harold P. Danz.
     p.   cm
Includes bibliographical references (p.   ) and index.
ISBN 0-8040-1014-5 (cloth). — ISBN 0-8040-1015-3 (paper)
QL737.C23D35 1999
599.75′24—dc21
                                                                    98-43497
                                                                    CIP

Softer than the light summer breeze upon your cheek, quieter than the sound of a snowflake's fall, the cougar strides through the forest and the countryside. One of the most successful of animal predators in the Americas, has the cougar now become a threat to humans?

This book is about cougars, but not only cougars; it is also about people—the people whose lives have been affected or influenced by the being and presence of this animal in their world.

I was born in an upper-Midwestern state where cougars were, and had been, an uncommon species for more than fifty years. We knew bear, lynxes and bobcats, and even wolves, but by that point in time the big cat was essentially a stranger to us. Reading about the cougar, or panther as we called it, extended to us a somewhat clouded and inconsistent mixture of information, but nothing with any real substance to it. The writings of former President Theodore (Teddy) Roosevelt and Ernest Thompson Seton characterized the cougar as a "sneak cat," a cowardly animal with a healthy aversion to humans and presenting no threat whatsoever to human life. But we also had access to a few of the more lurid novels of that day that excitedly portrayed the cougar as a cunning, merciless, and powerful killer, bent on human murder and mayhem.

The first time I saw a cougar in the wild was when I was assigned to Zion National Park, Utah, in the early 1960s. The beast fled across the road in front of my car, its body fully captured in the headlights as it continued on its unending search for prey, or surreptitiously to greet whatever else the future may have in store for it. Although I worked in and visited a considerable number of parks in the Southwest and the West that boasted cougar populations, the cats' presence was but indifferently observed through the finding of an occasional track or a deer carcass that a cougar had fed upon.

When we moved to Colorado in the early 1970s, a completely different image of the cougar began gradually to emerge. There were the usual accounts of cougars attacking and eating a variety of domestic animals owned by humans, but then there were also reports of humans themselves being attacked. In the midst of all of this were the sagacious comments of wildlife "experts" that these events were unusual, and that the cougar must have simply mistaken the human for a deer or one of its other common prey species.

As human attacks accumulated, or perhaps became more thoroughly reported, advisories were published stating what people should do if suddenly confronted by a cougar: don't run, stand up straight, look big, and control the movement of children. But once again, wildlife "experts" attempted to minimize potential risk, suggesting that one's chances of being hit by lightning, winning the lottery, or being assaulted by a deer, or the family dog, individually were far greater than those of experiencing a cougar attack. I don't believe that anyone could question the truth of this statistical observation, but the total number of verifiable cougar attacks that were reported seemed unbelievably small.

While I was working on a manuscript entitled *Of Bison and Man*, part of my research involved collecting information on all known bison adversaries and predators. I didn't expect to find a wealth of information with respect to past bison/cougar conflicts, but I was chagrined at the abject paucity of quality information, anecdotal or otherwise, dealing with the cougar.

The work of Stanley P. Young and Edward A. Goldman (*The Puma, Mysterious American Cat*), was outstanding, but this publication, published in 1946, is now more than fifty years old. Most contemporary literature was extremely species friendly, summarily dismissing the validity of all but the most blatant attacks by cougars on humans. Research that did touch upon human/cougar conflicts appeared to be selective, not to say subjectively biased: I noted that assaults in which the victim, or potential victim, was not physically touched had been discounted.

I can assure readers that, in this book, the information presented is fully reflective of actual circumstances and events surrounding the incidents of cougar/human conflicts that my research uncovered. I am also confident, however, that there have been a great number of attacks—attacks that received limited or no publicity—that I have not been able to identify. In addition, incidents involving tame cougars, defensive actions taken by cougars while they were escaping from hunters, or where the intended prey was another animal and the human was simply in the attack vicinity, have not been included.

❧

The human/cougar incident information that I acquired over a four-year period often required that I contact victims or family members, do extended research in innumerable libraries, communicate with a nearly overwhelming number of public officials and offices, as well as travel to an assortment of remote areas throughout the West and into Canada. Special thanks is extended to those wildlife officials in the United States and Canada who took the time to respond to my many inquiries, and especially for the helpful comments of Dr. E. Lee Fitzhugh, University of California, Davis Campus.

❧

The cougar is one of the slickest predators on the face of the earth. Operating alone it can capture the most wary of animals, but it most often selects its prey based on availability rather than preference. Palatability thus becomes secondary to opportunity. If a cougar is hungry it will kill and eat a skunk. Why then should it carry any scruples about attacking a human being?

Most of the past literature on *Felis concolor*, the cougar or puma, mountain lion or panther, ad infinitum, have seemingly carried, the same carefully crafted, but thinly veiled, message: all life has meaning, purpose, and direction—we must accept the cougar for what it is and make whatever allowances and accommodations necessary to ensure its survival. I have little argument with most of this. All life is important. We should hold dear the lives of all species, taking from each only what is necessary to ensure continuance and safety of the human species. However, if a cougar, or the sheer numbers of cougars near to human habitat, should threaten human life, then allowance and accommodation is no longer an acceptable or appropriate action for us to take.

In this world of contrast, reciprocity, savagery, and blemished but still unparalleled beauty, we all are temporal species. The inhumane former practice of electing to obliterate a species is a judgment that humans are not entitled to make. So let us try to learn as much about the cougar as it has been obliged to learn about us in order for it to survive.

Cougar!

Introduction

THE COMBINED AREA OF North and South America is more than 16 million square miles, representing 28.1 percent of the total land mass of the earth. Prior to the landing of Columbus and the later immigration of the Europeans, the human population of these two continents, referred to as *los Indios* by Columbus and now, in the English-speaking world, as Indians, were living not only in North, Central, and South America but also on the islands near both continents; and they had been doing so for thousands of years prior to Columbus. The Indian population as of 1492 has been estimated at approximately 53.9 million. However, only a small fraction of this total, fewer than 4 million, is attributable to the North American continent. By 1650, disease and genocidal efforts had reduced the total Indian population of both continents to 5.6 million. This would then suggest that when, in the early seventeenth century, the English colonies were formed on the eastern coastal area of what is now the United States, the native population at that time was rather limited and, as such, would exercise only minor impact on a bicontinental ecosystem.

The only animal that enjoyed a natural habitat in the New World nearly as far-ranging as that of the native *Homo sapiens* human beings was the cougar (*Felis concolor*), which at one time was found as far north as present-day British Columbia, Alberta, Saskatchewan, and Quebec in Canada, and as far south as the Strait of Magellan. The cougar's realm has since been reduced significantly by the inroads of civilization. Although now confined to the lesser populated areas, it still is the most dispersed of all the great cats.

In spite of what once was an extensive distribution of this magnificent carnivore throughout the Americas, even today we know very little about this enigmatic and sometimes paradoxical animal. Known by a variety of names—puma, mountain lion, panther, painter, catamount, deer tiger, and Mexican lion—the cougar furtively prowls the wild places of its remaining domain, avoiding contact with man whenever possible, and thereby earning its title Mysterious American Cat.

Like other large carnivores, the cougar is an electrifying animal, often feared and generally misunderstood. Its predations on domestic livestock made it nearly as unwelcome within the ranching community as the wolf; and even its taking of natural wildlife prey such as elk, sheep, and deer was considered to be particularly deleterious to the well-being of these animals. As a result of this unpopularity, the cougar's numbers were significantly reduced through assignment of bounties and aggressive reduction measures by official hunters, both state and federal. Retreating to remote wilderness enclaves the cougar was seldom seen, and by the late 1800s was considered to be an extinct species in most eastern states. Even today, predation of domestic livestock by charismatic megafauna such as bear and cougar is investigated by federal and state animal-control agencies. If it is determined that a bear or cougar—or in some instances a wolf or wolves—was responsible, only very few states will pay landowner claims for property damage or livestock losses. Colorado, for example, will pay depredation claims for property damage caused by bear, cougar, and elk, but not for that caused by any other species. Most states, however, will assume the responsibility for removal of a large predator, such as a cougar, or they may authorize the landowner to take the necessary control action.

Although an adult cougar obviously possessed the strength and capability to kill even a large man, it was not, in earlier years, regarded as a potential threat or danger to human life. The cougar was simply considered to be a rather cowardly animal that would flee from the sight or even the scent of a human. It was not until a number of attacks upon human beings in the early 1950s were irrefutably recorded that a differing perspective of the human and cougar relationship began to be developed. There is no reliable evidence to suggest that fear of humans by animals is an inherited characteristic; it needs to be learned. Much as did the bears of Yellowstone during an earlier generation, cougars living adjacent to human habitation have begun recently to associate humans with food and thus have become more willing to encroach upon what has been, heretofore, the exclusive domain of the urban human society. Pets—dogs and cats, for example—accordingly have become a less elusive and more dependable prey than the wild animals that cougars traditionally sought. Although increased human contact and familiarity with humans may not necessarily lead cougars to become contemptuous, this casual and gradually increasing awareness will certainly not inspire respect unless the cougar learns an object lesson from the encounters.

We need the cougar, just as we need all other creatures with which we share our environment. Experience has taught us that a discrete balance of nature exists that humans cannot intelligibly interfere with or manipulate without courting ecological disaster. Just as the introduction of exotic species to a new environment, without natural control mechanisms, invites overpopulation and the crowding out of native species, efforts toward predator control have also disturbed what had been heretofore the natural equilibrium. A prime example was the indiscriminate removal of predators from Yellowstone and other National Park Service areas prior to 1939—action that eventually created an enormous increase in the ungulate population and led to the undesirable outcome of starvation and disease.

The popularly espoused reasons for initiating predator control usually suggest that there are too many predators and insufficient wild game to satisfy an increasing predator appetite. Thus, in order to (1) protect domestic animals from becoming substitute prey, and (2) shield desirable game animals from continued harassment, the larger carnivores are either significantly reduced or eliminated. Although the cougar has been subject to constant persecution, classed as an undesirable, a varmint, we still have the cougar in many western states and perhaps also in a number of eastern states earlier believed to be cougar free. There is even evidence to suggest that the cougar population is expanding, and that, like the coyote, the cougar is accommodating itself to the human habitat. With this in mind, we need to take a fresh look at this exciting animal and how it appropriately fits into our environment.

This book is about the cougar—what it once was, how it has lived, its impact on humans, and how it now tries to survive in what has become a human-dominated world.

ONE Genesis of the Species

T HERE ARE ONLY five species of large predators left in the contiguous United States, and their numbers may be dwindling. The mighty grizzly bear *(Ursus horribilis)* is now found only in a few national parks and adjacent public lands in Idaho, Montana, and Wyoming. The smaller black bear *(Ursus americanus)* has fared considerably better than the contentious grizzly and can still be found in most western and several northern, eastern, and southeastern states. The grey wolf *(Canis lupus)* is still fairly common within Canada and Alaska, but it has been all but eliminated in the lower forty-eight U.S. states. A few wolves do occasionally take up residence in several of the northern states that are adjacent to Canada, but resident populations are usually restricted to Michigan, Minnesota, Montana, and Wisconsin. Efforts to seek approval for the reintroduction of the grey wolf to Yellowstone National Park met with strong resistance from local ranchers, but eventually approval was granted. Within the cat family *(Felidae)*, in the United States only two species are found that regularly prey on larger mammals: the jaguar *(Panthera onca)* and the cougar *(Felis concolor)*. The jaguar was probably never very common within the United States, and it is now seen only in the extreme southern part of states that border Mexico, and there only infrequently. The cougar, the only other large predator in the contiguous United States, is still determinedly stalking its prey.

Although classified in the animal kingdom by taxonomists as a "small" cat, there is nothing puny about a cougar. An adult male cougar most often will

The cougar is one of the largest predatory animals in the Western Hemisphere. Found in habitats as diverse as tropical rain forests, the rocky heights of western North America, and snowy Canadian provinces, this solitary hunter's primary adversaries are other cougars and man. © *Sharon Walleen/AccentAlaska.com.*

weigh more than 145 pounds, and some have even exceeded 200 pounds. On an average, the female is approximately 20 percent smaller than the male, but, provided with favorable environmental conditions, it has not been uncommon for the weight of an adult female cougar to better 120 pounds. The cougar's powerful legs and shoulders epitomize its extraordinary muscular development. Renowned for its agility and leaping ability, jumps of twenty feet and more (some even claimed to be in excess of forty feet) have been measured. Possessed of an awesome natural armory of weapons, the cougar will strike, slash, and drive its claws into the selected prey, clutching with an almost vice-like grip until it can conclude the attack by using its jaws—either strangling the victim by grasping the throat or biting the prey's vertebrae in back of the neck.

Public opinion regarding the wisdom of permitting large predators to roam at will, or even to let them exist within semiconfined wilderness areas, is still in a state of flux. Thus, public policies are continually subject to change, based on individual prejudices, indulgences, and fear. It is not easy to dismiss such arguments, proffered by these apprehensive people, because all have some basis of fact. Animal predators can, and occasionally will, injure and kill humans. When this infrequent event does happen, children or women are most often the subject of the attack; typically their injuries are the most gruesome. In spite of such tragedies, many of those who have studied this problem believe it is not appropriate or desirable to eliminate any species merely because its predatory or survival instincts threaten the human psyche—or the serenity some humans have assigned to the outdoor experience. Most people understand that, under duress or perceived danger, animals have the capacity to defend themselves, and possibly to inflict injury. Remove the predator, and its normal prey—which in fact is never a human being—could reproduce to a point where it becomes an even greater problem for humans than was the predator.

Economic considerations (e.g., concerns involving property ownership and the operation of cattle and sheep ranches) are likely motivations for some of the strong opinions in favor of the need for proactive predator controls. But the movement advocating control is wider than that: there are also still many individuals who dislike, and perhaps even fear, the wilderness: they perceive a constant danger and threat from large, free-roaming carnivorous animals. The fact that these carnivores must kill to live gives weight to a belief that predators are malignant; that they need to be excised, or at least closely controlled. On the other side are strong preservationist interests and activist lobbies that seek to protect and preserve all animals regardless of human concerns. Animal activist groups are quite often well funded and just as willing to pursue their goals as are their opponents, the ranchers, game hunters, and social urbanists. The actual fear itself, however—the innate fear of large carnivores—is expressed only through avoidance of direct involvement with the animal, or in tacit, if silent, support given to the more restrictive initiatives.

These fears notwithstanding, and apart from economic concerns, people seem to feel they have less to fear from the black bear than they do from the other three large predators now found in the United States. Perhaps this is because they have not actually been exposed to bear behavior and imagine that what they are dealing with is a living characterization of Smokey Bear, Gentle Ben, or their favorite childhood teddy bear. The 1997 bear incident in British Columbia, Canada, where a woman and the man who tried to save her were killed by a black bear in front of the woman's two young children, may alter this perception. Even those who should know better take the potential human risk from wild animals quite lightly. Early in this century, respected naturalist and wilderness pedagogue Enos A. Mills once stated: "Rarely does a bear kill a big animal, wild or tame. *They never eat human flesh.*" (1932, 150). I think that we can agree now, based upon the past performance of certain bears (Herrero 1985), that this is not an accurate statement, although some people still do not consider the black bear to be potentially dangerous to humans. There is a range of feeling in the human responses to the big predators. The reputation of the more truculent grizzly bear usually precludes any other human emotions upon uninvited contact other than that of apprehension and terror. Human aversion to the wolf is more likely predicated on its disrepute as an instrument of cruelty, treachery, and ruthlessness rather than on actual evidence that it represents a true, mortal threat. But the enigmatic and clandestine behavior of the cougar embodies entirely different human issues and concerns: Does it, or does it not, because of its mysterious ways and growing presence, constitute a greater danger than the other extant predators in the United States? This question—of the level of potential or prospective danger—is the focus of this book.

The cougar, like most of the other mammalian species of the American continents, has generic roots that go back to ancestors that migrated to the New World from Asia and Europe. In considering the genesis of species, we must note that through the more than 4 billion years of Earth history, there have been at least three major ice ages and a continuing geological phenomenon commonly referred to as continental drift (associated with plate tectonics). These events explain the existence of fossil similarities on different continents: there was potential for movement of mammals between continents that are now separated by oceans and seas. During Tertiary times, perhaps 60 million years ago, what once was a general tropical world climate began to contract toward the equator, creating latitudinal zones, or bands, with significant climatic changes.

There still were two principal land connections between North America and Eurasia. The first land connection—between Europe and North America —disappeared sometime during the early Eocene epoch, perhaps 50 million years ago, but the second connection, between Asia and North America, was available much longer because of a series of massive glaciers in the Northern

Hemisphere that occurred during the Pleistocene. The Pleistocene epoch was not a time of constant glaciation but saw a series of advances (glacials) and retreats (interglacials). During the glacial periods, ice sheets absorbed much of the Earth's water: oceans receded and continents expanded, and a land connection, which was up to a thousand miles in width, existed between Siberia and Alaska. This land bridge, and the lands immediately to the east and west of it, has been named *Beringia* by scientists.

Beringia attracted from Asia large resident herds of herbivores. For this to happen, the ordinary tundra vegetation that exists today would not have been adequate; it would not have provided a continuing and sufficiently nutritional diet for the large mammals that made the migration, such as bison, wooly mammoth, American mastodon, camel, musk ox, and horse; scientists therefore believe that a long, coarse grass covered much of Beringia's plains. The climate was predominately cool and dry, without extensive winter snow cover—conditions that would have been thoroughly to the liking of the aforementioned mammals during the Pleistocene period. Closely following these herbivores were the carnivores: the short-faced bear, the American lion, the saber-toothed cat, and the dire wolf. As climate changes permitted the herbivores to migrate into the body of the North American continent, the predators followed. Pleistocene carnivores were formidable adversaries, even for the largest of the land mammals. However, except for the short-faced bear, and perhaps the saber-toothed cat, the predators customarily traveled in packs or prides since it was unlikely that, alone, one of these intrepid hunters could overcome a healthy and mature bison or wooly mammoth.

The phylogeny, or evolutionary development, of the cougar has been as elusive for science as are the actual physical comings and goings of today's representative of this species. The cougar has been classified in the order Carnivora, which is a member of the Felidae family of fissipedia (carnivorous, or flesh-eating mammals that have separate toes). We do know that during the Mesozoic era, and conceivably in late Cretaceous times, about 65 million years ago, small animal-like beings, which were primarily insect eaters and gave birth to their young in the same way as most mammals do today, joined with the remaining saurians in populating this planet. Although not large—some perhaps not even as big as a small chipmunk—it is believed that from these little creatures two mammalian groups developed: those whose appetites favored plants and others that preferred to eat other mammals. These early and primitive carnivores of the Eocene and Paleocene times have been categorized as Creodonta by paleontologists. It is postulated that the Creodonta developed into two groups: survivors—those that could adapt to changing conditions; and nonsurvivors—those that were not adaptive. The latter just faded away. The survivors have been classified into a superfamily group, Uintacyonidae; and in this supergroup, the family Miacidae is presumed to be the source of today's felines *(Felidae)* and canines *(Canidae)*, the dog family.

The Felidae family is not without ancestral complications in genetic classification. To simplify the process, it is suggested that we accept as theorem that there were three subfamilies of Felidae, the Felinae, or true cats; the Machairodoninae, or saber-toothed variety; and the Nimravinae, or false saber-toothed. During the Oligocene geological time period, which began about 40 million years ago, and extending through the Miocene period, which ended approximately 12 million years ago, many of the higher forms of large mammal life first appeared. It was not until the late Pliocene, or perhaps even into the Pleistocene time period, that many of our current species of Felidae evolved. In addition to the American or California lion *(Felis atrox)* and New World saber-toothed cat *(Smilodon)*, a number of smaller feline predators during the Pleistocene kept busy with the abundant wildlife that was to be found in the Americas. Based upon paleontological research, a cougar-like animal, *Felis daggetti*, whose fossilized remains scientists extracted from the prolific Rancho La Brea tar pits, is purported to have had all the necessary genetic credentials to be the earliest common ancestor of the extant species of *Felis*. It is additionally believed by most scientists in the field that the cougar existed as a species at least three million years ago (Wayne et al., 465–94, suggest that this was more like six to eight million years ago) and by the time that the last North American glacier (Wisconsin) finally withdrew, perhaps eight to ten thousand years ago, the cougar had already firmly entrenched itself as the premier cat within the Western Hemisphere.

Members of the family Felidae, the cats, come in many sizes, shapes, and colors. Perhaps as a means of gross separation, zoologists have lumped most cats into just two family groupings: large (or Pantherini) and small (or Felini). Three cats—the clouded leopard, the snow leopard, and the cheetah—did not seem conveniently to fit the aforementioned two family groupings. The clouded leopard and the snow leopard have some of the characteristics of cats from both the large and small groupings, and thus are frequently identified as being "intermediate" cats. However, the snow leopard *(Uncia uncia)* has so many characteristics of the large cats that some taxonomists include it with other members of the *Panthera*, as species *Panthera uncia*. Other taxonomists prefer to split the Pantherini grouping into two genera: snow leopards *(Uncia)*, and all the other large cats *(Panthera)*. The cheetah *(Acinonyx jubatus)* is considered to be basically so different from other cats that it has simply been placed in a class all by itself. In addition to its unusual appearance—it is tall and lanky and has minimal ability to retract its claws and does not have claw sheaths—the cheetah's behavior, with its highly specialized method of hunting prey, is not replicated by any of the other cat species.

The primary difference between the two main groupings, in addition to the property of physical size, is whether or not the cat has the physical ability to roar. This is why there is some disagreement regarding the appropriate family grouping for the snow leopard: it does not roar. The roaring noise of the *Panthera* is generated by an elasticized band that is part of a bony, T-shaped protuberance, the hyoid, that is located at the base of the tongue. In smaller cats, the hyoid is completely bony; these cats voice either a scream, shriek, or cry. They also have the ability to make a purring sound when inhaling and exhaling. The larger cats *(Panthera)* can purr only when exhaling.

The cougar is the largest of the so-called smaller cats, and because individual cats within species vary considerably in size, some cougars are heavier than many jaguars or leopards. Thus, the inclusion of the cougar within the small-cat family grouping is based more on the cougar's behavioral manifestations, cranial/skeletal measurements, teeth, and vocal ability than on its size. The cougar does not make a roaring noise: its vocalizations can range from a whistle-like sound to that of a shriek or scream. When it is angered or in the process of snarling, a hiss and near growl have also been heard. Unlike the lion, tiger, and all other large cats, the cougar grooms itself like a small cat, licking its fur to a fine luster, and will similarly attend to the needs of its claws, sharpening them by drawing them across large rocks, trees, and the ground. Like the smaller cats, the cougar also crouches when it feeds and does not use its front cutting teeth or large canines to rip flesh from prey, as is customary with the *Panthera*, or so-called large cats. On the other hand, the cougar's pupils do not contract into vertical slits, as do the small cats, but remain round like those of the large cats. In view of these differences, we may sympathize with the zoologist's quandary, but for the layperson it is difficult to find logic in a concept that places the cougar, an animal whose weight often exceeds one hundred pounds, within the family of "small" cats.

The system that is currently used to facilitate the description and classification of all known species of plants, animals, and minerals (taxonomy) was the creation of Carl Linnaeus (1707–1778), a Swedish botanist. His efforts toward animals and minerals did not reflect the same rigor as that of his plant system, but in many respects he did accomplish his original objectives in a creative and reasonable manner. Over the years, the Linnaean system has been subject to a number of refinements and modifications by other taxonomists, and, conspicuously, many more species and subspecies have been subsequently identified and classified. What makes taxonomy somewhat enigmatic is that in this world the evolutionary process is ongoing and constant; all living species change as the environment around them changes. Thus, even modest or perhaps superficial changes can excite a taxonomist to declare the existence of a new species or subspecies. A good example of this is a recent subspecies proposal supported by the Dian Fossey Gorilla Fund, Zoo Atlanta, and researchers at the American Museum of Natural History. This reclassification proposal would basically separate from the world's remaining population of mountain gorillas approximately one-half of the estimated existing number, 620 animals, and establish a new and yet-to-be-named subspecies. The suggested reason for this reclassification is that the gorillas of Uganda's Bwindi–Impenetrable Forest National Park may have shorter thumbs and narrower trunks and skull, and that they spend more time in trees and possibly may not defecate as frequently in their night nests.

The *Brachiopoda lingula*, a shellfish, is said not to have changed in more than 500 million years because its ocean-bottom environment has not varied since the Paleozoic era, which is considered to be the period when marine invertebrate life initially began. However, the environment for most, if not all, the mammals has not proven to be such a constant, and they have found it necessary to evolve or, as a species, perish. There is general agreement that there are thirty-seven existing felid, or cat species; after that point taxonomists find little to agree about because of the seemingly prolific identification of subspecies. Kelsey-Wood (1989, 33) refers to thirty-one species of *Felis* or Felini (small cats) with 191 subspecies. When addressing *Felis concolor*, or cougar, it was suggested by Kelsey-Wood that there are twenty-nine subspecies. Young and Goldman (1946, 193–94), listed thirty subspecies, and Jim Bob

Tinsley, writer, hunter, and acknowledged cougar authority, has identified a total of thirty-five subspecies (1987, 112–16). There is little evidence of agreement in arriving at an accepted number of subspecies of cougar, even for the North American continent. Seton indicated that eight different "races" of cougar had been recognized (1929, vol 1, part 1, 42); but he goes on to say that "S. N. Rhoads considers that all of these North American cougars are races of one species. For purposes of life-history, at least, I prefer to accept this view." Hall and Kelson (1959, 957), and Young and Goldman (1946, 193–268) later described fifteen subspecies of *Felis concolor* in North America, and the aforementioned Tinsley identified a total of seventeen. These differences imply that identification of subspecies is an ongoing and endless process.

As people differ in facial features, coloring, structure, and form, so do all other mammals differ within their species. No two people are created exactly alike, and it is the same with all animals: it is not possible in nature to find a precise similarity between two individuals. Specific phenotype characteristics identify *Homo sapiens*, and in the same way other discrete phenotypes apply to other species. An individual difference—a morph—within a species (i.e., a single event) does not justify an announcement that there is a new subspecies. For such a claim to be made, the observed difference should affect whole populations and allow for a natural geographical distinction.

In view of the above, and in the interests of simplicity, it will be understood that it is not a purpose of this book to debate the number of subspecies of cougar that have been claimed, or to argue whether or not there are actually any legitimate subspecies. The ensuing chapters will focus on just the one species of cat, *Felis concolor*. It will not be assumed that any of the sundry subspecies, claimed or actual, would respond to given circumstances in manners that would differ from the responses of the others, except in those things that have been learned from individual experiences and environmental situations.

TWO A Cat of Many Names

T HE CAT THAT is called cougar *(Felis concolor)* once ranged over nearly the entire length and breadth of the North and South American continents. No other American mammal can claim such an extensive distribution and range. Because of this broad exposure to so many different human cultures and societies, this creature inevitably became the recipient of multitudinous names. Native Americans were all well aware of this large, tawny cat: of this we can be sure because of its depiction in countless works of prehistoric Indian rock art, and it must have been designated by numerous tribal names. When the Europeans "discovered" America, they, too, came up with a name for this unusual cat, as in their turn did later immigrants; in fact, some wildlife authors have suggested that there may have been more than forty such names. Some of the more common of these are cougar, puma, panther, painter, catamount, mountain lion, king cat, and tiger.

Without a name, any object, living or dead, animate or inanimate, is no more than a *thing;* a name is a shorthand way to describe it. Not knowing the accepted name for a given object or person can be quite frustrating if you wish to communicate. A few examples of this will demonstrate the problem: "Would you hand me that thing please?" "You know who I am talking about. Oh!— what is his name?" "I saw these birds—they were sort of black or maybe gray." With a name, however, communication becomes infinitely easier. The cougar—unlike most well-known species—being an animal with many names could present a problem. Fortunately, human identification of this creature is now not much of an issue.

The first person to see a cougar in the Western Hemisphere was likely one of the Paleoindians who crossed the Beringia land bridge, perhaps as long ago as forty thousand years, to hunt in and eventually populate the two newly dis-covered continents. There are no records to tell us what the Paleoindians may have called the cougar; nor does history say what the Norsemen under Eric or Leif Ericsson might have called the big cat, though they may have seen it during their five voyages to America around 1000 A.D. We do have accounts that early Spanish explorers found similarity in appearance between the cougar of the New World and the African lion. They referred to it as a "lion," lyon, or *Leon americano*. It was the fashion of the European "discovery" of the Americas—a more or less continuous process from 1492 until perhaps the early 1800s—for all features of the New World not previously identified or acknowledged by Europeans to be summarily given identifying names. Occa-sionally an object—animal, place, or whatever—acquired more than one name through virtue of its "discovery" by succeeding explorers; this probably added to the identity confusion. The interesting collection of identifying names of-fered for the animal we now know as the cougar is an excellent example of that past era of prolific name giving.

Amerigo Vespucci reported seeing "*leons*" on the beaches of Nicaragua in 1500. Christopher Columbus, during his fourth, and last, voyage to America, in 1502, observed "lions" along Nicaraguan beaches and the shoreline of Honduras. And an armed party dispatched by Columbus to explore the main-land of Costa Rica also recounted seeing deer, a turkey-like bird, and "lions." The Spanish were comfortable referring to the cougar as a *leon* and the jaguar as *el tigre*, a custom that is still generally followed in South America. One of the more interesting descriptions of this so-called American lion is that con-tained in a manuscript drafted by the Jesuit Juan Nentvig in 1762 and sub-mitted to the viceroy of New Spain (1980 trans., 28): "The quadruped called lion here—*naidoguat* in Opata—is not the king of beasts he is in other coun-tries. Almost as large as a yearling calf, this animal is so passive and cowardly that it does not fight when cornered but whines and cries instead. It is true that because of its size and strength it does damage and kills domestic animals, but it has neither the mane, color, nor claws of the real lion. Some call it leop-ard, also a misnomer." (The original manuscript, "A Description of Sonora and Arizona in 1764," was translated, clarified, and annotated by Alberto Francisco Pradeau and Robert R. Rasmussen. The description quoted above is from the translated manuscript, not the original, which was written in Spanish.)

Perusal of available literature of the fifteenth and sixteenth centuries reveals that it was indeed a rather common practice for the Spanish explorers and adventurers to identify as animals of the New World "lions" and "tigers." In attempting to describe the appearance of Indians at a particular point in time, Gaspar Perez de Villagra, in his *History of New Mexico* drafted in 1610 (1962 trans., 44), indicated that "some sought to resemble fierce a noble lion, dressed in the skin of that most royal beast; others covered themselves with the skin of striped tigers, or with the habit of the gray and hungry wolf; others appeared as hares, timid rabbits, great fish, eagles, and every other animal; in fact, every form of life that walks, swims, or flies was there, represented in most natural form." Francisco Vazquez de Coronado's account of the progress of his expedition, which had taken him and his men from Mexico City to the pueblos of New Mexico, was recorded in his August 1540 letter to Antonio de Mendoza, viceroy of New Spain. In describing what had happened to them thus far and what they had seen during their journey, he stated (Neider 1958, 26):

> They have many animals—bears, tigers, lions, porcupines, and some sheep as big as a horse, with very large horns and little tails. I have seen some of their horns the size of which was something to marvel at. There are also wild goats, whose heads I have seen, and the paws of the bears and the skins of the wild boars. For game they have deer, leopards, and very large deer, and every one thinks that some of them are larger than that animal which your Lordship favored me with, which belonged to Juan Melaz. They inhabit some plains eight days' journey toward the north. They have some of their skins here very well dressed, and they prepare and paint them where they kill the cows, according to what they tell me.

The cougar of the New World did have some of the appearance of the Old World lion. It had the same tawny color and basic appearance of the African lioness, and the absence of maned male lions was apparently not considered significant in this initial name-giving effort. One interesting explanation with respect to the male/female question was quoted by Seton (1929, 43):

> Adriaen van der Donck writes: "Although the New-Netherlands lay in a fine climate, and although the country in winter seems rather cold, nevertheless

Lions are found there, but not by the Christians, who have traversed the whole land wide and broad and have not seen one. It is only known to us by the skins of the females, which are sometimes brought in by the Indians for sale; who on inquiry say, that the Lions are found far to the southwest, distant 15 or 20 days' journey, in very high mountains, and that the males are too active and fierce to be taken. (*A Description of the New-Netherlands*, 2nd edition, 1656. Coll. N.Y. Hist. Soc., 1, 1841: 167) [this work is cited by Seton]

As previously noted, we now know that the relationship of *F. concolor* within the cat family (Felidae) to that of the African or Asian lion *(Panthera leo)* is not one of direct lineage, but this facet of taxonomy and genetics was not a serious consideration when our forefathers were deciding on a common name for this large cat of the New World. Their knowledge of large cats had been limited to that of Old World lions, tigers, and leopards, and given these parameters, their use of the term "lion" to describe this heretofore unknown cat becomes understandable. Hence, the terms "American lion" and "mountain lion" also became colloquial expressions of geographical descriptive function.

The word "American" in the binomial idiom "American lion" was obviously added to distinguish this particular "lion" from the better-known African species. The binomial term "mountain lion" was clearly fashioned to indicate this "lion's" territory In the Rocky Mountain and Western states, *F. concolor* is still frequently referred to as mountain lion, although the term cougar is also often used, especially in the Pacific Northwest.

Even though the cougar exhibits little resemblance to the Asian tiger, it has also been identified as a "tiger," "tigre," or "tyger." McMullen (1984, 372) suggests that these spotted or striped animals were "probably cougars young enough to still have their camouflage stripes and spots." Tinsley (1987, 9) theorizes that early travelers called any spotted cat a tiger, and thus the name was "falsely applied to all native American wild cats"—an observation of logic that appears specious if also applied to the unicolored cougar. The names tiger, tigre, or tyger were perhaps applied more frequently to the cats of South America and the southeastern United States than in any of the other New World cougar locations. Linnaeus classified but one race of cougar in 1771; he identified it as *F. concolor*, or "cat of one color." However, this same cat had earlier been identified as "tigre rouge," or red tiger, and Wawula (an Indian name), or deer tiger, and preceding this *Cuguacuarana Brasiliensibus, Tigre* (Young and Goldman 1946, 200). That the term "tiger" is still being used oc-

The cougar had been called "deer tiger" because of its particular liking for deer meat. Without predation, deer herds, growing rapidly, create environmental damage, and themselves face food shortages and eventual starvation.

casionally when referring to the cougar is possibly due to associated use of the name "tiger" for any large, flesh-eating feline, as well as to local culture and customs. It is noted that even the usually reliable *Webster's New World Dictionary* (3rd coll. ed., 1988) suggests that "tiger" is the appropriate word for "any of several similar animals; especially, a) the South American Jaguar, b) the African leopard, c) the Tasmanian wolf."

Most Latin Americans still use the name *el tigre* to denote the jaguar *(Panthera onca)*, whereas in the southeastern United States "tyger" and "tiger" were once commonly used for the cougar. Elsewhere chroniclers have identified the terms "red tiger," "brown tiger," "gray tiger," "deer tiger," "mountain tiger," and *Tigre poltron* (poltroon, or cowardly tiger) as synonymous with *F. concolor* in the Americas. It should be noted, however, that "tiger-cat" was also used by early explorers of the American West when referring to the American bobcat, or bay lynx *(Lynx rufus)* rather than to the cougar. In the journals of Lewis and Clarke, for example, where an effort was made to describe all the plants, birds, and animals they encountered during their 1804–1806 expedition, the write-up for the "panther" and the "tiger-cat" reads:

The tiger-cat inhabits the borders of the plains and the woody country in the neighbourhood of the Pacific. This animal is of a size larger than the wildcat of our country, and much the same in form, agility, and ferocity. The colour of the back, neck, and sides is of reddish brown, irregularly variegated with small spots of dark brown; the tail is about two inches long, and nearly white, except in the extremity, which is black. It terminates abruptly, as if it had been amputated; the belly is white, and beautifully variegated with small black spots; the legs are of the same colour with the sides, and the back is marked transversely with black stripes; the ears are black on the outer side, covered with fine, short hair, except at the upper point, which is furnished with a pencil of hair, fine, straight, and black, three-fourths of an inch in length. The hair of this animal is long and fine, far exceeding that of the wildcat of the United States, but inferior in that quality to that of the bear of the northwest. The skin of this animal is in great demand amongst the natives, for of this they form their robes, and it requires four to make up the complement.

The panther is found indifferently, either in the great plains of the Columbia, the western side of the Rocky mountains, or on the coast of the Pacific. He is the same animal so well known on the Atlantic coast, and most commonly found on the frontiers or unsettled parts of our country. He is very seldom found, and when found, so wary it is difficult to reach him with a musket.

In the Journals of Zebulon Montgomery Pike (Jackson edition, 1966, 1:87), reference was made to an incident involving a "panther" that occurred January 31, 1806, while the Pike party was exploring the Mississippi and had reached the northwest edge of present-day Cass County, Iowa: "Passed one very large meadow or Prairie, the course W. The Mississippi only 15 yards wide. Encamped about one mile above the Transverse of the Meado: Saw a very Large Animal, which from the leaps he made I should suppose to be a Panther; but if so, he was twice as large as those on the Lower Mississippi. He shewed some disposition to approach me. I squated down (miller being in the rear) in order to entice him to it, but could not." The name "panther" in referring to F. concolor was, and still is, a colloquialism that is more applicable to peoples from the eastern and southeastern United States than other locations in the Americas. Use of the term "panther" appeared more often than any other reference to a name for this animal in the journals and memoirs of early travelers to the West, perhaps because most of them had roots in eastern states. In cases where their historical accounts were indexed, encounters and experiences involving F. concolor are more often to be found under "panther" than any other name. An example is Gregg's *Commerce of the Prairies* (Thwaites 1966, 19:327). In a discussion of animals of the prairies, Gregg writes: "There are other animals of prey about the mountains, among which the panther is most conspicuous."

Another typical, and most interesting, use of the term "panther" can be found in John Townsend's *Journey Across the Rocky Mountains to the Columbia River* (Thwaites 1966, 21:274). During the latter part of August 1833, when Townsend was encamped in the Blue Mountains of extreme southeast Washington, he observed: "The panther is said to inhabit these forests in considerable numbers, and has not unfrequently been known to kill the horses of a camp. He has seldom the temerity to attack a man, unless sorely pressed by hunger, or infuriated by wounds." References to "panther" can also be found in the narratives of De Smet (*Oregon Missions* 1847, 214), Dodge (1959, 218–21), Farnham (1843, 204, 221, 226), Franchere (1854, 323, 325), Long (Edwin James 1823; Thwaites 1966, 77, 146), Nuttall (1821, 168, 210, 211, 325), Palmer (1847, 248), Pattie (Flint 1831, 43, 88, 194), and Woods (1822, 287).

Today, only one geographic area in the United States steadfastly continues to use the term "panther" when referring to the cougar: Florida and the extreme southeast. And this is only when alluding to the so-called "Florida panther" subspecies, *F. concolor coryi*. The Florida panther is listed as an endangered species, subject to the provisions of the Endangered Species Conservation Act of 1969. However, for this listing the law is somewhat difficult to enforce since, according to Alvarez (1993, 142–46), in addition to skull dimension, many of the characteristics attributed to the Florida panther (i.e., general pelage and coloration, presence of white flecks on the shoulder, neck, and head region, a middorsal whorl, and a crook at the end of the tail) are features now seldom found among the resident *F. concolor* population. The Florida Game and Freshwater Fish Commission has suggested that there are fewer than fifty, and perhaps as few as thirty, "panthers" in Florida. Unfortunately, it is also likely that some of these animals formerly were captive cougars that originated in the West but were later released in Florida; or that they are non-native *F. concolor* that have recently found their way to the Florida wilds. Regardless of the legitimacy of the subspecies claim for the Florida panther *(F. c. coryi)* any *F. concolor* found in Florida or the southeastern United States will probably always be referred to as a "panther."

One of the more idiomatic names given to *F. concolor* was that of "painter."

Florida's panther is an endangered subspecies of cougar. Found only in the remote areas of southwestern Florida, primarily in the Everglades, fewer than fifty of these animals reportedly now survive. *Photo: National Park Academy of the Arts; for use of her "Everglades Cougar" painting: Blanche Gassaway.*

Considering the colorful but generally unsophisticated and provincial nature of many of the people who transformed the wilderness of mid-Eastern and mid-Western America, the casual alteration of the term "panther" into "painter" is a grammatical outcome that could not be unexpected. Gregg (Thwaites 1966, 106), for example, relates a story in which a person who was more familiar with a city than the wilderness claimed to have been attacked by a "painter." The man said he beat the cat off by wielding his rifle like a club. People who heard the tale noted, however, that the shattered rifle exuded an odor strongly reminiscent not of "painter," but of previous encounter with a skunk. Authors of period literature that sought to capture the frontier mood of those pioneering days, such as James Fenimore Cooper, found the term "painter" suitably colorful for their purposes. Young and Goldman (1946, 2) quoted a particularly poetic passage of James Whitcomb Riley that further illustrates this point:

> "Yes—and painters, prowlin' 'bout,
> Allus darkest nights. Lay out

Clost yer cattle.—Great, big red
Eyes a-blazin' in their head,
Glitter'n 'long the timber-line—
Shine out some, and then unshine,
And shine back—Then steady! Whizz!
'N' there yer Mr. Painter is
With a hole bored spang between
Them-air eyes!"

What Chris'mas fetched the Wigginses (1913, 172)

Davy Crockett in his autobiography *A Narrative of the Life of David Crockett of the State of Tennessee* referred to the cougar as "painter" (1987, 19). In his writings it was also evident that he held the cougar's combative skills and spirit in high regard. In one instance, for example, in evaluating his bear dogs (Neider 1958, 142), he claimed that they were "as fierce as painters; so that a bear stood no chance to get away from them."

Col. Richard Irving Dodge contributed much to the literature of Western Americana. Unfortunately, he was seemingly of the belief that there were two distinctive and separate species of *F. concolor* in the Great West. In his *Plains of the Great West*, he describes the animals that frequented this region and he mentions both the cougar and the "Panther" (1959, 217–19). He reports that the cougar is "called variously the 'Mexican lion,' 'California lion,' and 'mountain lion,' is a habitual resident of many rough and broken parts of the plains," and that "he is not a good climber." The "panther," he claims, "is nearly the same animal on a smaller scale. The cougar is almost a lion." Expressing little regard for this "smaller" cat, he mentions that it is possible to pull its long tail without fear, and submits that "the animal is really very harmless to the hunter." Acknowledging the Eastern name of "painter," he further notes that "one becomes accustomed, as he grows older, to having the illusions of his youth dispelled; but after having killed fifty or more panthers, under a variety of circumstances, without ever seeing one show fight, it is difficult to account for the respect, even the terror, with which eastern professional hunters surround the 'painter' as they call it."

John R. Cook was one of those rough-hewn adventurers that hunted bison on the southwest plains in the 1870s. His published reminiscences, *The Border and the Buffalo*, describes his encounters with various Indian tribes that also hunted the plains of Texas and New Mexico, as well as the animal life common to these plains. Although the ongoing process of killing bison was the primary focus of his reminiscences, on three occasions he elected to mention his experiences with a "mountain lion," a "cougar," and a "panther." His first encounter occurred in the spring of 1874 when he was camped northeast of Santa Fe, New Mexico. Cook reported hearing the nearby cry of a "mountain lion." He describes it (1967, 71) as being "weird, almost human . . . like a cry of distress, which the brute kept up at intervals for nearly half an hour, without seeming to change position." In March 1875, while hunting bison along the Brazos in north-central Texas, Cook and his hunting partners caught sight of a "large panther," which they promptly shot and skinned. Some days later, after killing a small herd of bison, Cook came upon a "cougar" that was feeding on the carcass of one of the bison they had previously shot. Cook describes his next actions (1967, 183):

> The tawny, dirty, yellow-looking brute appeared to be totally oblivious of my presence. I streched out on my belly, and, placing a large buffalo-chip in freont of me, let the muzzle end of the gun rest on it, and then watched him for a minute or more. He would get hold of the flesh and try to graw and pull until he got a mouthful, then would raise his head and gulp down what flesh he had torn loose, and dive in again. After he had done this way twice and was busy getting another mouthful, I shot him, pulling for the butt of the left ear. He never knew what hurt him. I went down to where he and the buffalo lay, and taking my ripping knife out of the scabbard, I scalped the cougar, taking both ears and the frontal hide down to the lower end of the upper jaw, including the lips. Then I also amputated one of the forelegs at the knee, and hurried back to the wagon.

Some weeks later, while within the same general area, one of Cook's partners followed an unknown animal into a nearby gulch and in his efforts to identify it he said it "snarled at me . . . and the thing lashed its tail and had red eyes." Cook advised his partner that he should not have entered the gulch without a good working gun because the animal "is either a panther or a cougar." One of the hidemen, who just happened to be in the camp, then showed everyone the scars he was carrying on his chest that he received "from a painter in Arkansas." Cook and several others from the hide camp immediately decided to kill the beast. After sighting the animal, it was identified by Cook as "one of the largest panthers, as I thought, that ever was." They all shot this animal, and with entrails dragging on the ground it disappeared into cover, where it later died (1967, 201–3).

Not to leave the impression that Cook and his cohorts just singled out bison and cougar for their hunting efforts, Cook also mentioned shooting an eagle because he "had heard that eagle-oil was the best kind of gun-oil" (1967, 177–78).

One of the more interesting, although fallacious, explanations of the differences between a panther, or cougar, and a mountain lion was an article by Frank Mossman that was published in September 1901 in *Outdoor Life:* "The Cougar and Lion of the Pacific Coast." Mossman wrote:

> The cougar and the mountain lion (felis concolor) are one and the same species, and yet they differ a great deal in size, color, and general appearance, the lion being larger-limbed and far larger in every way than the cougar or panther. While the legs of the lion are shorter, they are vastly more powerful than those of the cougar, which greatly accounts for the fact that the former is more destructive to stock. They differ in their habits of breeding in that the female lion will keep her two kittens (and sometime three) until they are a year or more old, and sometimes they are seen together when the kittens are full grown. From close observation of the habits of the female lion I am forced to believe that they do not breed every year but every second year. The cougar breeds every year, as far as I have observed in some twenty years of close study of the animals in all phases and under all conditions, both alive and dead.

Similar in derivation to "painter" is the name "catamount." Young and Goldman (1946, 3), Tinsley (1987, 11) and Hansen (1992, 2) claim that "catamount" is an acronym for cat-of-the-mountain, and was used for *F. concolor* more often in the Eastern states—particularly in New England. The indefatigable *Webster's*, while defining catamount as any of various wildcats; especially (a) the puma, cougar, and (b) lynx, goes on to offer as a definition for catamountain "any of several wildcats, especially the leopard or the European wildcat." Consequently, if it was not a universally acceptable substitute name for the cougar, its use was then apparently common, at least, for people of the northeastern United States.

Another example of confusion in early reports of animals of the *F. concolor* species can be found in Gabriel Franchere's narrative of his 1811–1814 journey to the Pacific Northwest. Franchere lists what he considers to be the principal quadrupeds of the country; among many other animals, he names "the panther, the catamount, the lynx"—implying that these three cats are separate species (Thwaites 1966, 323). In a similar vein, John Russell Bartlett, in attempting to identify all known quadrupeds and birds that he noted on his Western journey from 1850 to 1853 *(Personal Narrative of Explorations and Incidents in Texas, New Mexico, California, Sonora, and Chihuahua)* names both cougar and panther. Bartlett states (1965, 555) that "among the former may be mentioned the leopard [probably referring to the jaguar], cougar, ocelot, lynx, panther." Although he mentions cougar rather than catamount, along with panther, Bartlett implies, like Franchere, that the panther is somehow different. Parenthetically, to raise another point, I found Bartlett's mention of the lynx to be surprising, for this is a northern animal that would not reasonably be expected to be found south of the Colorado Rockies.

Another interesting name that was given to *F. concolor* was "king cat." King cat is more like a title than a name, and like most of the remaining names that this cat has acquired it is not in general use. Nevertheless, for North America this name, or title, may not be a misnomer: it refers to a species that has perceived preeminence over all other native cats. In a more plebeian tenor, the cougar has also been referred to as "big cat," "wild cat," and just "cat."

A name that has received a certain measure of scientific acceptance, by more than a few zoologists, is that of puma. It is also to be noted that some taxonomists—a limited number—proposed the designation *Puma* as a mammalian subgenus of *Felis;* and, to take this one step further, some of these classifiers had even suggested a species transfer from the genus *F. concolor* to *Puma concolor.* The reasoning behind these proposals is somewhat enigmatic: we have been told that the word "puma" is derived from the Quechua language of the South American Inca tribes and means "a powerful animal." We have also been told that another language of the Central Andean highlands, Aymara, also uses "puma" to identify *F. concolor.* Based on these two language examples and the general use of the name "puma" in many areas of South America, it was apparently proposed that "puma" be used as the common name for *F. concolor.* Anderson (1983, 1) adds to the above reasoning (1) that "puma" is not a product of mispronunciation, and (2) that it has the advantage of brevity.

According to linguistic scholar Morris Swadesh (1962, 1262–91), Indians were speaking in excess of 2,200 different languages when Columbus arrived in the New World. In addition, there is evidence to suggest that all tribes that had experienced contact with *F. concolor* had a term—a specific word or words —that referred to this animal. Tinsley (1987, 12) provided several examples of Indian names, as did Hansen (1992, 1–2), Seton (1929, vol. 1, 37), and Young and Goldman (1946, 2–4), as have many other knowledgeable writers. It thus seems that the name "puma" is certainly not used exclusively in Indian languages; nor is it, nor has it ever been, the most commonly accepted name for this cat among peoples now residing in the Western Hemisphere.

Vying in popularity with "mountain lion," "puma," and "panther" as a common name for *F. concolor* is "cougar." Not as geographically limited in usage as the foregoing names, "cougar" is universally recognized as referring to just one specific American cat species. It is certainly not a lion; nor is "cougar" always a habitue of mountains. In "cougar's" favor, it may be noted that "panther" could equally refer to the leopard or the jaguar, or perhaps suggest a species relevance to the genus *Panthera*. Although the name "puma" is common within certain geographical areas of South America when referring to *F. concolor*, so also are a number of other names, including that of the previously mentioned "lion." Incidentally, it is also to be noted that the occupational name for those hardy people who are paid by Andes ranchers to hunt the large tawny cat is *leoneros,* or lion hunters.

In conducting research regarding estimated cougar population for this book, it was necessary to contact a number of state wildlife agencies for current data. Of sixteen states known to have cougar populations, seven state agencies referred to *F. concolor* as a mountain lion, eight used cougar, and one used panther. None referred specifically to *F. concolor* as a puma, although supplemental literature later furnished by two of the states included a general statement that the mountain lion, as they named it to be, is also commonly known as cougar, panther, or puma.

"Cougar" is said to have originated in the Guarani Indian (Paraguay and Brazil) word for this cat, *cuguacuarana.* However, even in this supposition we seem to have little agreement. Tinsley (1987, 9) and Young (1946, 3) offered the explanation that the correct Guarani term was *sussuarana,* but was incorrectly transcribed. In 1761, Georges Louis Leclerc de Buffon, a French naturalist, is reported to have distorted or abbreviated this word in writing it as *cugouar*—which then became the derivative of "cougar." Another suggestion is that the name was arrived at because it sounded somewhat like the cry often made by this creature.

Regardless of its origin, "cougar" is the name of choice for most Americans, including wildlife authors. Ernest Thompson Seton, for example, referred to the animal as a cougar, although he recognized that other names were also being used. Theodore Roosevelt was more specific: "The Spanish speaking people usually call it simply lion. It is, however, sometimes called cougar in the West and Southwest of our country, and in South America, puma. As it is desirable where possible not to use a name that is misleading and is already appropriated to some entirely different animal, it is best to call it cougar" (1905, 1990 edition, 17). Kevin Hansen, in association with the Mountain Lion Foundation, pauses in his recent publication *Cougar* to recognize that there are other names of common use but he continues to identify this cat as a cougar, as does the work of Cahalane, Turbak, Milne, Hancock, Andy Russell, Harley Shaw, and that of many others.

Literature and news accounts that deal with *F. concolor* are excellent sources for seeing what has now become a common practice—joint or interchangeable name usage. Authors who go to great length in explaining to their readers why the appropriate name should be puma, panther, mountain lion, or cougar, then go on to use all of these names in their article or book. News articles that touch upon cougar/human encounters use all of the common names: cougar, mountain lion or lion, and, although less frequently, panther and puma. From this interchangeable use, it appears that mountain lion, cougar, and, to a lesser degree, puma are all readily acceptable names for the public. "Panther" remains somewhat vague, perhaps even in Florida. For many readers, "panther" might call to mind an image of a stealthy and savage black leopard.

From the foregoing, I believe that there are fewer objections to the use of "cougar" than to that of the other names. In the following chapters, *F. concolor* will consistently be referred to as a cougar, except where I quote other writers who use another name.

> They call him "puma" in the zoo;
> Down South he's known as "panther," too;
> In many places way out West
> Folks think that "cougar" suits him best.
>
> So you can give him any name
> And still he'll look and act the same.
> He's just a great big yellow thief
> That likes to steal the rancher's beef.

With slinking stealth and sudden leap
He catches calves and colts and sheep.
He prowls the rocky canyon sides
And knows right where the mule deer hides.

He's very much afraid of folks;
Most tales of his bad deeds are jokes;
And one old dog can bark and whine,
And chase him up the tallest pine!

David Newell. From *American Animals.*
Reprinted in his article "Panther!"
in *Saturday Evening Post* 208 (July 13, 1935): 10.

THREE **Characteristics of the Cougar**

WHAT DO WE really know about the cougar? If we answer truthfully, we would have to say that we actually know very little about this animal. Authors of one of the better research works ever compiled on *F. Concolor*, Stanley P. Young and Edward A. Goldman, entitled their 1946 work, *The Puma: Mysterious American Cat*. I don't believe they could have chosen a better word than "mysterious" to describe the lifestyle of the enigmatic cougar. Independent, shy, and secretive, the cougar has been referred to as "the ghost of North America" (Hornocker 1992, 52), "a ghost" (Caras 1969, 23), "a seldom-seen ghost of the farther places" (Waterman 1973, 132), and "ghost walker" (Lawrence 1983); it has also been disdainfully labeled "sneak-cat" by many early North American big-game hunters—a name subscribed to even by wildlife luminary Ernest Thompson Seton. The cougar has also been identified, paradoxically, as (1) a craven coward, timid, and unwilling to defend itself and easily treed by the smallest barking dog; and (2) a brutal and merciless assassin, nighttime livestock marauder, and latent man-killer. Which characterization is accurate? Conceivably both could be. But as representative of a species? Perhaps neither.

The dilemma we have in correctly identifying just what cougars are all about is related more to how humans envision the proper function of nature, after due consideration of primal human needs, than what it is that the cougar does or does not do. The human species seems to prefer a tidy process that will label all living organisms either good or bad. In Genesis, the first book of the Bible, God is said to have created everything by the sixth day, "and he found it good." Man was then said to have been given dominion over all creatures, but man has been busy ever since attempting to adjust what are perceived to be flaws in the creative process. Some of the "adjustments" were deemed necessary so that a burgeoning human species could better utilize land resources—without the assumption of any rights for other living organisms to suitably occupy and utilize planet Earth. The bison, which formerly occupied the plains and grasslands of America, were judged expendable in order for the land to be more efficiently exploited. Elimination of the bison meant the Native Americans could then be more easily assimilated into a dominant white society and their lands could be utilized for ranching, farming, and other aspects of national growth. The lifestyles of a number of other wild species were also incompatible with an urbanized and "civilized" society; thus, some are now quite extinct; others have been identified as being either threatened or endangered.

Although anthropopathy is a somewhat common and usually harmless notion, unfortunately it has intensified a human perception that there are both "good" and "bad" animals—a judgment based on their behavior as measured against human standards of conduct. J. Frank Dobie noted that even Ben Lilly, the pragmatic but supremely individualistic hunter of bears and cougars, attached certain moral attributes to animals: bravery to the grizzly, loyalty to the wolf, cowardice to the cougar (1950, 185). With the possible exception of the irascible bison, wild herbivores have, in the main, been nominally categorized as passive, gentle beasts; they are thus usually the recipients of a reasonable level of human compassion. Notwithstanding that the entire deer family has been vigorously hunted over the years, it would be fair to say that the general human feeling toward these animals is positive. If we could possibly consider such films as *Bambi* as representative of true human sentiment, we might further suggest that public opinion borders on the solicitous. Carnivores, on the other hand, do not find human favor. Although we humans are considered primarily to be a carnivorous species, we seem to find something particularly repugnant about the predation and eating habits of the other carnivores. However, we do not elect to cloak all predators with the same villainous robe. We save our deepest censure for those that we perceive as being ugly or those whose motives we find to be thoroughly clandestine; and thus we determine their purpose to be probably sinister.

The African lion would certainly be numbered among those predators that present danger to human life, and many terrifying experiences are accordingly published that fully support this contention; however, the lion is also perceived as courageous, and humans place high value on courage. The hyena, on the other hand, is considered by many people to be a disgusting, obscene creature. Two very different reputations—yet the lion and hyena will actively compete for the same prey. The grizzly bear of North America, in those areas where it still can be found, is an acknowledged wilderness menace—a potential threat to human life; however, the grizzly has also acquired a reputation for nobility, great strength, ferocity, and courage. Conversely, although it presents a lesser threat to human life, the American cougar's reputation has sometimes been one of cowardice, cruelty, and deviousness.

James Capen (Grizzly) Adams, who was born in 1807 in Midway, Massachusetts, and who hunted and captured a variety of wild animals that included cougars, wolves, and bears, had great respect for the grizzly but only contempt for the cougar. While tracking a grizzly through what is now Yosemite National Park, Adams was startled by the screech of a cougar and exclaimed: "For a moment my very bones quaked with terror; but I soon reasoned myself calm. What a fool, thought I, to be thus startled by the cry of a panther, a cowardly brute, which dare not stand face to face and fight with a man; while here I am, inviting combat with a grizzly bear, the savagest beast that ranges the forest!" (Hittell 1926, 196).

There is a great deal of complexity and unpredictability in animal conduct. Eckert (1983, 285) suggests that all animals, including the human species, behave in accordance with outputs of the nervous system as modified by stimuli from the environment. Because of vagaries and the dynamics involved, it is thus not practical, logical, or even reasonable for us, even when dealing with human beings, to attempt to chart a possible singular outcome when emotion or behavioral action becomes the primary agent. There is a similar range of complexity in the conduct of other creatures, particularly that of the predators, that calls into question the dependability of generalizations about behavior; perhaps all generalizations are simply fallacious. No one can accurately predict how an animal will behave under circumstances of need or stress, and any decision that it may arrive at involving flight or fight could also depend upon factors other than its past conduct or assumed species behavioral patterns. Even the seemingly timorous deer can, and will, occasionally attack and fight ferociously with its sharp hooves and horns. These animals, so often considered meek, can be formidable, and their occasional determined onslaughts have led to a number of human victims.

The cougar does not possess the same temperament, belligerence, or territorial instincts as those of the grizzly. But it is equally as capable of defending itself, or perhaps of initiating an assault should it happen to decide on that course of action. The grizzly depends upon its size and great strength to overcome its prey, which usually are much smaller animals. The cougar depends upon stealth and agility, coupled with an array of teeth and claws that, in their actual use, would be the envy of any other American carnivore. Although a cougar does not possess the great strength of a grizzly, a cougar can, and often does, kill animals that are more than double its own weight, and then move the carcass some distance from the kill site to feed.

Because it is basically a nonsocial animal, the cougar demonstrates only limited protective instincts. In most cases, an adult female maintains a home range that can vary in size from five to twenty-five square miles, but she will travel through a territory that can be as large as four hundred square miles; the size of the home range depends on the territory's ability to satisfy the cougar's physiological needs. An adult male cougar usually requires a larger personal territory: it can be as little as fifteen square miles or as much as thirty square miles, but transient animals may travel through a territory as large as five hundred square miles. Often there will be some minor overlapping of the selected home ranges of female and male cougars, but this does not seem to solicit significant aggressive responses from either animal. Male cougars are usually quite careful to avoid encroaching upon the marked home range of another male cougar, but when this does occur the subordinate male most often will retreat. There are times, however, when conflicts do occur. Maurice G. Hornocker, who conducted studies in the San Andreas Mountains of New Mexico between 1985 and 1990, placing radio collars on cougars that he captured and later released, monitored several fights between male cougars. He was able to tell if the encounter resulted in a mortality (Hornocker 1992, 58). One big male, that Hornocker named Atilla because of his level of aggression, was so belligerent that he even killed three female cougars that had home ranges near his.

Cougar family life can also become violent. "Buffalo" Jones indicated that the large males, or toms, would eat the kittens so that the female could quickly come in heat again (Easton 1961, 156). Probably for this reason, most cougar mothers attempt to prevent a male from getting near her litter. All cats, however, will behave somewhat similarly in this regard: When an African male lion assumes control over a pride, his first act is to kill all the young cubs conceived by the previous male or males (Young and Goldman 1946, 138). And Victor H. Cahalane (1961, 266) mentions an incident that occurred some years ago in Colorado (1925): a male and female cougar stayed together even after she gave birth to kittens; after a Forest Service hunter killed the female, the male returned to the den and promptly ate the kittens. The male returned to the den many times, presumably still searching for his mate, until he, too, was killed.

Since the cougar is a solitary animal, unlike the African lion, it has not acquired, and seemingly has not had a need to develop, skills in communal associations. Only rarely is there an observed pairing of cougars, and this normally occurs only when they are actively mating or when the female and/or her adolescent young are still functioning as a family group. Cougar hunter Ben Lilly expressed the belief that young cougars have a pack instinct (Dobie 1950, 190), but by the age of fourteen to twenty-four months they have already established individual ranges and are completely detached hunters. Cougar researchers Harley Shaw and Maurice Hornocker observed that antisocial behavior was a decided characteristic of cougar adulthood, but that aggressiveness is not a uniformly distributed trait. Shaw indicated that he had radio-tracked one mature male cougar over a six-year period, and this particular animal was never able to establish his own territory; he was continually displaced by more dominant cougars (1989, 17).

Although cougars in their natural habitat would not normally seek a community arrangement with others of their species, except for purposes of breeding and the expected and occasionally extended maternal association of the mother with her progeny, cougars in captivity have been able to adjust quite well to conditions associated with group living. One of the more unusual exhibitions of communal living developed at the Frankfurt Zoo. A cougar family, consisting of parents and three of their near-adult-sized kittens, were trained by their keeper to perform for visitors in a manner similar to that of circus felines such as lions and tigers (Kirchshofer 1968, 137). Another example of a seemingly compatible cougar relationship occurred at the Arizona-Sonora Desert Museum. Two adult cougars of different sex were placed together within one of the museum's natural-habitat enclosures. Both cougars were

Two cougars—a spayed nine-year-old female native Arizonan and a five-year-old imported male from Colorado—playfully share accommodations in their view-free enclosure in the Sonora Desert Museum, west of Tucson, Arizona.

lifetime zoo habitants. The nine-year-old female cougar was spayed. After recovering from her surgery, she was placed in a generous enclosure with a five-year-old male cougar. The enclosure was environmentally attractive and included nearly all accoutrements necessary to satisfy cougar territorial requirements. The two cougars had shared only limited familiarity with one another previously, but, according to museum staff, this arrangement has thus far worked out quite well.

The Denver Zoological Gardens, although it does not provide its exhibition cougars with anything resembling a natural habitat, currently has three cougars, one male (Sundance) and two females (Squash Blossom and Nellie Kim), successfully sharing the same "estate." The cougars are related, and that is most significant in their getting along. The cougars are held in a rather small and uninspiring caged enclosure that fronts a pseudo cave arrangement where they usually spend most of their day. This is not to suggest that these three cougars are more deprived than those held in the Arizona-Sonora exhibit, but only that the visiting public has a lesser opportunity for participating in a natural viewing experience.

Unfortunately, or perhaps fortunately depending upon the circumstances

At the Denver Zoo—cage and minimal habitat enclosure for three captive cougars.

that may surround such an encounter, a zoo may well be the only place most people will ever see a cougar. Moreover, public perception of what cougars are all about may be further distorted because zoo environments allocated to predators are frequently more like prison cells than natural habitats. This is not necessarily a fault of zoo management, but one of the realities dictated by space availability, budget restraints, and the result of precedence associated with the international Species Survival Plan (SSP), which suggests that zoological gardens offer special treatment for species that are threatened worldwide (Koebner 1994, 125–26, 129–31). Consequently, many zoos in the United States will exhibit native species only if they are threatened or endangered.

Adjacent to one of the many casinos in the Las Vegas area of Nevada is the Southern Nevada Zoological–Botanical Park. Identified as a "children's zoo," this little park surprisingly offers a marvelous variety of animals and birds, many that are indigenous to the southwestern desert region. Contained in one of their spacious cages is their resident cougar, Cougie. This healthy specimen was brought to the zoo by state wildlife officials when he was a small kitten.

The Sonora Desert Museum has provided a superb artificial territory for each of the southwestern species it displays. The cougar enclosure incorporates water, sheer rock cliffs, and plenty of vegetative cover and rocky outcroppings.

Coupled with the neighboring deer, coyote, badger, and cottontail exhibits, this section of the zoo presents to its bright-eyed young visitors views of animals that they might otherwise never see, even though the creatures are quite common.

One of the most remarkable private assemblages of cougars that I have seen is that maintained by Michael Jurich in his Prairie Wind Wild Animal Refuge. A Denver native, Jurich had been fascinated by wild creatures since he was a boy, and now a childhood dream of his has come true: he operates his own, private, animal refuge. In it he provides sanctuary for a variety of wild animals that, without his intervention, would have been destroyed. In addition to providing a home for an agglomeration of coyotes, wolves, foxes, lions, tigers, and bears, Jurich also, at the time of my visit in 1995, happened to be the custodian of nine cougars.

Prairie Wind Wild Animal Refuge is located in a somewhat secluded area, off a little-used county road, approximately twenty miles northeast of Kiowa, Colorado. I made prior arrangements with Jurich to meet him at his refuge

Cougie in his enclosure at the Southern Nevada Zoological–Botanical Park in Las Vegas. Note the distinctive toe and plantar pads on front and rear feet.

Mike Jurich with Coe, a one-year-old male cougar. Coe was one of three kittens born to Savanna in the Prairie Wind refuge in 1994.

and was fortunate to have selected one of that year's warmer November days. In compliance with Colorado state law, all of the animals at Prairie Wind are in cages, but the limitation does not trouble these animals whatsoever: their cage becomes "their" territory and they have no interest in further freedom. In addition to receiving an obvious high level of loving care from Mike, unlike most wild carnivores they are assured of living out the remainder of their lives with dignity and serenity.

When I arrived at the refuge, Mike had just completed making a few temporary housing arrangements at the refuge in order to accommodate a new cougar guest. The former owner of this cougar, a four-year-old female, had brought her to Prairie Wind because he was unable to meet government licensing requirements for personal possession of the animal; she would stay until he could—an event that in all probability would never occur. The arrival of this new tenant appeared to be quite an event for all the other animals: they were in constant motion in their cages, offering vocal comments on the proceedings. The two cougars housed in cages adjacent to the newcomer's let her know by their snarls and hisses that they would be keeping an eye on her, and she, in turn, busied herself in berating them and abusing her accommodations by tossing around the provided animal shelter. This adjustment process is very important, as Mike explained: Cougars are primarily solitary animals; they do not eagerly welcome other cougar company, unless they themselves seek it—and then it is essentially only to mate; many captive cougars have never seen another cougar before and are unable to accept a symbionic relationship. In addition, changes in routine, particularly if the alterations are dramatic, are unwelcome and stressful.

Jurich is convinced that captive cougars, as well as most animals, are creatures of emotion. He rejects the notion that cougars are cowardly animals, and believes that they will react to humans based upon how well they have been treated in the past. He does, however, feel more comfortable with solid-color cats, and finds spotted and striped cats are harder to handle.

The Out of Africa Wildlife Park at Fountain Hills, Arizona, is an unusual wildlife exhibit that offers a somewhat different perspective on the cougar. Co-owners Dean and Bobbi Harrison maintain more than twenty-five species of mammals, reptiles, and birds in a compound that attracts more than one hundred thousand visitors a year. Animals are both on display and in performance. In addition to white tigers, tigers, lions, leopards, jaguars, a caracal, servals, and bobcats, the Harrisons also have five cougars.

Savanna when she was eight years old. All the cages at Prairie Wind Wild Animal Refuge were spacious and clean and the animals were all in apparent good health.

Coe expressing his displeasure at the author's intrusion into his assigned habitation at the Prairie Wind refuge. In the background is Shiloh, a male aged two and a half years.

Bobbi Harrison and the author at the Harrisons' Out of Africa Wildlife Park, Fountain Hills, Arizona. Although not native to Africa, five cougars were on display at Out of Africa, but only one of them actually participated in the park's wide variety of animal performances.

A cougar is used in a "show" with two bears and three wolves. The objective of this mixed-species performance is to demonstrate that trained animals of different species can get along together. Although in the performances that I witnessed the cougar seemed somewhat diffident or aloof, I was told that on occasion they have been able to get a cougar to participate more actively with the wolves. There were some obvious levels of human discomfort, however, in working with the cougars. The reasons for this will be discussed in chapter 8, "Danger to Humans."

Under captive conditions, it seems that the behavior of any wild species of animal is affected not only by its environment but also by its day-to-day routine. Additionally, we should expect genetic influences—that is, instinctive behavioral patterns—to exert at least moderate impact upon captive animals. Noted outdoorsman Clyde Ormond described an incident of instinctive behavior on the part of a captive yearling cougar that could have led to serious injury for Ormond's wife. In 1954, the Ormonds and four other couples on a fishing and floating excursion along the Middle Fork of the Salmon River in Idaho camped overnight near a ranch that boasted ownership of a "pet" cougar. The party decided to visit the ranch. The cougar was a male, approximately a year old, that had been caught as a kitten and had since been kept at the ranch. The cat was secured by a collar and chain to a wire, one hundred yards long, that permitted it access to the ranch's large lawn, which had a railing around it. After obtaining permission from the ranch owners to touch the cougar, Ormand's wife reached down and began to stroke the cat. Clyde Ormand describes what followed (Ormond 1958, 205):

> Quick as a flash, [the cougar] had her hand into its mouth, with the wicked teeth on either side. In the same movement, it rolled over on its back, doubled all feet into a knot under her hand, and manifested all the symptoms of a cat fighting an enemy.
>
> "Don't pull back!" the owner commanded suddenly. "Don't resist!" My wife let the cougar have her hand, limp. He didn't bite deeply, but let her hand go, as the owner scolded him. I'm positive that, had she resisted at all, her hand would have been torn to pieces.
>
> In the realization that we'd done a foolish thing, and wondering just how to make the cat let go, should he decide to maul her hand, I'd bent over the railing in an effort to get at him, if necessary.
>
> In a flash, too sudden to thwart, the cat let go of her hand, and in the same movement had my red jacket. He jerked it from over my arm, had it on top of himself as he rolled back upon the ground, and, in a series of snarls and teeth, tried to tear it to pieces. Only the beating of the cat with the owner's denim coat made him let go, and scamper off to the other end of the wire tether.
>
> It didn't dawn on me why the young cat had let go of flesh to take that woolen jacket until later. Then I remembered. The autumn before, I'd worn that jacket deer-hunting, and had actually had it on while dressing a deer. Enough of the dried blood, or scent, had remained to turn that young cat into a frenzied, instinctive killer.

Although Ormand's later assessment of what may have triggered the cougar's attack on his wife is questionable, the attack certainly does suggest an action of instinctive behavior.

In *Love Affair with a Cougar*, Lyn Hancock affectionately reminisces about her experiences with five cougar kittens that briefly shared her home and her life before those involved went their separate ways. In spite of these animals receiving almost constant supervision and being treated with caution, instinctive behavior on the part of the cats led to two incidents of human injury. Hancock, although reluctant to suggest that cougars, whether captive or free, are a potential danger to humans, acknowledges that establishing eye contact with a cougar may not be a smart thing to do. After relating several occasions where her young cougars had acted aggressively when eye contact was made, she quotes the comments of Gary Bogue, a researcher from the Alexander Lindsey Museum in Walnut Creek, California, who was raising cougars and observing their behavior (Hancock 1978, 76):

This is a case where looks can kill. I started things out by staring at a sleeping kitten. They seem to sense your eyes. One eye quickly opens, it makes hard contact with yours, then suddenly the cat is up, crouched and ready for the game. It looks straight into your eyes. Only you really don't want to play, so you break contact and glance away. The cat simply walks around to the side you are facing and you can actually feel those eyes trying to pull yours down to meet them.

One time I had trouble trying to introduce a young female cougar to a male. Up till then he had at least given me some grudging respect, but when I brought in the female cat he seemed furious with me. Instead of instantly charging me he tried to make eye contact. But man, oh man, let me tell you this wasn't any little old cub game. He tried everything short of running up and grabbing my face to get me to look him in the eye. I looked up at the sky . . . over at the house . . . at a tree . . . the grass . . . bushes . . . anything. The cat's whole body was in a tense, ready-to-attack position. Every move I made, his head swiveled and followed. I finally even moved carefully within the restrictions of his chain, approaching as close as ten feet, close enough so I couldn't have gotten away. But even with his intense dislike at that moment he respected my not making eye contact with him. Incredible! Finally I withdrew beyond the end of his chain and made eye contact with him. Instantly he visibly tensed all over, his hind feet quickly moving under his body in readiness, the black tip of his tail flicking back and forth. His glance sent hot and cold flashes down my back. It was a moment of utter fear for me. I'd never felt a thing like that in my life and I never want to feel it again. I couldn't help myself. I broke eye contact. He didn't charge. He knew I was far beyond the limits of his chain. But to the last day we had him, I couldn't trust myself within his range.

An animal in captivity is subject to enormous pressures: they can't run, they can't hide, and one thoughtless human action can induce an attack. James

Alldis, former head keeper of the London Zoo, considered a large male cougar, Sabre, to be a special friend of his, but since the cougar had lost whatever fear he may have had of humans, he presented problems in handling. On one occasion he injured himself in an attempt to seize his keeper and thereafter was affected with a slight limp (1973, 49–50). His temper cooled over time but he still demonstrated rather strong likes and dislikes. Although Sabre showed little tolerance for other zoo animals, he readily accepted a female cougar in his cage and mated with her twice prior to his death at the age of sixteen.

In their book *Cougar—Ghost of the Rockies*, Karen McCall and Jim Dutcher described an observational research project in Idaho that involved placing a recently bred captive three-year-old female cougar in a five-acre fenced enclosure. Three kittens were soon born to the female cougar. When the kittens had reached the age of adolescence, one of the small cats escaped the fenced enclosure, only to be promptly killed by a wild adult male cougar that happened to be nearby. In accordance with the original design of the research project, the remaining two kittens were eventually released to the wild. However, it was not appropriate to release the adult female as she had become too familiar with humans and would either become an easy target for the guns of hunters or present a threat to human life.

The McCall/Dutcher research project crew had named the adult female Catrina, and although they had obviously grown attached to this cougar, they maintained a healthy respect for her and her capability and willingness to inflict serious injury on team members. One such incident involved an attack on cameraman Franz Camenzind (1992, 127–28):

> Her increasingly erratic behavior was testimony to these fears. She stalked the crew more frequently and responded less submissively to our shouts of 'No!' when she tried to jump on one of us. . . . Regardless of the reasons for Catrina's dangerous behavior, she continued to attack at unexpected times. The most serious attack was on my second cameraman Franz Camerzind, just two evenings before we released the cubs. We had closed Catrina in the small pen during a filming session so we could work without worrying about her antics. After completing our work, Jake released her. She dashed down to the pond, then back up the hill, stopping suddenly by my side. After batting her paw at me and curiously gnawing on Franz' leg, she raced away. I knew she was acting up and told everyone to cautiously head for the gate. Franz backed about ten yards off the trail, positioning himself downhill to film if she charged us. Catrina's view of him must have been fragmented by bushes

or the angle of the sun. Sparked by his motion, she raced toward Franz and sprang through the air, knocking him and the Arriflex to the ground. She grasped his neck and head in her jaws and wrapped her forelegs around his torso. I ran to Franz, booted Catrina once, and she backed off. She had lanced Franz' skull with a sharp-pointed canine tooth and ripped his ear. His body was covered with claw marks. Catrina's attack was triggered by Franz' distance from the rest of the crew and his quick movements that she was unable to decipher. She certainly had no fear of him nor any of us as a wild cougar would.

Obviously there are worlds of differences between the behavioral attributes of captive and wild animals. Most of us, of course, would probably never see one of the more elusive and clandestine animals such as the cougar unless it was being held captive. Observing one of these heavily muscled and superbly graceful caged cats stoically accepting its future as a captive may arouse in humans feelings of pity and compassion. But if we may look at it from the cougar's standpoint, the human pity is a misspent emotion; although absolute freedom certainly has its values, the captive cougar lives a far more comfortable and longer life than its free-roaming relatives. Moreover, captive cougars also tend to overcome the instinctive reactions of apprehension and fear they are believed to hold for humans. Although it is often claimed that captive cougars have demonstrated some level of affection for their keepers, it is to be noted that when the cougar reaches adulthood, it is usually, because of its unpredictability, disposed of or maintained in secure confinement.

In order to avoid any appearance of incongruity, I here must make clear that in describing the following characteristics and traits of the cougar, I have identified only general expectations with regard to the noncaptive animal; these characteristics may, of course, be equally applicable, in some instances, to the captive animal.

THE COUGAR AND ITS COLOR

When in 1771 Carl Linnaeus classified the one race of cougar, *Felis concolor*, "cat of one color," he would have been unaware that identification of the *F. concolor* subspecies eventually would become an ongoing process. In terms of the total species, the "one color" aspect is not correct, but it is generally apropos if we consider only the individual cat. In other words, except as kittens, cougars are not mottled, or striped; they only come plain in color. However, just as the so-called black bear can come in diverse hues from coal black to straw brown, *F. concolor's* pelage comes in an assortment of subtle and varying shades. Cougars are mostly described as being red, brown, gray, buff, cinnamon, or even black, while the ears and tip of the tail are said to be normally either dark brown or black. On the underside of the cougar, the coloration is generally whitish, including the muzzle, chin, throat, rump, and from the rump mid-way to the foot on the interior sections of the back legs. Erudite, or more detail-orientated, observers will identify cougar color more precisely as reddish-fawn, terra cotta, grizzled gray, tawny brown, and so forth.

At birth, cougar kittens have distinct dark brown to blackish spots or blotches arranged in an irregular fashion on their bodies, and quite visible streaks or stripes of a similar darker pelage ringing the tail. The spotting and rings begin to fade by two months of age, and when the kitten is aged around eight months it will then shed its kitten fur; thereafter, the blotches and stripes are hardly visible. By the age of one year, the cougar's youthful markings generally will be completely gone.

Although there is a wide variety in coloration, the pelage of the cougar often tends to evolve toward a color that is most compatible with the geographical area in which the animal lives and with that area's primary cougar prey. Thus, in some areas one color would be predominant, but with minor variation. It is still possible that very rare specimens of albino or black cougars will turn up from time to time, but a cougar pelage that features the quite simple gray, reddish, or brown hues are what we normally expect to see.

THE SIZE OF COUGARS

An adult cougar can vary as much in body mass from its peers as can specimens of any other mammalian species. It has been commonly accepted that the largest North American cougar ever killed in the wild was taken by J. R. Patterson, a government hunter of animal predators, near Hillside, Arizona, in March 1917. This cougar, a male that weighed 276 pounds even after the intestines had been removed, measured eight feet, seven and three-quarter inches from the tip of his nose to the tip of his tail. Formerly, it is asserted, cougars that inhabited eastern North America may have been "up to nine feet

Cougar kittens retain their spots until they are about eight months old, when they shed their soft kitten fur and the spots and tail rings become almost invisible. The kitten shown is a mounted specimen in the Denver Museum of Natural History.

long and 280 pounds in weight" (Wright 1972, 113). Claims of cougar hides that after measurement were anywhere from eleven to thirteen feet long are usually the results of enthusiastic and vigorous hide stretching. Famous cougar hunter Ben Lilly suggested that "the fresh hide of a full-grown male lion will stretch about three feet" (Dobie 1950, 186). Perhaps it is for these and associated reasons that the Boone and Crockett Club, which lists North American big-game records, ranks cougar size by the length of skull (without lower jaw) and greatest skull width—figures that mean little to most people since it is difficult to visualize total mass of an animal based upon skull size, and particularly since a cougar's head proportionately is small in relation to body size. In *Nooksack Tales and Trails*, P. R. Jeffcott cites the following (1949, 340):

> A probable record of all time in the country in hi-as pus-pus (big cat) stalking, was the record of two "Jam" (Ferndale) hunters as recorded in the "Bellingham Bay Mail" in October, 1874. The two nimrods, Messrs [D. E.] Follett and [B. J.] Haward were credited with having killed a cougar of momentous size. It was a typical mountain lion and, according to the report, tipped the scale at four hundred pounds. In ridding the Mt. View country of that giant predatory beast, they proved themselves public benefactors.

If we consider average documented size for the species, an adult male would weigh approximately 140 pounds and a female about 30 percent less, or about 100 pounds. The length, from tip of the nose to tip of the tail (with hide still on the cat), would be around 7 feet for an adult male and 6.3 feet for an adult female. This average takes into account the cougars of the north and northwest and those found in the southwestern states of Colorado, Utah, and Arizona, which tend to be larger than those found in other locations. It is interesting to note that the captive cougar, which generally has all the food it needs at its disposal, does not as a rule reach other than average size. Cougars in the wild will go though periods of feast and famine; as a result, the truly large and the diminutive are those cougars that roam the wild and depend upon availability of prey and hunting skill.

THE COUGAR'S PHYSICAL CHARACTERISTICS

Appearance

Perhaps the most striking physical oddity of the cougar is the size and shape of its head, relative to the rest of its body. The head is rounded, with a short muzzle and features that are almost like those of a house cat. According to a number of past recorded cranial measurements, the length of the skull for an adult male cougar can range between 6.8 and 9.3 inches, and the width between 4.9 and 6.4 inches. In body weight, the cougar is only slightly smaller than the jaguar, or approximately the same size as the leopard, yet the skull size of the cougar is significantly smaller than both of these other cats. The skull of the average adult male jaguar, for example, will be approximately 40 percent larger than that of the average adult male cougar.

The adult male cougar's tail is quite long, usually measuring between 27 and 38 inches in length for an adult, or approximately one-half the length of its body from nose to terminus at the root of the tail. This tail length is also one of the cougar's distinguishing characteristics: it is long enough to create a drag mark when the cougar is traveling on snow.

The stature of the cougar's heavily muscled and blocky forequarters is in marked contrast to its long-limbed and imposing hindquarters, offering a body silhouette somewhat suggestive of that of a cheetah on steroids. The shoulder height of the adult male cougar will often exceed 28 inches, and its hindquarters may be as much as 2 inches higher. These powerful leg muscles can propel the cat through levels of physical achievement that seem near miraculous. Bounding leaps of more than twenty feet are rather common, and in cases where the cougar pounced from some height, springs of more than forty feet have been recorded. Stanley P. Young indicated that he knew of one cougar startled by a camera flash that jumped thirteen feet in reflex action from simply a normal stance (1946, 94).

The Cougar's Speed

Like most cats, the cougar is capable of great speed for short distances, but it tires quickly and, because of its limited lung capacity, requires time to catch its breath before it can resume further exhaustive activity. Since the cougar has not been accurately clocked, it is not possible to determine its maximum acceleration potential, but most people who have seen a cougar in full run or participated in a cougar hunt using dogs agree that the cougar is far faster than dogs for short distances; hunters also say that the cougar is at least equal to, if not faster than, a horse over such distances. This would place the sprinting speed capability of a cougar somewhere between 40 and 55 miles per hour. Unfortunately for the cougar, it can keep up such near-maximum bursts of speed for distances of only two hundred to three hundred feet, and never for more than one-quarter of a mile. For this reason, the cougar is easily treed by dogs.

Power and Strength

In a selective synopsis of North American Indian myths and legends, Rose A. Palmer mentions a California tribe, the Karok, that passed on to succeeding generations a folk tale describing how the cougar acquired its great power (1944, 236–38). This "Fable of the Animals," recounts how the world and all creatures were made by Kareya, the supreme being. Since all the animals were alike in power, and it was necessary to determine which should be food to others and to man, man was given the task of making bows and arrows and of giving the longest weapons to the beast that should have the most power and the shortest to the one that should have the least. The coyote, who was considered by the Karok to be the most cunning creature, planned to stay awake the night before the weapons were to be handed out, so that he would be the first to arrive and be able to select the longest. But his scheme failed because coyote finally dropped off to sleep, awakening only after all the other animals. The coyote was then the last to arrive and accordingly received the smallest bow. The longest bow was given to the cougar, so he had the greatest power of all. The bear was given the second largest bow, becoming thereby second only in power to the cougar.

The strength of the cougar is certainly legendary. Many tales, besides Indian legends, have been told and retold over the years about the phenomenal power of this elusive cat of the American wilderness. It is well documented that a cougar can kill an animal that outweighs it by more than five hundred pounds, and then move the carcass some considerable distance prior to feeding. An article by Will F. Evans in *Outdoor Life* (1922, 344–45) described one such incident. Evans's dad, who was a small cattle rancher in Texas in the 1880s, discovered the carcass of a valuable two-year-old heifer, her head twisted under her, wedged into a hole from which one of the springs serving the ranch flowed. Although the rancher was a large man, he was unable to move the six-hundred-pound cow and went back to the ranchhouse to get a team of horses. Unable to return until the following day, he then found the heifer gone and an abundance of claw prints indicating that a large cat had taken the heifer. Suspecting that an escaped African lion might be the beast responsible, he cautiously followed drag marks up the side of a nearby mountainside, shortly finding the body of the partially eaten heifer. Wisely, he decided to return to the ranch for a gun and his dogs. The dogs easily tracked and subsequently treed the cat, which proved to be not a lion but a large cougar.

Young and Goldman (1946, 60–61) cite numerous instances, involving both males and females, in which a cougar, after making a kill, evidently carried the victim on its back for some distance while holding the body firmly in place with its teeth. The cougar has such remarkable dexterity, superb muscular ability, and swift reactions that no anecdotal account of cougar accomplishment in this area can be easily dismissed.

Curiosity and Playfulness

There is an old aphorism stating that "curiosity killed the cat," but there is no evidence that the cougar's penchant for inquisitiveness has brought it harm.

Human activity in particular, for one reason or another, seems to trigger an irrepressible curiosity on the part of the cougar. Michael Jenkinson mentions an incident involving a cougar trailing him and his companion for four miles, and he concludes his tale by stating: "But as is the case with the vast majority of people who have been trailed by cougars, our cat was merely curious and meant us no harm" (1980, 93). The annals of most sporting magazines and journals are replete with stories of wilderness travelers being followed by cougars, without resultant harm. One of the better stories is provided by Enos A. Mills, nature guide par excellence (1932, 46–47):

> Looking back along the line of my ski tracks, I saw a mountain lion leisurely cross from east to west. Apparently she had come up out of the woods for mad play and slaughter among the unfortunate snowbound folk of the summit. She stopped at my tracks for an interested look, turned her head, and glanced back along the way I had come. Then her eyes appeared to follow my tracks to the boulder pile from behind which I was then looking.
>
> Playfully bouncing off the snow, she struck into my ski prints with one forepaw, lightly as a kitten. Then she dived into them, pretended to pick up something between her forepaws, reared, and with a swing tossed it into the air. Then her playful mood changed and she started on across the Divide. After several steps she stopped, looking back as if she had forgotten something but was a little too lazy to retrace her steps. But finally she came back. She walked along my ski tracks for a few steps, then began to romp, now and then making a great leap forward, and rolled and struck about with the pretence of worrying something she had captured. She repeated this pantomime a few times, and then, as if suddenly remembering her original plan of action, again walked westward. Arriving at the summit she hesitated, and when I saw her last she was calmly surveying the scenes far below.

Tracks and Scat

The cougar has four toes on each rear leg and five on each foreleg. The fifth toe on the forelegs is a semifunctional dewclaw located in an inner-rear location slightly above the foot proper, and thus it will never touch the ground or leave a tracking indentation. The prominent impressions of a cougar foottrack are a bilobial lead and trilobial trailing heel pad and four toes arranged asymmetrically above the pad. The front foot is somewhat larger than the rear and will accordingly leave a larger impression upon the trail surface, but the most distinctive difference in appearance will be found through examination of

FRONT FOOT   REAR FOOT

Drawing of front and rear cougar footprints. The prints are not to scale. Depending on the age and size of the animal, front tracks can range from two and a half to four inches in width, and slightly less in length. The rear track is usually smaller. The wide trilobed plantar pad is distinctive of the cougar. Although claw marks are not usually present, if the cat is moving at a rapid pace or moving uphill, they may now and then show. If the cougar is simply walking, the stride between the front and rear tracks may average about twenty-four inches, but like the size of the pad marks, stride is dependant on the size of the cat. The straddle (distance between the left and right leg units) can be up to twelve inches.

heel-pad markings. The heel pad impression made by a rear foot is decidedly smaller than that of the front, but its trilobial image is more defined.

Like all cats, the cougar's toes are covered with hair, or fur, providing a wider surface padding and contributing to the separation between toes, and between toes and heel pad. The toes themselves have distinguishing characteristics; hence, it is possible, through examination of a well-defined impression, to determine precisely which foot made the track mark. If the trail surface is not sufficiently malleable to hold tracking features, such as the trilobing trailing edge of the heel pad, impressions will not be clear and it may be necessary to follow the track for some distance before a more distinct footprint can be inspected.

It is often assumed that the absence of nail or claw marks indicates that a track was made by a cat with retractable claws, but a number of canines have significantly worn or severely cut nails that leave no markings. Conversely, if the going is particularly tough or slippery, a cougar may use its claws to obtain additional purchase. However, should this occur, the cougar claw marks will appear in its track as slits rather than as the blunt impressions that are normally left by canine nails. The typical canine track would also show a heel pad with two lobes on the trailing edge and toes nearly of the same size, arranged symmetrically, with little difference in size between the front and rear feet.

In snow, the cougar's long tail can create an unmistakable drag mark that could appear on either side of the foot prints, usually in alternating order. This feature is particularly helpful in distinguishing cougar tracks from those of a large bobcat.

There actually is, believe it or not, a branch of science, referred to as scatology, that is devoted to the study of feces and fossil excrement, and in tracking a cougar, or learning about the habits or recent history of such an animal, the observation of scat does in fact have considerable significance. Most cats will attempt to cover their droppings by scraping or scratching up the surrounding ground material. Along cougar trails, and often near their kills, fecal materials and urine can be found in "scratch hills," or litter heaps, that can be as large as six inches high and six inches wide. Poking through such markers can yield a wealth of information about the cougar's possible size, how long ago it was at the site, and what it may have eaten.

For the cougar, these scratch hills or scrape marks are important informational signposts; they can be used to identify territorial boundaries, notify potential sexual partners of availability, or warn off interlopers. We can readily see examples of the animal information-exchange process in the activity of domestic dogs and cats: they regularly search for fragrances from their contemporaries.

Vocal Communication

An important item in the list of cougar attributes and characteristics is its method of and the degree of its vocalization. Communication in the animal kingdom embraces individual actions and behaviors as well as a creature's capacity to convey information to others of its species in a language expressed through sound. Of the assortment of sounds in the cougar's vocal repertoire, it is the scream that generates the most human attention.

Because the cougar conducts itself in what seems to us to be a sinister and surreptitious manner, New World explorers knew very little about its true habits and behaviors, and they often embellished the few and fleeting encounters that they did have. Thomas J. Farnham, in describing some of the more exciting events experienced during his travels through Oregon Territory in 1839 (Thwaites 1966, vol. 28: 226), recorded hearing the scream of a cougar as follows: "About the middle of the night the panthers on the mountain gave us a specimen of their growling capacities. It was a hideous noise: deep and broken by the most unearthly screams! They were gathering for prey; for our horses and ourselves. We drove up the animals, however, tied them near the camp, built a large and bright fire, and slept till daylight." John K. Townsend, who published a narrative of his experiences during 1833 and 1834 while traveling across the Rocky Mountains to the Columbia River (Thwaites 1966, vol. 21: 274), was equally dramatic and fanciful in describing what he presumed was the cry of a cougar: "Early this morning, a large panther was seen prowling around our camp, and the hallooing of last night was explained. It was the dismal, distressing yell by which this animal entices its prey, until pity or curiosity induces it to approach to its destruction. The panther is said to inhabit these forests in considerable numbers, and has not infrequently been known to kill the horses of a camp. He has seldom the temerity to attack a man, unless sorely pressed by hunger, or infuriated by wounds."

Surprisingly, a number of usually otherwise well-versed wildlife experts held the opinion that the cougar did not scream, and in fact was given to little, if any, vocalization. John James Audubon and John Bachman (*Viviparous Quadrupeds of North America*), for example, offered the following pronouncement regarding the cougar and the sounds it was said to make (Cahalane 1968, 128):

> The tales related of the cry of the Cougar in the forest in imitation of the call of a lost traveller, or the cry of a child, must be received with much caution, and may in many of their exaggerations be set down as vulgar errors. In a state of captivity, we have never heard the male uttering any other note than a low growl; the female, however, we have frequently heard uttering a kind of mewing like that of a cat. . . . All the males, however, of the cat kind, at the season when the sexes seek each other, emit remarkable and startling cries as is evidenced by the common cat, in what is denominated caterwauling. . . . The cries, however, to which persons have from time to time directed our attention, as belonging to the Cougar, we were well convinced were uttered by other animals.

The noted English naturalist and scientist Charles Darwin in describing the puma [cougar] wrote: "It is a very silent animal, uttering no cry, even when wounded, and only rarely during the breeding season" (True 1889, 605).

Victor H. Calahane, former chief biologist of the U.S. National Park Service, while keeping an open mind on the subject of the cougar scream, points out that Jay Bruce, perhaps one of the most renowned and experienced of cougar hunters, had never heard a cougar scream (1961, 268). Calahane also indicated, however, that he had heard a female cougar in the Washington Zoo shriek repeatedly on several occasions, but he qualifies this observation by stating: "Most of the screams attributed to the mountain lion prove, on investigation, to come from a lovelorn bobcat or from various species of owls. . . . A number of times in the Chiricahua Mountains of Arizona, I have heard screams that seemed to sound exactly like those of the lion in the zoo. But not being face to face with the animal at the time, I suppose I should not swear that they were mountain lion screams" (1961, 269).

It was not only certain so-called wildlife "experts" that had expressed the belief that cougars did not issue the scream or cry that they were being given credit for. *Outdoor Life* devoted a complete article to "The Cry of the Mountain Lion," concluding that it "doesn't cry nearly so often as some people would have us believe" (Frost 1912, 143–44). W. E. Humphrey wrote an article for *Outdoor Life* (April, 1928, 102) in which he stated that Herbert H. Pidcock, a noted cougar hunter from Vancouver Island, B.C., advised him that he had "never heard the cry or scream of the cougar and does not believe that it makes any such noise. He thinks this is one of the fictions that have grown up around this animal." To counter several articles that it had previously published suggesting that a cougar doesn't scream, *Outdoor Life* then printed one that stated "I Heard a Cougar Scream" (Davis 1935, 39, 63, 73). According to J. Frank Dobie, even the much acclaimed bear and cougar hunter Ben Lilly had never heard a cougar scream (1950, 185).

Jerry A. Lewis *(The Longwalkers)* claims to have "lived in cougar country all my life . . . and never heard a cougar scream"; but, he says, he still believes that it happens (1995, 275). Notwithstanding those few who may still harbor doubts regarding the cougar's ability to initiate its famed scream, the extent of testimony and sheer number of eyewitnesses (McCabe 1949, 305–6) to the contrary have, to my mind, clearly erased the controversy.

One sound that the cougar cannot make is the resounding roar of the lion, tiger, leopard, or jaguar. However, the cougar is capable of issuing a number of other vocal sounds in addition to a scream. The feline hiss is rather common, along with a low-pitched growl and a soft mewing tone. These noises, along with just plain caterwauling, are similar to what may be expected from a house cat. Since the cougar can weigh more than twenty times the weight of a house cat, these sounds are, as is to be expected, much louder than the common cat's. Like the house cat, the cougar can, and does, purr. And, also as with its diminutive cousin, the purring is seemingly a natural reaction that denotes enjoyment or satisfaction.

When calling its young, a mother cougar emits a chirp-like whistle, which is usually responded to in the same way by the kittens. When I was visiting Mike Jurich at his Prairie Wind Wild Animal Park, he made this chirping sound and it was immediately responded to by at least one of the three yearling cougars that were born at the refuge. Whenever I hear the chirping or whistling sound that a cougar can make, it reminds me of a comparable vocalization that is commonly made by the cheetah. It is interesting that these two cats are analogous in so many respects, but so vastly different in others.

LIFE SPAN

I have no way to prove it, but it seems rather doubtful that any wild cougar has died peacefully in its sleep. Principal causes of cougar death are (1) starvation, (2) injuries and accidents, (3) predation of young by other animals, (4) predation of adults by humans, (5) territorial combat with other cougars, and (6) parasites, rabies, and other diseases. Although it has been reported that a few cougars have lived as long as eighteen years in the wild, life span only infrequently exceeds ten years.

Certain zoologists, a few writers of natural history, and some strongly opinionated cougar hunters are of the belief that cougars in the wild live as long as, or perhaps longer than, those in captivity. The evidence, however, does not support this contention. Maurice Hornocker began his study of cougars in January 1963. He began by marking fourteen animals within a hundred miles of Missoula, Montana. By spring, he reported that most of the fourteen had been shot by hunters (1992, 54). Subsequent experiences in New Mexico and Idaho confirmed the current fragility of cougar life in the wild. Captive cougars, on the other hand, while more receptive to disease, definitely are recipients of far better care; consequently their life span can be as long as twenty or twenty-five years.

BREEDING AND FAMILY LIFE

The female cougar is usually ready to breed when she reaches two and one-half years of age. The male will become sexually active at about the same time, or perhaps a little later than the female. All of the so-called superior animals follow certain seasonal procreative rhythms, but the female cougar does not really have a specific breeding season and mating can occur at any time. The female is in estrus for approximately nine days, and during this period any available male cougar will compete for her favor. An interesting observation with respect to the cougar breeding cycle was mentioned by Mike Jurich of Prairie Wind Wild Animal Refuge. Mike had an adult female cougar that had recently completed her estrus period, and not more than a week later it became necessary to house an adult male cougar tempoarily in her cage. The male was not kept in the female's cage for more than three days. Mike claims that the female cougar apparently returned to an estrus condition almost immediately. The pair quickly mated, as evidenced three months later by three newborn kittens.

A female in estrus can attract a number of aspiring suitors. They will actively compete for this mating opportunity, and as a result some of the males may be seriously injured. The mating relationship can last for as long as two weeks, or it can be even shorter. When the male departs, the female may elect to mate again with a new partner should the opportunity present itself.

In its wild state, the female cougar will give birth to from one to five kittens, ninety to ninety-six days after a successful copulation. Because the cougar is not considered to be a member of the *Panthera* species (the great cats that have the ability to "roar") its offspring are called kittens rather than cubs. Immediately after the young are born, the female will again start an estrus cycle, with the usual nine-day period. If this condition should attract a male near to the den site, it could lead to the death of the kittens. The adult male would have no compunction about eating all of the new arrivals. After mating takes place, the male assumes no further role. The female becomes totally responsible for the care of the young.

The selected den site can be as crude as a simple bed within brush or ground cover or be as formidable as a rocky crevasse. The female usually keeps the den neat and clean and exercises extraordinary care in maintaining its secrecy and concealment.

Cougar kittens can weigh up to one pound at birth, but if more than two or three kittens are born alive in the same litter, their weight could be as little as eight ounces. They immediately begin to nurse and continue to do so until they are discouraged by the mother from this practice. This usually occurs when the kittens are from five to six weeks of age. Although meat soon becomes the staple diet for the young cougar, scatological analysis and review of cougar stomach contents reveal that berries, some form of vegetation, and even insects are occasionally eaten. The kittens usually stay with their mother for at least a year, sometimes longer, but unless they leave on their own by the time they reach maturity, they will typically end up being driven off by one of the mother's new sexual partners.

Because it is the nature of carnivores to establish territorial boundaries that exclude others of their species, young cougars striking out on their own usually find themselves in a constant travel status until locating a suitable unoccupied area. In many instances this will be an area where the former cougar occupant has been killed. In the cougar world, territorial possession is widely accepted as being nine-tenths of the law, so disputes are mutually avoided wherever possible.

HUNTING AND PREY

Within any given area of cougar habitat, there may be any number of animal species that are, or can become, acceptable prey for resident cougars. The main food source is deer herds, which the cougar will follow throughout his or her territory. This does not mean that other animals do not, or could not, become victims, because in circumstances of hunger a cougar will basically eat anything. Young and Goldman (1946, 127) compiled a listing of the stomach contents of cougars reported by Fish and Wildlife Service hunters. These reports were assembled from field and laboratory examinations of cougars that were taken throughout the western United States for a five-year period, from 1918 to 1922. Deer meat was found most often (approximately 48 percent of the time) but beef came out a close second (37 percent). Other food items identified were horse, sheep or goat, elk, bait, vegetation, pork, antelope, rabbit, ground squirrel, and carrion. It is presumed that if such a listing could be made today, the food items would reflect a similar variety of diet, but those cougars taken near urban areas would also be found to be eating domestic pets.

The cougar has a voracious appetite and can consume huge quantities of meat at one meal. It will usually return to the kill a number of times as long as the meat is still reasonably fresh. For this reason, large animals are the cougar's first choice, and since a healthy cougar has extraordinary killing powers, the size of the prey gives it but little pause. Estimates of the number of deer that an average cougar kills in a year range from as low as five to a high of one hundred, but this seems dependant upon the quantity and quality of other game available. In captivity, a male cougar will eat anywhere from three to ten pounds of meat a day, depending on its size and occasionally on the time of year; a captive female eats somewhat less, but her activity and needs are considerably less than that of a cougar that has to expend energy and effort to provide for itself.

The cougar is not necessarily the frugal conservator, taking only what is actually needed or required for it to exist comfortably. It can also become a ruthless killer, consumed with destructive passion. Reports by stockmen of wholesale slaughters of domestic animals were once quite common. One unforgettable incident mentioned by Young and Goldman occurred in Glade Park, Colorado more than seventy-five years ago. A cougar entered a herd of bedding ewes and during a single night killed 192 of them (1946, 142). Durward Allen (1962, 233), wishing to capture the essence of the thoughts of a typical rancher and outdoorsman of the early 1900s, quoted Theodore Roosevelt's description of a cougar treed on the rim of the Grand Canyon in 1913: "The big horse-killing cat, the destroyer of the deer, the lord of stealthy murder, facing his doom with a heart both craven and cruel" (1913, 264).

Some writers, however—to my mind naive individuals—espouse the Pollyanna viewpoint that the cougar kills only what it needs. To quote one, the cougar "never kills more than he can eat. Once he has killed a roe deer or stag [the author was referring to our white-tail deer and elk], he remains with the booty until he has eaten the last remnants" (Sletholt 1975, 47). Even Gary Turbak suggested that "if the kill is left undisturbed, the cat *may* continue to feed on the carcass until almost nothing is left" (1986, 21). Turbak, who expressed little regard for the cougar as a potential threat to human life and limb, after citing an incident of a cougar attacking a human being advised his readers: "Incidents like these are rare aberrations in the cougar's otherwise secretive lifestyle. Most people now know that they have nothing to fear from the great cat" (1986, 29). Cougars thus seemingly kill on an opportunity basis; if they are hungry and prey is immediately available, they will attempt to kill

and eat from this immediate quarry; failing this, they will go back to the remains of an earlier kill.

One tale that I particularly like and that may throw light on the cougar's
hunting habits comes from Ben East, who was senior field editor for *Outdoor
Life* for many years and published an astonishing number of true-life wilderness adventures. In this story (1960, 223–37) East chronicled a cougar hunt
in Montana involving cougar hunter Roy Murray. Murray began tracking this
particular cat one cold February day, traveling on horseback. He took with
him only one dog. He soon found the cougar's first kill, a two-point buck.
Nothing had been eaten but the tastier part of the entrails. Camping out,
Murray came upon a second kill the next day, a big doe. The cat had eaten
only the liver and a few odds and ends. Camping out again the second night,
the following morning Murray came upon the cougar's third kill, a six-point
buck mule deer. After a third night's camp, Murray found the cougar's fourth
kill, a big cow elk. The elk had a calf, but the cougar didn't molest the calf; it
just ate the liver of the cow elk. Following his fourth night out, he discovered
the cougar's fifth kill, a yearling cow elk. Again the cat ate only the liver. Later
this same day, the cat killed a yearling steer, and again ate only the liver—this
time beef liver. Murray stayed out another night and in the morning came
upon the next kill, a yearling mule deer, a doe. After playing with the deer a
while, the cat eventually killed her and ate the liver and part of her ham. Murray stayed out one more night and the next morning found a calf elk that had
just been killed; the cat again had eaten only the liver. Following the fresh trail,
Murray's dog startled a large male cougar from a thicket and the cat was subsequently cornered on a slab of rock and quickly shot. Nearby, Murray found
the carcass of yet another animal the cougar had killed that day—a two-year-
old elk; the cougar had eaten only the elk's liver.

A final measure of testimony with respect to the cougar's ability and nature as a hunter is provided by Enos A. Mills, veteran wilderness prowler and
environmentalist: "The mountain lion is something of a game hog and an epicure. He prefers warm blood for every meal, and is very wasteful. I have much
evidence against him; his worst one-day record that I have shows five tragedies.
In this time he killed a mountain sheep, a fawn, a grouse, a rabbit, and a porcupine; and as if this were not enough, he was about to kill another sheep
when a dark object on snowshoes shot down the slope near by and disturbed
him" (1909, 9–10). Mills also mentions his discovery of the carcasses of a
whole herd of deer, nine in number, that had been killed by a single cougar

operating in deep snow. He notes that the cougar "had eaten but little of their flesh" (1915, 265).

There is no general agreement by cougar experts with respect to prey selection on the part of the cougar. Some experts say that the cougar will take only the sick, the old, or the very young because these animals are the easiest to catch and kill. Others, of equal credibility, maintain that the cougar will take whatever animal presents itself as the more convenient of choices, regardless of age or condition. And still others take a more malevolent posture, suggesting that the cougar will take only the finest and best—particularly if it happens to be a prize domestic animal. I tend to agree with those who think that, lacking a choice, a hungry cougar will take whatever prey is convenient, but that if choice presents itself, the cougar will take what appears to be the less formidable prey.

The cougar kills by stalking as well as by ambush. Its killing technique has been well defined and abundantly documented. Small prey are dispatched with a blow or blows from its paws. Large prey are usually hit high on the shoulder and neck with a great deal of force, and the cougar will sink its long canine teeth into the back of the neck or the base of the skull. The animal usually dies from catastrophic damage to the spinal cord, either from the force of the impact and its fall to the ground or by the bite. Depending upon the actual size of the prey animal compared with that of the cougar, death can occur quickly or, in some instances, after a short, but limited, struggle. Should this attack method fail to kill the prey promptly, the cougar may move to grasp the throat in its mouth and attempt to crush the windpipe. This can be somewhat more hazardous to the cougar because of flailing hooves. Young cougars are often less accomplished and occasionally the result of their attack is not as quick or as efficient as that of the more experienced cougar. Occasionally, a cougar will attack an intended victim and come out second best. A large deer or elk, for example, whose rack of horns and sharp hooves are lethal weapons, every now and then may successfully drive off an attacking cougar.

THE COUGAR'S DEMEANOR

Quite often I hear people express the opinion that animals (that is, animals other than human beings and perhaps some of the higher primates) lack the ability to reason, that they are not endowed with conscience of a moral code, and that they react solely on instinct; therefore, they cannot be held accountable for their behavior or actions. Consequently, in this opinion, when humans become involved with other members of the animal kingdom, judgment of fault or degree of guilt may not be weighed and measured. The only consideration should be whether or not the animal presents a clear and present danger to humans because of the experience of this particular involvement or incident.

Ben Lilly, bear and cougar hunter extraordinaire, was an anomaly in that he professed that he was not one to anthropomorphize, but he obviously held strong feelings about what he felt were the sinister and diabolic nature of bears and cougars. Frank Hibben spent some time with Lilly and came away with the impression that Lilly regarded himself as a policeman of the wild, and he considered cougars as "the Cains of the animal world. They were slayers and should be killed in their turn" (1948, 4). Hibben recalls how Lilly believed that he could speak the language of the animals and recounted to him an incident where he had brought a bear to bay on a rock and before killing the animal he addressed it in a courtroom manner: "You are condemned, you black devil. I kill you in the name of the law." And the bear is reported to have answered: "I cannot escape and I die" (1948, 5).

Most decisions and policies that are made with respect to wildlife are, fortunately, not made by individuals like Ben Lilly; they involve some form or level of government. In dealing with incidents involving humans and bears in National Parks, park management considers the circumstances of the encounter, and intent. A mother bear with cubs that attacks a human is perhaps only being protective of her young, and accordingly is perceived to be acting in an acceptable manner. A bear that may attack and later feed on a human, however, cannot be accepted and is permanently removed from the park ecosystem. Since cougars tend to be more reclusive, whenever and wherever an unprovoked attack on a human takes place it is considered an extraordinary event, and swift action is taken to destroy the cougar.

We know that the cougar is mainly a nocturnal animal; that it is seldom seen; and that it is a relentless hunter with a voracious appetite for meat; we also know that the liver, as well as the blood, of its victims is highly prized. Now these are not necessarily endearing qualities, to be sure, but we must admit that among carnivores it differs from others only in its extreme efficiency and hunting success. Is a cougar unnecessarily cruel? Perhaps, by human standards, it is, but human standards mean nothing to a cougar. By carnivore standards, the cougar is an efficient professional; its kills are swift and there is very little pain for its victim. The frequent claim that the cougar is a cowardly beast is an absurd observation when we consider that, more often than not, it is frequently outweighed substantially by its prey. The claim of cowardice appears to be generated simply by the cougar's unwillingness to participate in a contest that it clearly cannot win.

James Capen (Grizzly) Adams was an intrepid mountaineer and bear hunter. Throughout his life, Adams carried an extremely poor opinion of the cougar. During the winter of 1853–1854, Adams and his partner were hunting in Yosemite Valley. His partner Solon was attacked by a cougar, and by protective instinct Solon pulled the cape of his buckskin coat over his neck and called to Adams for help. The cougar was shot at by Adams but it escaped. In his review of the incident later, Adams comments:

> How he came to have such forethought [covering his neck with his coat] was strange; some others might have done so, but most men would never have thought of it; I, for one, would have sooner drawn my knife and fought. I asked why he did not fight; he replied that he was afraid to move, supposing that it would only infuriate the animal. Such a caution, said I, would have been good in the case of a bear; but the panther is made of different stuff. By nature a coward and a sneak, he has the cruelty of cowardice, daring the combat only when he has a sure advantage, and wreaking a bloodthirsty ferocity most upon an unresisting victim. A determined stroke with a knife, though it may not have killed would have terrified and put him to flight. (Hittle 1926, 208)

A different perspective appears in an account of an encounter experienced by mountain man and explorer Christopher (Kit) Carson. Carson and a companion were camping along the streams that flowed westward from the Rockies to the Great Salt Lake. While Carson was checking traps set near a camp, he was preparing to shoot a wild turkey with his large-bore rifle when he spotted a large cougar not more than twenty feet away. Expecting an attack, he fired at the cat, but his shot was deflected by tree roots and the cougar was struck by the bullet only in its left shoulder. The cougar was quickly upon Carson, who was obliged to defend himself with a knife. When Carson failed to return to camp, his partner searched for him and found him badly injured and unconscious, a dead cougar next to his body. Carried back to camp, Carson eventually recovered (Polley 1978, 183–84).

The noted nature writer and artist Ernest Thompson Seton spent most of his life studying animals, noting and commenting on their behavior. In his *Wild Animals at Home*, he entitled one chapter "Sneak-cats—Big and Small," and when he discusses the cougar he indicates that "the cougar is the most elusive, sneaking, adroit hider, and shyest thing in the woods. I have camped for twenty-five years in its country and never yet seen a wild cougar" (1913, 189-90). Some people might assume that the term "sneak" is meant to convey that the cougar behaves in a stealthy, underhanded, or cowardly manner. I don't believe that it was Seton's intent to impart this sort of message.

It is perhaps expected that normal cat traits could be mistaken for cowardice. The cougar, being similar to all cats in many respects, is cautious when confronted with an unfamiliar or potentially dangerous situation. When startled, all cats are inclined toward flight, but if pressed, even in the face of overwhelming odds, they will give a good account of themselves. Perhaps far better than any other animal of its size, the cougar takes full advantage of its hunting and predatory skills. It can move silently and finds no need to disclose its presence; its muscles are designed for power and sudden explosions of energy, and it is equipped with teeth that are quite different from the omnivore's. In fact, it is perhaps the most specialized of all North American carnivores. Its evolutionary passage and current physiological state was earned through years of savage contest, stealth, and its use of superior tactical strategies. Call it a loner; call it a night stalker; but don't call it a coward.

RELATIONSHIP WITH HUMANS

There is a common belief that the cougar is simply fascinated by humans and will follow a wilderness traveler for many miles, or will otherwise surreptitiously study the actions of human beings. There have been more than enough incidents to support such allegations, and, anyway, the cougar is curious about a lot of things. The human/cougar relationship, however, is one between observer and subject. The cougar is little interested in forming a lasting friendship or bond with humans, although occasionally contact may be tolerated.

There are, however, stories in support of the notion that the cougar is something of a friend to, or at least tolerant of, humans. Two tales especially are frequently mentioned in this regard, both of them dealing with events said to have occurred many years ago. The first, recounted in a folk tale of the early 1500s, concerns a young Argentinean girl, Maldonada, and her disobedience of an order from the Spanish commander of her community. In spite of specific instructions forbidding anyone to leave the immediate vicinity under penalty of death, she slipped into the jungle to look for food. Later found in the company of a tribe of Indians, she was taken back to Buenos Aires, the town she had earlier left. As punishment for what was considered willful disobedience, Maldonada was tied to a tree outside the colony; it was presumed that wild beasts would soon devour her. After several days, she was found to be still alive and quite well. She indicated that a cougar had stayed with her and given her protection.

The second tale tells of a group of Jesuit missionaries in the wilderness of southern California in the late 1600s. Frustrated in their efforts to raise domestic animals because of the number of cougars thereabouts, the Jesuits tried to solicit support from the local Indian tribes, offering to give them cattle if the Indians would kill the predatory cougars. The tribes, however, considered cougars to be their friends because in times of need they often scavenged meat from cougar kills and because they considered the cougar to be benefactor and patron. They refused to help the Jesuits. Although the story goes on to infer that over time the Indians were converted to Christianity, surrendered their pagan beliefs and superstitions, and assisted the Jesuits in control of the cougar population, the tale does give interesting insight into a different view of human/cougar relations.

All humans, I believe, harbor strong, or at least latent, feelings about members of the cat family in general. Cats are independent, and many people respect and appreciate them for this uniqueness and self-reliance. Cats are also viewed as something of an enigma; rarely do they behave in an expected manner: occasionally they will demonstrate playful, almost frolicsome behavior; the next moment they can be aloof or even present a threatening posture. The cougar is an authentic, card-carrying member of the cat family, and humans perceive it to present traits and characteristics that are the ultimate of feline evolution.

Each animal has its own values and worth. Animals bring with them gifts of resplendent beauty and they offer measures of wonder and excitement that brighten our lives. Along with other phenomena, they make the Earth on which we live a fascinating place. Prior to the European discovery of the New World, Native Americans treated the cougar—as well as all other animals—with courtesy and respect. The culture of the new immigrants did not permit such acceptance, and most felt only discomfort, fear, and abhorrence.

We need the cougar, just as we need every other creature that we share our environment with. How dull would our American wilderness become without the wolf, the bear, or the cougar. The cougar may not need humans, but humans and the spirit of the wilderness needs the cougar.

FOUR

Relationships within the Animal Kingdom

THE WORLD COMPRISES a virtually uncountable number of ecosystems and ecotones (transitional zones), each of which contains its own unique system of interacting populations of different species. Within these complex units, each and every day, critical, and often desperate, struggles take place. These are part of a species equilibrium process. The objective is always to achieve balance, but often—all too often—the environment is altered or compromised by human intervention.

The North and South American continents once teemed with wildlife. The native people who lived on these continents took only what they needed from the wildlife populations, and therefore a natural equilibrium resulted. When European immigrants arrived, they introduced a new and different culture and presented an ever increasing demand upon the preexisting environment. Quite rapidly, massive ecosystem challenges and changes developed as human populations swept westward. Forests were cut, grasslands and plains were occupied by domestic herds, wilderness areas were opened to exploration and settlement, and indigenous species were gradually displaced from their habitats. Some species were able to move elsewhere and adjust, but many were reduced substantially in number, and a few were completely eradicated.

The relationships of species to one another are an integral ingredient of the ecosystem function; one example of this is that when native hoofed mammals move to new locations, the carnivores that prey upon them usually follow. Thus a system of checks and balances served to keep the population of

In their search for graze and browse vegetation, elk and deer will move to lower elevations, and the carnivores that prey on these species usually follow.

the victims within forage limits and to provide predators with a food supply. The vegetative cycle also played an important role in this natural balance of nature. Plants assimilated energy from the sun and necessary minerals from the soil. The plants were then consumed by grazing herbivores, who in turn were preyed upon by carnivores; and both of these groups were part of an organic recycling process that returned nutrients to the soil to be used again by the plants. The carnivores also served to keep animal species healthy and vigorous, nature showing no sympathy: the weak, the sickly, and the old were among the first victims. But neither did nature show sympathy to the physically incompetent or incapable predator: they would die through starvation or eventually become prey themselves.

When deer, elk, and vast herds of bison were no longer present in their former numbers, or not in their former habitat areas, it was only natural that the predators who had fed on these animals would turn their attention to the domestic herds for their survival. The human owners of these herds found this an unprofitable and unacceptable practice and moved to destroy the predators. First to go were the wolves; then the historic ranges of the coyote, cougar, and bear were gradually compressed into more limited and isolated western locations. Only in the past century has the human species begun to waver from its desolate path of aggressive use and plunder of natural resources. Because of this, possibly we can consider that there be some measure of sanctity for established wildlife ecosystems. And, further, from this, possibly we can consider the relationship of cougars to other animal species—species that may now safely share, without overt human manipulation, a somewhat stable and common environment.

Correctly, an animal is defined as any living creature belonging to the animal kingdom. However, since the word "animal" is often used, albeit incorrectly, to denote only the mammal, that will be the way in which we will use the term (i.e., limited to mammals) in this chapter. Among animals, the cougar is a solitary creature of the wilderness, found with other members of its species only when mating or when still part of a family unit. It has no need for, or interest in, other animals except with regard to edibility or whether the animal currently presents itself as a potential threat to the cougar. Thus, the relationship of most animals to the cougar will be as prey or potential prey; that of the others will be as competitive carnivores or potential adversaries.

OTHER COUGARS

Young cougars from the same litter usually get along quite well, and with the exception of minor sibling squabbles, conflicts have not been observed. The young will remain with the mother until they reach full maturity and are encouraged to leave. Adult female cougars are somewhat more tolerant of other females than are adult male cougars of other males; thus, most intraspecies battles and fatalities are instigated by males.

In the wild, nuances associated with declared territorial boundaries suggest that mutual avoidance is preferable to combat wherein serious injury may result. However, in captivity the close proximity of other cougars does not appear to be a continuing irritant. But even here, for a cougar to share his or her cage amicably with another cougar would require that the animals involved have had a prior cordial relationship.

Cannibalism is apparently not an infrequent occurrence. Young and Goldman (1946, 137) cite two incidents of cannibalism they were aware of; John Lesowski (1963, 586), too, cites two cases: one in which a female cougar fed on the body of a male that Lesowski had killed, and a second in which a large adult male killed and partially ate a smaller adult male. Jim Bob Tinsley (1987, 60) refers to six other cases; Robinette et al. (1961) provides additional incidents; and Erwin Bauer (1988, 18) reports that veteran researcher Maurice Hornocker had once "found the bloody place where a male cougar had killed and eaten a young cougar, proving that the species is sometimes cannibalistic." As was pointed out in chapter 3, adult males represent a constant threat to the lives of the young cougar; they will kill and eat kittens if given an opportunity. The eating of young by any of the cat species, however, is not uncommon. Although this is a trait usually observed in the adult male, Hartley H. T. Jackson in his *Mammals of Wisconsin* (1961, 400) indicates that the female is not exempt. He tells of a female lynx giving birth to five kittens, and "when the first was born she at once prepared to clean it, and seemed fond of it. After a short time, however, it gave vent to a weak squeal, which caused her to eye it curiously for a moment, when another squeal was delivered, this settled the kitten's doom—it was at once devoured." All of the other kittens also died, either from being injured by the mother or after removal from the cage. Eating of young has also been observed among African lions and Asian tigers (Knottnerus-Meyer 1928, 110).

DEER, ELK (WAPITI), AND MOOSE

The deer family (Cervidae) in the United States and Canada is composed of four distinct species, the elk, or wapiti *(Cervus canadensis)*, the moose *(Alces palces)*, the mule deer *(Odocoileus hemionus)*, and the white-tailed deer *(Odocoileus virginiana)*, along with a number of subspecies such as the Coues deer *(Odocoileus couesi)* and coast black-tail *(Odocoileus columbianus)*. Whereas the ranges for elk and moose in the United States are now small, the range for white-tailed and mule deer is still quite extensive. The white-tail is still found in most, if not all, states, the southern border area of Canada, and into mid-continent South America. The range of the mule deer generally extends from the Pacific Ocean to the Dakotas, and south to Texas.

One of the cougar's names was at one time "deer tiger" because of its fondness for deer meat; wherever there were deer, there too you would find the cougar. The deer is still the favorite food of the cougar, presumably because of

This interesting panorama—a scene displayed in the Denver Museum of Natural History—shows what is in fact an unlikely circumstance: a mother cougar brings a freshly killed deer to her den site—but the kitten shown may still be a little young to eat meat. Cougars will accept meat after they are six weeks of age.

its size and its abundance. During the 1800s, deer were slaughtered by Eastern market hunters to such an extent that they were almost exterminated. To protect the remaining animals, hunting pressure was gradually decreased. Since most animal predators had been eliminated, this meant that all obstacles to population growth had been effectively removed. Deer are satisfied to live on a limited range; they usually can find plenty to browse on and, under these conditions, mature females will normally have two fawns each year. Because of these favorable circumstances, the white-tail deer has rapidly overpopulated a number of areas throughout its current range. Although the hunting of either sex is now being permitted in many states, the absence of a constant predator, such as the cougar, acerbates the problem.

The size of the white-tail deer varies from one area to another. Other variables also govern its weight (e.g., availability of food and certain environmental conditions), but an average weight of 160 pounds can be anticipated. Specimens weighing more than three hundred pounds are occasionally reported, however. The cougar usually approaches the deer from the rear after stalking the prey at a distance of not more than fifty feet. With a quick rush, which will include bounds of more than twenty feet, the cougar strikes the deer with a great deal of force, which nearly always knocks the animal down; then, holding the deer with its front claws, the cougar rakes with its rear claws while severing the spinal cord, separating the neck vertebrae, with its canines. On occasion the cougar may be obliged to dispatch a particularly fractious victim by crushing the windpipe or the opening of the jugular vein of its prey.

The mule deer is larger than a white-tailed deer, has bigger ears, and antler tines that are pronged or branched. It displays a black tip on its tail. Terrain permitting, the cougar will hunt the mule deer in the same manner that it does the white-tail—creeping close to it by use of whatever cover is available and then pouncing on the back or side of the victim. Once in a while, a cougar may seek out a preferred viewing site, which may then become a fortuitous and pivotal ambush platform.

Feeding, the cougar typically will open the upper paunch first (next to the rib cage) and eat the liver, and then perhaps some of the other organs. After that it may start on the breast meat, loins, and hams. The cougar likes fresh blood and will lap up whatever quantity is available. As soon as the cat has completed its first meal from the carcass, it will usually attempt to cover any remaining portion with whatever forest or ground debris may be available. It is generally believed that this is an effort to "hide" its food cache, but a different, and interesting, opinion has been offered by Stanley Graham, Colorado writer and outdoorsman (1918, 94): "Prior to leaving a carcass (usually a deer) a lion will claw out most of the hair and then rake this, together with sticks, pine needles or snow over the body so that the whole effect is quite weird and scary. This, I believe, serves the double purpose of preserving the meat, and also of frightening away any scavenger animals like the coyote, fox or lynx, which would otherwise depredate his food."

It should not be inferred that the cougar/deer relationship is such that a cougar need only to locate a deer and his next meal is assured. Many times the hunting and stalking leads but to a flash of tail and a distant deer.

The elk, or wapiti, is a large animal. Its height can exceed five feet at the shoulder and it may weigh between seven hundred and a thousand pounds. The female, like all members of the deer family, is usually about 30 percent smaller than a male, or bull, elk. At one time, elk ranged over most of the United States except for Florida and arid areas within the Great Basin. Elk can still be found in the Canadian provinces of Alberta, Manitoba, and Saskatchewan, and all eleven of the most western United States, exclusive of Alaska. Some restocking has also taken place, and small herds are now being maintained in Arkansas, Kentucky, Michigan, Pennsylvania, and Wisconsin.

The taking of elk by the cougar is not a very meaningful figure when compared with the much larger number of white-tailed and mule deer that will fall victim. However, there are considerably more deer than elk to be found within the known range of the cougar. In those areas where there are a lot of elk, such as Yellowstone National Park, elk may be favored over deer. A team of researchers that studied cougar activities in Yellowstone National Park in the winter of 1985/1986 concluded that elk "may be the dominant prey item" within the park (Despain et al. 1986, 67). In chapter 3 we saw that a cougar tracked by Roy Murray killed nine animals over a seven-day period; four of them were deer, four were elk, and one was a yearling steer. It seems that availability rather than preference determines whether a cougar takes a deer or an elk.

Although the elk is substantially larger than the deer, the kill method is basically the same. Some observers believe that the cougar will also grab the muzzle of the deer or elk with its front leg, or its claws, pull the head back, and break the neck either by force or as a result of a fall. A recent article in *Outdoor Life* (Brandt 1996, 18) offered that "mountain lions bring down elk by leaping on them and wrapping one front leg under their chins and pulling back, breaking the elk's neck."

As already noted, cougar offensives are not always successful: the cougar's timing may have been bad or the intended prey may have been alert or too elusive. Moreover, whenever a cougar selects a prey animal larger than itself, the risk of injury, or even death, to the attacking cougar becomes a distinct possibility. Consequently, although deer and elk are natural prey animals for the cougar, they should not be regarded as certain victims. Their antlers and sharply edged hooves can be devastating weapons (Manville 1955, 476–77). And their endurance is far better than that of the cougar if the contest becomes a chase.

The moose is the largest antlered mammal that now lives, or may have ever lived, on planet Earth. It can weigh as much as one thousand pounds and stand more than seven feet at the shoulder. Its huge palmate antlers are as impressive as its body size, reaching and occasionally exceeding six feet from tip

The Rocky Mountain elk is vulnerable if attacked by a cougar. Although a mature bull may be too large an animal even for an adult cougar, this young bull is likely prey, as are cows and calves.

to tip. Even the smaller Shiras moose, which is common to the United States, possesses an antler rack that is nearly five feet across. A bull moose also comes fully equipped with a dreadful temper. During the rut, which lasts from four to eight weeks in late fall, the bull is ready to challenge anything that moves, including a human. When I was working in Grand Teton National Park (Wyoming) in the early 1950s, I enjoyed fishing the beaver ponds adjacent to the Snake River, just below our home on what was then called the Black Tail Ranch site. To reach the beaver ponds, it was necessary to walk some distance through tall grasses and brush. I still can recall the trepidation I felt on discovering a fresh moose bed, and how grateful I was when I reached the beaver ponds safely without having disturbed one of those short-tempered denizens of river bottoms.

Wolf packs are the principal predators of moose. However, a cougar can, and will, kill a moose if conditions are favorable. Since moose are now generally found only in Alaska, Canada, and a few of the northern and mountain states such as Minnesota, Idaho, Montana, and Wyoming (they are also seen in Colorado, Utah, and perhaps one or two other states, but only in limited numbers) opportunities for cougar predation are limited.

THE AMERICAN BISON

Although the moose is a very large and powerful animal, the massively con-structed bison would be an even more formidable project if it were to be added to cougar cuisine. The burly North American bison *(Bison bison)* has two rec-ognized subspecies, *Bison bison bison* (plains bison) and *Bison bison athabascae* (wood bison). Although some bison still range within state parks, national parks, and national refuges, most of these animals now graze on private lands and are raised for purposes similar to that of domestic beef herds.

The cougar is little considered as a possible predator of the bison. This I find to be interesting since at one time a considerable number of cougar in-habited both North and South America. I would have thought that a young bison calf would present itself as a rather tempting morsel to a hungry cougar. John Dunn Hunter, who claims to have observed a number of attacks by cougar on bison, relates the following incident that he once observed in West-ern Arkansas (1973, 66–67):

> In one of my excursions, while seated in the shade of a large tree, situated on a gentle declivity, with a view to procure some mitigation from the oppressive heat of the midday sun, I was surprised by a tremendous rushing noise. I sprang up, and discovered a herd, I believe, of a thousand buffaloes running at full speed towards me; with a view, as I supposed, to beat off the flies, which at this season are inconceivably troublesome to those animals.
>
> I placed myself behind the tree, so as not to be seen, not apprehending any danger; because they ran with too great rapidity, and too closely together, to afford any one an opportunity of injuring me while protected in this manner.
>
> The buffaloes passed so near me on both sides, that I could have touched several of them merely by extending my arm. In the rear of the herd was one on which a huge panther had fixed, and was voraciously engaged in cutting off the muscles of its neck. I did not discover this circumstance till it had nearly passed beyond rifle shot distance, when I discharged my piece, and wounded the panther.

Hunter claims to have later killed the cougar, removed, smoked, and dressed the skin, and later arrayed himself in it to "surprise the herds of buffaloes, elk, and deer, which on my approach fled with great precipitation and dread." In-terestingly, Hunter's description of a cougar attack on a bison is analogous to a similar incident purportedly observed by noted frontiersman Daniel Boone

Bison prefer flat open ground. The likelihood of a cougar being able to snatch a bison calf is remote: reports from past days of cougar attacking bison involved forested areas, not open plains.

(Young and Goldman 1946, 97–98; quoting from Timothy Flint's 1856 publication on Daniel Boone). While returning to his Kentucky home from one of his frequent backcountry sojourns, Boone recalls meeting an enormous herd of bison that were obviously quite agitated. As the herd approached, the reason for their fury became apparent: a cougar was situated on the back of a large bison and was clawing and biting the animal so fiercely that the bison's blood was running down on all sides. Boone indicated that he then shot the cougar, who "released its hold and came to the ground."

Although the above incidents are supported only by anecdotal testimony, they both fall within the realm of possibility, and for that reason I have elected to consider that the cougar was once a potential predator of bison.

MOUNTAIN (BIGHORN) SHEEP, MOUNTAIN GOAT, AND ANTELOPE (PRONGHORN)

Three ungulate species, mountain (bighorn) sheep, mountain goat, and antelope (pronghorn), although only related in the animal kingdom by broad taxonomic order, do have one thing in common: they are occasional prey for an experienced and capable cougar.

The pronghorn antelope, family Antilocapridae, species *Antilocapra americana*, is found in most of the western plains area from Canada to Mexico and Nebraska to California. Great speed and flaring patches of white rump hair are the two pronghorn characteristics more commonly noted because they are part of the pronghorn's personal flight program. Primarily a resident of plains, prairies, and the sagebrush flats, its search for the more tender and succulent grasses may send it into mountain areas during the warmer summer months. That is where the pronghorn is more likely to encounter a cougar. Smaller than a deer, the antelope seldom weighs more than 125 pounds. Its sharp hooves and horns can be effective weapons against coyotes, but they are of meager help when the antelope is challenged by the cougar's superior size, strength, teeth, and claws. It is an infrequent victim because its outstanding vision and speed usually permit it to avoid capture by cougar ambush or even the most painstaking stalking.

The white and bearded mountain goat is not a true goat; in habitat and physiology it appears to be more comparable to the European chamois, although the chamois is a much smaller animal. The mountain goat, family Bovidae, species *Oreamnos americanus*, is found in the higher mountains of northwestern North America, and an adult male may weigh between 250 and 300 pounds. Although these rocky perches may serve as a welcome haven from most predators, the goat will periodically fall victim to a cougar. Ernest Thompson Seton once suggested that the "principal enemy of the bighorn sheep and mountain goats" was the cougar (1929, 106). This is a most logical observation since the cougar is an outstanding climber, and these rocky and craggy masses, which so effectively shield the goat from other predators, affords the cougar with both hiding places and places from which to attack. Douglas H. Chadwick, in his study of mountain goats, writes: "Cougars are wonderfully quick, strong, stealthy predators, at home in rock-rimmed country. Evidence of the big cats killing mountain goats comes from a number of different investigators. Traveling through open stands of timber close to goat cliffs I found goat carcasses bearing unmistakable marks of the puma's work: deep tooth punctures in the neck from the cat's favorite killing hold, and shoulder meat cleanly removed by its specialized flesh-shearing teeth, the carnassials" (1983, 83–84).

The pronghorn antelope is usually found in groups and herds that occasionally number in the hundreds. Speed is their most effective defense—and extreme curiosity their weakness. Only infrequently do they wander close enough to areas that offer cover adequate for the cougar to mount a successful attack.

Although not a true goat—it is actually an antelope—the mountain goat is generally safe from attack while in the high country. The golden eagle may occasionally pick off a very young kid, but older goats have little to fear from an eagle. Cougars will climb for goats, and sometimes they are successful, but it is when the goats descend into the valleys that they are most vulnerable.

Rocky Mountain bighorn are grass eaters. If the grass and browse becomes too sparse, they will descend from their mountain ledges and steeper slopes, which puts them at greater risk of attack from the cougar.

When high country forage is not adequate to support all of its nourishment and mineral needs, the goat becomes obliged to move to lower elevations, to the grassy slopes, and occasionally even to mountain valleys. It is then that the goat is more susceptible to attack from other predators, such as the grizzly and black bear.

There are two species of wild sheep in North America: the Rocky Mountain bighorn, family Bovidae, species *Ovis canadensis*, and the northern sheep, *Ovis dalli*. There are two varieties of the latter species, the Dall, or white sheep, that are located throughout the greater part of Alaska and also in the Canadian Yukon, and the stone, or black sheep, that are also found in the Yukon, and south into British Columbia.

The Rocky Mountain bighorn are found in most mountainous areas of western North America, from northern Mexico to North Dakota, including the dry mountains of the southwestern deserts, southwestern Alberta, southeastern British Columbia, and along the Pacific coast to northern California. Smaller than the mountain goat, an adult male bighorn will usually weigh between 175 and 200 pounds. Its impressive horn construction and nimble

In the high mountain country, traveling along rocky ridges and ledges, Rocky Mountain bighorn are secure from all but the most skilled hunters.

hooves can inflict severe punishment on any of the smaller predators should the opportunity present itself. While in its mountain home, bighorn are usually safe from most animal predators, with the exception of the cougar, the eagle, and perhaps an intrepid bobcat. Like the mountain goat, the bighorn will occasionally move to the lower elevations for better feed, and it is at lower elevations and at water holes that it is at greater risk of predation by a whole host of waiting carnivores such as the coyote, bear, bobcat, wolf, and wolverine.

In the arid southwestern mountainous areas, the shortage of suitable vegetation, with regard to both quantity and quality, limits the number of deer and bighorn that the land can support. Since the cougar's meat demands are high, a cougar would have a hard time surviving on a small resident ungulate population. Gale Monson and Lowell Sumner (1985), in their research on the desert bighorn, identified several incidents in which cougar predation had nearly wiped out small resident communities of desert bighorn. One such incident, in the summer of 1968 near Hawthorne, Nevada (Mount Grant), involved the establishment of an enclosure for the purpose of reintroducing desert bighorn to the area. In line with the policy of the U.S. Fish and Wildlife Service at that time, the service "conducted a seven-month effort to rid the vicinity of predators" (1985, 192). Six bighorn were released into the enclosure in June 1968. On July 30, two were killed by cougars, and the following day another was killed. As a consequence of these attacks, four cougars were killed in the vicinity of the enclosure, and an electric fence was added to further protect the sheep from cougar attack. Other evidence of predation on desert bighorn has also been uncovered in southern California (Cronemiller 1948, 68).

Noted wilderness wanderer Enos A. Mills observed cougars taking mountain sheep on a number of occasions (1909, 9–10). Mills noted that "the mountain lion is a prowler, a cowardly rapacious slaughterer, and may visit the heights at any time. Though apparently irregular in his visits, he seems to keep track of the seasons and to know the date for spring lamb, and he is likely to appear while the sheep are weak or snowbound. He is a wanton killer and is ever vigilant to slay. He lurks and lies in wait and preys upon all the birds and beasts except the bear" (1915, 107).

Young and Goldman are also among those who advance the opinion that cougars are an "enemy" of mountain sheep, citing one instance where eighteen sheep skulls were found at one mountainside location (1946, 134). Several prominent outdoorsmen and hunters are of the belief that, if given a choice, cougars will select sheep over any other meat (Keith 1948, 220).

Commenting in his *Mountain Lion Field Guide* on predation of lions [cougars] on bighorn sheep, pronghorn, and peccary, Harley G. Shaw writes: "Kills of bighorns and antelope have been documented but are relatively rare." It was not, I'm sure, his intention to imply that cougars are not an effective predator of the bighorn or the antelope. Wild ungulates will always constitute a major portion of cougar diet. If a cougar is sufficiently hungry, it will eat most anything—from grass and bugs to mice and moose. Enos Mills once observed a cougar catching and eating grasshoppers (1918, 125).

From time to time, useful information regarding cougar diet has been obtained by analysis of prey items found in cougar scat and stomach contents. Through precise laboratory examination of these materials, food selection can be scientifically established. Preference patterns can be determined with respect to frequency of choice and availability. When the prey is a smaller animal, however, it is not so easy to confirm the selection; sometimes all that may be found in dung or stomach are tiny pieces of fur, a particle of skin, or a claw.

Scat studies by a variety researchers over many years have revealed considerable information about cougar diet. I was impressed with scat analysis provided by Frank C. Hibben in his study of the cougar in 1937; although the

This exhibit in the International Wildlife Museum, Tucson, Arizona, depicts a cougar about to pounce on a pronghorn antelope. Uusually, however, the cougar has little opportunity to include antelope in its diet: the swift pronghorn likes to range on the open plains; the cougar prefers rocky areas and good ground cover.

work is detailed, its presentation is very understandable. For each of the two regions (Arizona and New Mexico) and the nearly thirty collecting stations, scat indicated the expected preference of deer as the most common cougar prey, but the number and variety of smaller mammals taken was less expected: jack rabbit, cottontail, gray fox, skunk, porcupine, badger—all were there.

Kitchener (1991, 127–28) reports the analysis of the contents of two cougar scat studies. In the first study, published by Yanez in 1986, cougar scat was collected from two sites in Chile. The scat contents indicated that regardless of time of year the predominant prey species was the European hare (*Lepus europaeus*). The second study, done in Big Bend National Park, Texas, by Leopold and Krausman, covered two different periods: 1972–1974, a time of high deer population, and 1980–1981, a period when the Big Bend deer population was at a low point. Leopold and Kaufman discovered that during years of high population, deer, followed by peccary, were the primary prey species for the cougar. Lagomorphs (rabbits and hares) were of only minor dietary importance. In the years of low deer population, the taking of peccaries increased significantly and so did cougar harvesting of lagomorphs.

A chart showing the frequency with which cougars take a particular prey was developed by Hansen (1992, 44). The information was assembled from six different studies: three involved study sites in Florida, Oregon, and Utah; one was in the Canadian province of British Columbia; one was in Peru; one was in Chile. Rabbits and hares were common prey items in the British Columbia, Utah, and Chilean studies, but of only minor importance in Florida; they were totally absent in Oregon and Peru. Other studies of cougar stomach contents and/or droppings over the years reflect basically similar findings; if deer are present, they are the first prey choice; if they are not readily available, most anything else present and edible that can be captured will subsequently be taken.

It follows that the absence of mountain sheep, mountain goats, and antelope in feces or stomach contents does not mean that these animals are not prey; only that they are not plentiful or were not commonly found in that particular cougar's travels.

COLLARED PECCARY

The collared peccary, family Tayassuidae, species *Tyassu tajacu*, is, simply stated, a piglike animal. Although the peccary is in the same zoological order as the deer family, the bighorn sheep, the mountain goat, and the pronghorn antelope—(Artiodactyla, even-toed ungulates)—it is piglike in appearance and behaves like a creature altogether different and far-removed from the aforementioned herbivores. The peccary, or javelina, will eat just about any plant in its path, as well as reptiles, eggs, bugs, worms, small animals—and more. Traveling in bands of from fewer than half a dozen to occasionally more than twenty-five, favor running more than fighting; if cornered, however, or if they otherwise become aggressively inclined, they will put up stiff opposition and severely can punish an inexperienced predator.

Studies of cougar scat and stomach contents from areas in which peccaries and cougars happen to share an environment reveal that the peccary is one of the more popular prey items in the diet of the cougar. Although the jaguar may prefer a diet featuring fresh peccary more than the cougar does, the jaguar's range does not reach very far into the arid southwestern United States. This pretty much leaves the peccary for the cougar, the bobcat, the coyote, and a few feral wolf/dog species that are still to be found in that territory.

Rabbits, hares, and the little pika were once included in the order of rodents (Rodentia), but because they have six incisor teeth rather than four, they were taxonomically placed in the order Lagomorpha, and the family Leporidae. Those two additional incisors cannot really be seen unless the mouth is pried open. They are located directly behind the two large incisors in the upper jaw and are of only limited use to the animal. Hares and jack rabbits (genus *Lepus*) are larger than the typical cottontail rabbit (genus *Sylvilagus*); they also have longer ears and longer rear legs. With the longer legs, some species of hares can reach a running speed of forty-five miles per hour and leap more than five feet vertically and twelve feet horizontally. There are a considerable number of species of hares and rabbits, all varying to some degree from the others but all more or less taking the same basic form and appearance.

Rabbits and hares are prey for nearly all the species that include meat in their diet: snakes, predatory birds, most members of the order Carnivora, and of course human beings. Any rabbit or hare that happens to die of old age in the wild has obviously lived a charmed life. Since even the largest hare will weigh less than fifteen pounds, a cougar is hard-pressed to subsist solely on hares and rabbits. The cottontail rabbit, our so-called bunny, is not much more than a mouthful for most of the larger predators, and unless the cougar or other carnivore can successfully follow the prey into its burrow or dense brush, the rabbit has a fair chance of avoiding capture. On balance, the ex-penditure of energy may often not be worthwhile for a cougar.

Rodents fulfill a similar role in the cougar diet as do rabbits and hares: they are not the prey of choice if larger prey, such as deer, are available. But if the opportunity avails and nothing more favorable is readily available, rodents will be eaten. Known cougar diet has included numerous members of the order Rodentia: mice, rats, gophers, squirrels, beaver, and porcupine are but part of the list. Cases of cougars catching and eating the smaller rodents such as mice and ground squirrels are well documented, but the taking of beaver and por-cupine is perhaps of greater interest.

The beaver, family Hydochoeridae, species *Castor canadensis*, is the largest rodent in North America; worldwide, only the South American capybara is larger. Valued for its fur, the beaver was the eagerly-sought-after object of many explorative and entrepreneurial expeditions on the American western and northwestern frontier. Although the beaver receives considerable acclaim for its purported skill as a hydraulic engineer and waterfront architect, it is in fact one of the more witless of animals now in existence. It would become rather easy prey for any enterprising carnivore were it not for the refuge of deep water and its submerged passages into and out of its lodge home.

A cougar will usually pounce upon the slow-moving beaver when it is busy gathering branches for a dam or traveling from one place to another over land. It may also strike even when the beaver is in its pond, prior to it reaching deep water. Although the beaver's strong jaws and imposing front teeth may dissuade smaller, less-determined predators from attack, these modest weapons are but a hollow defense against the skill and strength of a cougar.

An interesting tale about beavers is told by Enos A. Mills, who as outdoorsman, naturalist, and author-observer of wildlife in the Colorado Rockies may have no equal. Mills, unlike many of his contemporaries, was not averse to interfering in so-called natural events: he would protect a docile prey species from anticipated or actual attack of a predator. On one occasion, after watching for some time a colony of thirty or forty beavers harvesting aspens, he observed that both a coyote and a cougar were sneaking up on the unsuspecting dam-builders. Before he could warn the colony (a small one for a group of beavers), the coyote quickly killed three. Mills leapt into the fray, shouting and flailing around with his feet. The coyote fled, but not before showing his intense displeasure by baring his teeth at Mills (1911, 29). The cougar simply faded into the woods. Shortly after this episode, Mills discovered evidence that a cougar had killed and eaten beaver from this colony on two succeeding days (1911, 35-36).

The porcupine, family Erethizontidae, species *Erethezon dorsatum*, is similar to the beaver in at least one respect: it is not exactly a cerebral giant. The negative impact of the porcupine's mental sluggishness, however, is substantially mitigated by its possession of a formidable protective array of sharp and barbed body quills. When a porcupine assumes its defensive posture—shielding its head, arching its body, and raising its tail—only the impetuous or the uninformed fail to take necessary caution. Embedded quills often become a serious matter for an animal stuck with them, and it is not unusual for such a tormented creature to die from either starvation, infection, or the penetration of a vital organ by continued movement of the quill though the animal's flesh. However, Frank C. Hibben referred to a male cougar he observed as the "porcupine cat." He reported that this cougar seemed to specialize in eating porcupines, yet it had acquired only a few permanent quill "souvenirs" in all its many porcupine conquests (1948, 85).

Another carnivore that seems to have learned how to breach the porcupine's spiny defense with efficiency is the fisher—family Bassariscidae, species *Martes pennanti*. The fisher, a weasel-like mammal, is now only very rarely found in the United States, but it once was instrumental in keeping porcupine populations under control. Its method of attack was an assault upon the head or the unprotected underbody of the porcupine; it would then burrow through the flesh. Porcupine carcasses found with the head completely eaten off have probably been killed by a fisher; a cougar usually eschews the head.

A cougar simply flips the porcupine over, rips open its soft underbelly, and eats whatever portions of the body it may fancy. The cougar, however, can still receive damaging injury from quills if they become embedded. Cougars that have learned how to dine on porcupines successfully usually avoid receiving quills in the facial area. Erwin Bauer mentioned in his *Predators of North America* (1988, 20) that a noted cougar hunter and taxidermist from Sheridan, Wyoming, reported that almost every cougar carcass he had examined "has had porcupine quills embedded in it somewhere." A study of cougars on the Uncompahgre Plateau in Colorado (Anderson, Bowden, and Kattner 1992) indicated that of fifty-seven cougars captured by the study team, twenty had suffered injury, but only two carried porcupine quills. Apparently swallowing quills presents the cougar with but little difficulty: they have been found in some abundance in cougar scat.

BIRDS AND FISH

Most domestic house cats will instinctively stalk and pounce upon any bird they believe they can kill, and their large cousin the cougar is no different. For obvious reasons, larger birds are preferred to small ones, but if the cougar is hungry enough, any bird will do. When Karen McCall and Jim Dutcher were studying cougars held in a five-acre fenced enclosure (1992, *National Geographic*, July 1992), ducks that landed in a beaver pond within the enclosure were attacked by an adult female cougar that had never hunted in the wild. After she caught one of the ducks, she immediately began to pull off its feathers and then gave it to her three kittens.

Wild turkeys and grouse, and even the small quail, will become prey from time to time. In practice, it is more common for a cougar to climb roost trees at night and swat the grouse or turkeys, rather than to attempt to catch the birds unaware during daylight. Renowned cougar hunter Ben Lilly indicated that he found the meat of grouse in cougar stomachs along with that of other victims (Dobie 1950, 196). Enos A. Mills noted that the cougar of the Rocky Mountains had no difficulty in catching grouse (1909, 9–10). Wild turkeys were pursued by cougars with such vigor in certain New Mexico and Arizona localities in the 1870s that the cougars were said to be depopulating the turkey-breeding places, to such an extent that "in a few years the race will become extinct in this region if measures are not taken to prevent the wholesale slaughter" (Young and Goldman 1946, 139).

The aroma of fish appears to have as much allure for a cougar as it does for a house cat. It has been claimed that cougar trappers use, with considerable success, a lure the base of which is decomposed fish (Young and Goldman 1946, 139). Stanley R. Graham, a Chicago entrepreneur and wildlife author, hunted cougars in New Mexico, Colorado, and Arizona from ca. 1915 through the 1920s. Graham claims that during spawning season the cougar will snare fish from creeks with its front claws and "with a dexterous jerk, will flip a fish from the water upon the bank. The smaller victims it usually cuffs and slaps around, tantalizing and playing with them as we have often seen a cat do with a mouse" (1918, 41).

Ernest Thompson Seton mentioned in his *Lives of Game Animals* (1929, 132) a somewhat interesting story about a cougar and his interest in trout. It seems that after catching a large trout, a guide by the name of Terrioux threw the fish in back of him so that it couldn't wiggle back into the stream. Hearing a noise behind him, he turned around and as he reached for his fish spied one of the largest cougars he had ever seen. Terrioux claims that "he was only a few feet from me and was sneaking up to get my fish; when I saw that beastly cat trying to make away with my fish, I was so mad that I did not stop to think of the consequences, but brought my fishing pole down on his head with all my might." The cougar was so surprised that it promptly fled—without the trout.

Clyde Ormand *(Hunting Our Medium Size Game)* relates another story about a cougar and a fisherman. Apparently this cougar had been following a man who had been fishing Yellowstone's Snake River. The man heard a cougar scream, turned, and saw a cougar not a hundred yards behind him on the trail. Since he was carrying a creelful of rainbow trout, he concluded that the cougar smelled the fish and wanted them. He threw the creel and trout into the brush and quickly left the area. The next day he reported that he went back with a friend and a rifle, but could find "neither the cougar nor any trace of trout or creel" (1958, 207).

OTHER CARNIVORES

Grizzly and Black Bear

The cougar does not normally seek confrontation with any of the larger carnivores, but when confrontation does occur the cougar can certainly hold its own. When its opponent is the North American black bear, it often is the victor.

The common black bear (family Ursidae, species *Ursus americanus*) is found in most of the woodland areas of Canada, Alaska, the Rocky Mountain and West Coast states, along the East Coast, and within several of the states of the Southeast and upper Midwest. Although it is referred to as being a "black" bear, it can be brown, somewhat light hued—almost yellow or silver, and even cinnamon. When I was with the National Park Service and stationed in Yosemite National Park, California, in 1963, a mother bear regularly brought her three cubs around to the front of our house to feed on acorns. All three of her cubs were a different color: one was so light it appeared almost to be blond.

Since black bears and cougars often share the same habitat, it is possible for confrontations occasionally to occur. Although it is obliged to feed on vegetation for most of the year, the black bear is omnivorous and also relishes meat in its diet—and that is when it becomes a competitor and potential adversary for a cougar. The weight of an adult black bear ranges between two hundred and five hundred pounds. All bears pack a mean wallop in their front paws, and their teeth are capable of piercing the thickest metal cans, so they are not a foe for the cougar to take lightly.

One writer of the old West, Natt Dodge (1963, 458) expressed some doubt that a lone cougar would ever attack a black bear unless the latter was sick or wounded. Although bear meat is, every now and then, found in the stomach or scat of cougars, there is little other evidence that says conflicts are any other than infrequent. Probably the greatest field expert ever on bear and cougar behavior was the late Ben Lilly; he spent virtually his whole lifetime hunting and studying the bear and the cougar. Although Lilly has not only been widely quoted but also himself put some of his thoughts on bear and cougar in writing, I am not aware of one single statement he ever made regarding cougars and bears fighting in the wild.

One oft-mentioned tussle between a black bear and a cougar was apparently observed by Major John C. Cremony, who served with the U.S. Boundary Commission in the Southwest between 1849 and 1851. Cremony, accompanied by Apache guides, had been hunting cougars along the Pecos in the vicinity of what is now Ft. Sumner when the group heard a dreadful but unidentifiable sound. Curious as to what could be making such noises and seeking out the source, they came upon a life-and-death battle between a large cougar and a middle-sized black bear. The bear was quite evidently not enthused about the encounter and would have liked to have broken off hostilities and gone away, but the cougar was apparently deeply intent upon killing the bear. After a number of skirmishes, the cougar successfully clawed through to the bear's vital organs. After despatching the bear, the cougar licked its wounds, took hold of the bear's carcass, and dragged it to a more secluded place, where it began to cover the carcass for a later meal. It was at this point that one of the Apache guides killed the cougar (Cremony, *Life among the Apaches*, 1951, 225–26—a reprint of the 1868 edition).

Another instance of deadly confrontation between a cougar and black bear took place some time prior to 1800 near Schuylerville, now Saratoga, New York. An early settler, Mynheer Barhydt, had just built a cabin within Bear Swamp and witnessed the battle. Barhydt indicated that the bear had discovered the cougar's den and, in the absence of the mother cougar, killed the cougar's young. Soon thereafter, the cougar arrived and attacked the bear, reportedly with an awesome display of fury. The cougar eventually implanted her claws so deeply in adversary's body that the bear could not throw her off. In the struggle, which Barhydt claimed lasted more than an hour, the two animals rolled over each other into a ravine, and when all became still Barhydt looked down, over the edge, and saw that both animals were dead (Stone 1975, 137–39, and Bradley 1940, 116).

The grizzly (family Ursidae, species *Ursus arctos horribilis*) once occupied most of the North American continent. Now it is found only in Alaska, the

Canadian Northwest Territories, and south through most of British Columbia and western Alberta to the Rocky Mountain areas of the United States; the major United States population is within the greater Glacier and Yellowstone National Park ecosystems. This is a big and powerful bear—a beast that knows its strength and fears no other animal, with the possible exception —*earned* exception—of the human being.

Ernest Thompson Seton (1929, 90–91) writes that G. W. Ferguson "recorded" a fight between a grizzly and a female cougar that was witnessed by two miners working a claim near Murray, Idaho. It was reported that a female cougar had a den and kittens in the vicinity, and when a grizzly, apparently unknowingly, approached the den, the mother cougar attacked the grizzly. During what the miners described as a fierce battle, the combatants fell off a mountain ledge and both were killed by the resultant fall. The miners claimed that the cougar was still hanging on to the grizzly's cheek with her teeth; the bear's back and throat were torn and lacerated and "his belly hide ripped into ribbons, mute evidence of the fact that all her paws with their 18 sharp claws had not been idle" (612).

However, no one has yet suggested that a cougar would, or ever has, successfully challenged a grizzly over the rights to a carcass or to priority passage on a woodland trail. The cougar is much smarter than that. Enos Mills, the original wilderness wanderer, often had an opportunity to observe the grizzly while it still roamed throughout the Colorado Rockies. Mills indicated that "bears and lions are not neighborly, and at best each ignores the other; but one bear I knew followed a lion for weeks, and others have occasionally done likewise, profiting by the food-supply—the excess killing of the lion" (1919, 31). As further evidence of the commonality of this practice, Mills further once observed a grizzly usurp the carcass of a deer killed by a cougar: the cougar "leaped toward the grizzly with a snarl, struck at it and dashed into the woods. The grizzly, without even looking round to see where the lion had gone, commenced eating" (1918, 126).

Coyote, Fox, and Wolf

Has there ever been two animal families with so much rancor and enmity toward one another as the cats and the dogs? An adult cougar is physically superior to any wild or domestic member of the dog family in America, yet it

The coyote can be found throughout much of North America. Like the raccoon, it seems comfortable foraging near human habitation. This specimen is in the North American display in the Denver Museum of Natural History.

will usually flee from a single barking dog nearly as quickly as it would from an obstreperous pack. One theory, often expressed, is that cougars flee from a barking dog because of an instinctive, ancestral fear of voracious wolf packs. Examination of the literature reveal little that would suggest that the relationship between cougar and wolf is a significant one; therefore we must conclude that this instinctive dislike is of evolutionary origin.

Perhaps it is because the cougar operates in such a surreptitious manner that it dislikes the clamoring pronouncements the wolves make of their of their presence. Whatever the reason, if the dog doesn't bark the cougar is not inclined to flee, and is likely to dispose of the dog quickly.

The coyote, fox, and wolf are all members of the dog (Canidae) family. Although sharing the taxonomic relationship, they have no family fondness for one another. The wolf will kill the coyote as well as the fox; the coyote will kill the fox; and the fox is usually smart enough to try to keep its distance from both larger canine species. The coyote *(Canis lantrans)* is about half the size

The coyote—more of a scavenger than a hunter—is usually careful not to disturb the carcasses of cougar kills lest it too becomes a meal for a cougar.

of a wolf, only rarely weighing more than sixty pounds. It is found over most of western and central North America and, unlike its larger cousin the wolf, its population and range is increasing. The coyote kills the bobcat at every opportunity, but it is well aware that it stands little chance against the cougar. Not only does the cougar serve as an imposing predatory competitor for the coyote, the cat also readily hunts the coyote as if it were no different than other prey.

The coyote is a scavenger; it will enthusiastically feed on carcasses left by other predators, but it will not disturb a cougar kill for at least four days, and perhaps as many as six, for fear the cougar will return and catch the coyote on the carcass. Trappers indicate that if any trap becomes scented with cougar urine, coyotes leave the area as quickly as their legs can carry them. In *The Voice of the Coyote*, coyote researcher J. Frank Dobie offers a number of quotes and observations about cougars killing a coyote and promptly eating it (1949, 78–79). Unlike the case with somewhat vague relationship existing between the black bear and the cougar, there is no doubt whatsoever about the prey/predator relationship between coyote and cougar.

The common American fox is occasionally eaten by the cougar. Exclusive of the smaller and somewhat rare kit, or swift, fox, two fairly common species of fox, the red fox *(Vulpes fulva)* and the gray fox *(Urocyon cincereoargenteus)*, are distributed throughout the United States, Canada, Alaska, and Mexico; the gray fox is also in Central America and northern South America. Reynard, of course, is the villain of numerous tales and fables, but it really is not much bigger than a good-sized alley cat. A big adult male usually will weigh under fifteen pounds, and more often its weight is closer to ten pounds. Not a big item on the cougar menu, fox meat has nevertheless been found in cougar stomach contents and in scat. Fox carcasses, stripped of their meat and revealing evidence of cougar predation, have also been found.

The largest member of the Canidae family on the North American continent is the gray, or timber, wolf (Canis lupus). Other wolf subspecies populated sections of the United States at one time or another, but now they are all but completely extirpated from their former haunts. The range of the wolf is now primarily confined to Alaska and Canada, with a few limited packs still operating in Idaho, Michigan, Minnesota, Montana, Wisconsin, and Yellowstone National Park, Wyoming. Wolf size varies quite a bit. Like most mammals, they are sexually dimorphic: the male is substantially larger, occasionally weighing upwards of 170 pounds. Although both wolves and cougars were classed as vermin and subsequently victimized by a variety of state predator-control acts, the cougar has survived while the wolf has been all but wiped out. The reasons for this difference in control outcomes are many, but probably the major causes are that (1) the cougar is a loner and does not announce its presence as readily as does the wolf; (2) since it does not favor carrion, the cougar usually will shun dead animals left as bait, as well as carcasses baited with strychnine and arsenic; and (3) only infrequently is a cougar spotted in an open area.

It is repeatedly pointed out that the cougar is a fresh-meat eater; however, if it is sufficiently hungry it will eat even the oldest of carcasses rather than starve. A cougar was once trailed in Olympic National Park and was found to have dug out the remains of a previous kill and "gnawed on the old bones like a dog" (Petersen 1912).

In his outstanding work The Wolves of Mount McKinley, Adolph Murie mentions the cougar only in reference to research previously conducted by Frank Hibben in Arizona and New Mexico (1937, 42–44). This was with regard to the cougar taking of animals with abnormal or subnormal characteristics. While I was with the National Park Service and assigned to Grand Teton National Park, in the mid 1950s, Adolph was a biologist on the Grand Teton park staff. In a number of conversations "Ade" expressed the opinion that the wolf had little impact upon the grizzly in their Alaskan environment, and he couldn't recall a single cougar/wolf conflict from his research experiences in either the United States or Canada.

In *The Puma—Legendary Lion of the Americas*, Jim Bob Tinsley, who devoted several paragraphs to specifics about the cougar's relationships with bear, coyote, jaguar, and other predators, offered only a speculation about the wolf: "Perhaps the worst enemies of the puma at one time were the wolf packs that roamed the countryside at will. Few, if any, wild animals could survive the relentless onslaught of these dreaded hordes" (1987, 64). Frederick W. True, former curator of the Department of Mammals, U.S. National Museum ("The Puma, or American Lion: Felis Concolor of Linnaeus," which appeared in the 1889 National Museum report) noted that it had been previously asserted by Pennant (*History of Quadrupeds*, 3rd ed., 1793, p. 290) "that the wolf serves the puma for prey," a statement with which he disagreed. He did note, however, that the museum of the Royal Society of London had housed "the skin of a puma which was shot shortly after it had killed a wolf" (601).

Documented incidents suggestive of confrontations are but few. Thomas Nuttall, who conducted a more or less scientific exploration into Arkansas Territory in 1819, offered the following on an encounter between a cougar and a wolf:

> Panthers are said to be abundant in the woods of the Red river, nor are they uncommon on the banks of the Arkansas. A somewhat curious anecdote of one of these animals was related to me by my guide. A party of hunters in the morning missed one of their dogs from the encampment, and after a fruitless search were proceeding on their route, when one of the other dogs obtaining a scent, discovered to the hunters, dead beneath a tree, the dog which had strayed, together with a deer and a wolf in the same condition. It appeared, that the panther, having killed a deer, and eat its fill, got into a tree to watch the remainder, and had, in its own defence, successively fallen upon the wolf and the dog as intruders on his provision. (Thwaites 1966, 210–11)

A more recent cougar/wolf encounter occurred sometime in either December 1995 or January 1996 in western Montana. To initiate a wolf-reintroduction program in Idaho, a number of adult wolves were captured in Alberta in early 1995 and they were moved to selected Idaho wilderness areas. According to Yellowstone National Park staff, the carcass of one of these wolves, an adult female, was found in February 1996 covered by several layers of snow near Drummond, Montana, in the Rock Creek drainage, by a Mike Jimenez. Mike told me later, over the telephone, that the wolf was still wearing its identifying collar. The carcass was later examined by a forensic laboratory, and although it was badly chewed up by coyotes, the wolf, it was determined, had been killed by a cougar.

"Grizzly" Adams, an admirer of the big bears, had little use or respect for the cougar. In Hittell's biography of Adams, an episode describing the exploration of cougar dens by Adams, his partner Gray, and two unnamed Indians provides information about what cougars had dined on. One den, which was located in a precarious rocky perch, was described as follows: "The place itself, as we found upon reaching it, was of most gloomy description, but exactly calculated for the dens of ferocious beasts. It seemed a perfect Golgotha of the animal creation; for the bones of deer, antelopes, wolves, coyotes and birds, together with feathers and hair lay scattered about in every direction. Some of the bones were yellow with freshness, others perfectly bleached, and many crumbling with age" (1926, 247). Although Adams's description may well be factual, it is not consistent with the housekeeping conditions commonly found around cougar dens. Most have been described as rather neat and clean and devoid of bones, decaying food matter, and the like.

Bobcat, Jaguar, and Lynx

All continents, exclusive of Antarctica and Australia, possess an array of non-domestic members that belong to family Felidae, the cats. Within the North American continent, seven specific species can still be found: the bobcat, cougar, jaguar, jaguarundi, lynx, margay, and ocelot. The jaguarundi, margay, and ocelot are associated more with Mexico and the tropical areas of Central and South America than they are with the United States. Their numbers are few, and information as to the possibility of their contact with the cougar is almost nonexistent.

The jaguar (Panthera onca) is an accomplished traveler, and although it now makes only limited forays into the United States from Mexico, the potential for contact with the cougar still exists. Since the jaguar is a bigger and stronger cat than the cougar, enjoying a weight advantage of up to seventy-five pounds, the cougar would probably prefer avoidance over confrontation. Although we do not have much information as to what actually may happen when these two large cats meet, a great deal has been offered over the years in the realm of opinion: writers and other cougar "experts" suggest that the cougar would eventually win a battle because of its "superior speed and ability."

An adult jaguar is generally larger than a cougar, but the cougar, reportedly, has often been the victor in direct confrontations. This photo is of a nineteenth-century Kuhnert print, *Jaguar Killing Tapir*.

Naturalist in La Plata, by William H. Hudson (1929, 35) is frequently cited in support of the cougar-superiority theory. Hudson says he had often heard that the resident cougars of Argentina and Paraguay were the aggressors and that they would defeat the jaguar in face-to-face combat; hunters had found that some jaguars they had killed had significant scarring on their backs, and it was presumed that these scars were the result of fights with cougar.

Alan Rabinozitz studied jaguars in the Belizean jungle from 1983 through 1984. His studies indicated that "pumas might be avoiding areas where they overlapped with jaguars and where jaguars were relatively abundant. It seems possible that in these same areas they were selecting among types of prey that they fed upon in order to reduce competition" (1986, 247).

The lynx *(Lynx canadensis)* is a prowler of the colder northern venues. It is common only to the upper northwest of the United States and to higher elevations of the Rocky Mountains, but is also occasionally seen in a few states of the Midwest and New England, bordering Canada. Sometimes confused with its smaller cousin the bobcat, the lynx is stockier, with long, dense fur and somewhat more heavily padded and larger feet. It is not believed that the cougar is particularly interested in these more evident differences between lynx and bobcat; it will react to both of these cats in the same way, killing and eating them when it can.

The bobcat *(Lynx rufus)* is found only in North America. It is the most widely distributed and geographically disbursed wild cat of the United States. Not a large animal, an adult male usually weighs somewhere between fifteen and twenty-five pounds. The bobcat does not tackle prey much larger than itself. Stanley P. Young's *The Bobcat of North America* provides what is perhaps the best reference to bobcat/cougar confrontation:

> Fish and Wildlife Service hunters have found that a puma [cougar], which can move more swiftly than a bobcat, may kill its smaller relative when these two meet. This is particularly true in mountainous areas of heavy snowfall. This might be a case of 'cat eat cat.' With respect to the enmity between a bobcat and a puma, Robinette [Fish and Wildlife Service hunter] says:
>
> "On December 12, 1949, Tony Sutich of the Nevada Fish and Game, found the remains of a bobcat which had been killed by a cougar in the Duck Creek area of eastern Nevada. The bobcat had been covered over almost completely by snow which the cougar had raked over it after eating his fill. I visited the place the following day and found that the entire midsection of the bobcat, including the backbone had been eaten except the stomach, intestines and some hide connecting the front and hind quarters."
>
> "In addition to the foregoing, I have analyzed one cougar stomach that contained bobcat remains. The cougar was an adult male killed by federal hunter Willis Butolph in Cedar Canyon, Iron County, Utah, July 27, 1950. There was one pound one ounce of bobcat remains in the stomach." (1958, 38–39)

Young goes on further to mention another incident where a cougar "had chased a bobcat up a tree, tore it to pieces, and ate it in the tree" (1958, 40).

Raccoons, Ringtails, and Coatimundi

The masked and band-tailed little creatures of the family Procyonidae do their scurrying around at night, and as a consequence, they are apt to run into other nocturnal predators—predators we humans might find less comical in behavior and appearance than the raccoons, ringtails, and coatis.

Not as widely geographically distributed as the raccoon or the ringtail, the coatimundi *(Nasua narica)* can be found in the United States only in the extreme southwestern areas: Arizona, New Mexico, and Texas, along the

Mexican border. A svelte version of the raccoon, but with a much longer tail, an adult male coati will usually weigh between twelve and twenty-five pounds, but somewhat larger or smaller specimens are seen occasionally. Coati meat has been identified in cougar scat, but not to any great extent because of the coati's preference for a desert habitat.

The ringtail *(Bassariscus astutus)*, with its big eyes and foxlike face, is a real charmer; it is also perhaps the most inquisitive of all the members of *Procyonidae*. Found along the Pacific Coast from Oregon through California, southern Nevada, western Colorado, southern Kansas, Arizona, New Mexico, Oklahoma, Texas, and down through Mexico into South America, the ringtail is different from the raccoon and the coati in that it has a light-colored rather than black mask. This midget midnight marauder is so small, customarily weighing less than three pounds, that it is eaten by cougars only infrequently, and then perhaps just as recreational diversion. A researcher who was working on his master's thesis at the University of Utah uncovered an incident in which a cougar had killed eight animals, including five ringtails, without bothering to eat from any of these carcasses (Tinsley 1987, 61).

The raccoon *(Procyon lotor)* is the bigger of the three *Procyonidae* species. An unusually large adult male can weigh more than forty-five pounds. The raccoon is noted for its courage when facing a dog or a pack of dogs, but it doesn't have much of a chance against the dog's master or a cougar. Raccoon meat is found in cougar stomachs and scat more often in areas where deer and other big game are not as prevalent or immediately available.

The Weasel Family

A whole host of animals fit into the weasel family, Mustelidae. They are carnivores, with a set of anal scent glands that secrete an odor that ranges from a musky aroma to a foul stench that can be almost overpowering. Each species included in this family takes aversion to every animal it comes in contact with, and the combination of its odor, behavior, and sharp teeth spells trouble for the other species—unless it is a cougar. A cougar looks upon most of these little beasties as just another light snack. What perhaps is one of the more interesting aspects of the relationship of the cougar to the animals in the weasel family is that, unlike other species, none of these creatures have changed significantly in the last ten thousand years, or maybe even longer.

The distributional range of the raccoon in North America places it in cougar habitat everywhere but in a few areas of the northern Rocky Mountains. This specimen is part of the North American exhibit, Denver Museum of Natural History.

Weasel types that have been identified in cougar stomachs or scat are marten *(Martes americana)*, all three species of weasels, the badger *(Taxidea taxus)*, the common striped skunk *(Mephitis mephitis)*, the spotted skunk *(Spilogale putorius)*, and a number of others. The fisher *(Martes pennanti)* is now seen so rarely in the wild that, in terms of its survival, cougar predation is an insignificant matter. As to skunks, most of us are rather incredulous at hearing that a cougar, or any animal, could be interested in eating one. Theodore Roosevelt once stated, early in his hunting career, that he had only "seen a wild cougar alive but twice, and both times by chance. On one occasion one of my men, Merrifield, and I surprised one eating a skunk in a bullberry patch; and by our own bungling frightened it away from its unsavory repast without getting a shot" (1893, 337). Ben Lilly is said to have commented that a cougar would give preference on a trail to a grizzly, but that the grizzly would leave a trail to avoid a skunk; the cougar, however, would not leave a trail because of a skunk, but would eat the skunk (Haynes 1966, 255–56). In *Animal Life in the Yosemite*, Grinnell and Storer report on a cougar/skunk encounter:

On November 8, 1916, Mr. McLean, senior, was riding on horseback along the road about 8 miles east of Coulterville. His shepherd dog was scouting along the adjacent sidehill through the manzanita and ceanothus brush. At one place there was a strong odor of skunk, and shortly the dog began to bark in tones which indicated that he had treed something. Mr. McLean rode to the spot and found up in a golden oak what he first thought was a bobcat. . . . Presently Mr. McLean saw a long tail hanging below a limb and realized that the animal was a Mountain Lion. Promptly he shot it, the rifle ball passing through the lion's neck. The animal "smelled powerfully" of skunk, and later its stomach was found to contain flesh, skin, and black and white hair of a striped skunk. (1924, 98)

The badger and the wolverine *(Gulo luscus)* are both pretty tough characters, and only a large cougar would consider taking on either one if it were angered. The badger is perhaps the easier target, being smaller, but it could cause fearful damage with its long claws and sharp teeth before succumbing to a cougar's attack. As for the wolverine, some observers believe it is more than a match for a cougar, and even perhaps for a large bear. Not commonly found anymore in the United States, an adult male wolverine can weigh as much as fifty pounds, but what it lacks in size (relative to, say, a cougar) it makes up for in tenacity and ferocity. Victor H. Cahalane, former National Park Service biologist, identified a number of occasions where a wolverine has attacked cougars, taken over cougar kills, and generally bullied cougars. Since the cougar is not inclined to take unnecessary risks, there is no reason to believe that it would actually attempt to prey upon the wolverine, and, since the wolverine is slower and a more awkward runner than the cougar, it is doubtful that the wolverine could do other damage than to just drive a cougar away from its kill.

DOMESTIC ANIMALS

Perhaps the major factor in the disappearance of the American wilderness was the pioneering growth of domestic animal herds and flocks. When domestic animals are brought into territory previously occupied by native species, the policy adopted by humans is that all native creatures incompatible with livestock rearing have to leave voluntarily or be permanently removed.

Not as unwelcome perhaps as the wolf, the cougar was nevertheless one of

Wolverines—now only infrequently found in the United States, primarily in the extreme northwest. Although not as yet an endangered species, the few that remain are more often seen in the Arctic and sub-Arctic areas of Eurasia and North America. The specimens shown are part of the North American display in the Denver Museum of Natural History.

the first predators subject to a variety of control measures, sometimes being summarily targeted for elimination. Since it is not endowed with human reasoning ability, a cougar is unable to differentiate between animals that humans would protect and those that are fair game. The cougar has preyed upon virtually all domesticated species, and suffered the consequences. However, in spite of the temptations of an easy meal offered by domestic animals, the cougar's preference is still wild game. A cougar epicure, I imagine, would always consider nature's *pièce de résistance* to be members of the deer family.

Over the years, cattle, sheep, goats, hogs, domestic fowl, and numerous exotic ranching species have all been sampled by cougars. What is considered by livestock owners to be particularly abhorrent are not the random and occasional killings, but those few incidents that have involved wholesale slaughter. Perhaps it is because sheep and chickens tend to cluster together and behave erratically when attacked that they are more often the victims of these murderous frenzies.

The one domestic animal that seems to have found especial favor as a prey species for cougars is the horse. The cougar will take greater than normal risks to obtain horseflesh. It has even been suggested that some attacks on human beings occurred because the human was riding a horse at the time and the cougar was simply after the horse. A few writers have discounted the widespread claims of cougar attacks on horses (Schueler 1980, 259), but accounts of such predation, especially on colts, were so frequent and flagrant in the late 1800s and early 1900s that many ranchers claimed that it was economically impossible to raise horses in cougar country. In fact, one subspecies of cougar native to Rocky Mountain localities was named *Felis concolor hippolestes*, or horse killer.

In addition to its interest in livestock, the cougar has also gone after household pets—cats and dogs. To the cougar, this level of predation may seem to be essential for its survival; in practice, it is suicidal, because loss of a beloved pet leads to such human emotional trauma that it usually requires the death of the cougar responsible. This critical and sensitive issue and related matters to do with the urbanization of America and the future of the cougar will be considered in later chapters.

In its continual search for food, the cougar is the quintessential predator. Very little that is still alive and quivering is overlooked. In addition to the species mentioned above, the cougar has also fed upon such diverse creatures as alligators, armadillos, opossums, frogs, and turtles. Whatever is edible, vulnerable, and available has a good chance of appearing on the cougar menu.

The Native American and the Cougar

The ground on which we stand is sacred ground. It is the dust and blood of our ancestors. On these plains the Great White Father at Washington sent his soldiers armed with long knives and rifles to slay the Indian. Many of them sleep on yonder hill where Pahaska—White Chief of the Long Hair [Colonel George A. Custer]—so bravely fought and fell. A few more passing suns will see us here no more, and our dust and bones will mingle with these same prairies. I see as in a vision the dying spark of our council fires, the ashes cold and white. I see no longer the curling smoke rising from our lodge poles. I hear no longer the songs of the women as they prepare the meal. The antelope have gone; the buffalo wallows are empty. Only the wail of the coyote is heard. The white man's medicine is stronger than ours; his iron horse rushes over the buffalo trail. He talks to it through his "whisper-ing spirit" [telephone]. We are like birds with a broken wing. My heart is cold within me. My eyes are growing dim—I am old. . . .

(Crow Chief Plenty-Coups, farewell address, given on council grounds of the Little Bighorn Battlefield site in 1909. Joseph K. Dixon, *The Vanishing Race*. Doubleday, Garden City, NJ, 1913, 189)

T HE ABOVE WORDS, which were so movingly spoken and eloquently descriptive, express sadness and despair over the passing of what was the former unconstrained and simple way of life for Native American tribes and the eventual demise of a distinctive and unique culture. The land, the animals, the rivers, forests, grasslands, and the Indian were all one.

Respectful of the Earth's natural resources and the many and varied forms of life that these resources supported, the Indian favored each with value and honor. Although some creatures may have been held in a somewhat higher level of esteem than others, none were worshipped as a deity because Native Americans, like the European immigrants to America, believed in the existence of only one true and all-powerful God.

According to some rather carefully prepared estimates (Mooney 1910, 390), there were approximately 846,000 Indians residing in the United States in 1492 upon the arrival of Columbus. Thomas E. Mails (1972, 12) claims that by 1800 "all of the Plains tribes together numbered no more than 200,000 people." Conceivably, their practice of maintaining small-to-medium-sized mobile communities served the Indians well by reducing the spread of disease and avoiding possible environmental contamination. When various Indian tribes were forced from areas of natural habitation and placed on reservations, the confinement proved to be devastating. Disease, coupled with the lack of adequate health care, significantly reduced their numbers.

Current scientific thought has it that ancestors of the myriad tribes found in the United States migrated across the Bering land bridge from Asia more than forty thousand years ago, in much the same fashion as did the mammals they hunted. The possibility also exists that some of these new Americans may have come by sea, landing countless years ago on the eastern and western coasts. Indian legends, folk tales, and even certain anthropologists and archaeologists suggest that some tribes may have always been here—that they did not have to come from somewhere else (Goodman 1981). The significant differences in physical characteristics and culture seem to support the common contention of multiplicity of ancestral source. Whatever the circumstances may have been, the early immigrants were primarily itinerant hunters; they pursued the animals, found the hunting good, and perhaps left and returned with others. Eventually, most of the people stayed.

Within Indian culture, mythology, and religion, animals and animal spirits are iconic figures of the first magnitude. Each animal possessed an ability or characteristic that, if emulated by a tribal member, was believed to lead this member to a better life or preferred social status. Consequently, names of animals were not only commonly bestowed on individuals, they were also adopted by clans, societies, and cults.

To most tribes, names mean everything. For an individual it could impart historical, and perhaps even mystical, significance: it might refer to an exploit or encounter that an ancestor had had with a particular animal or animals. The individual's name or the name of the tribal membership grouping or clan could also express the wealth and status of a tribal family; for example, through membership in a clan and possession of the right of association with the clan's named animal defender. It might also be through the names of other animal protectors—perhaps names that the member's ancestors had purchased and so secured for the family the right to hand them down to succeeding generations.

Belonging to a clan was more than just social fellowship: some sort of family connection was usually a prerequisite to tribal clan membership. Besides the clans, some tribes also maintained a variety of societies, some of which, because of their ceremonial customs and actions, were considered secret. Many of these tribal societies were basically militaristic in nature. They were arranged by member age into a number of divisions. Prior battle accomplishments or individual acts of courage, daring, or heroism could entitle a society member to other special honors or status. A few of the more specialized tribal membership groupings were not only militaristic but were also cultlike in part.

The Bear Cult is a prime example of the combining of tribal societal structure with mysticism. In nearly every Plains tribe, small numbers of men believed that they had obtained supernatural bear powers through dreams. They painted bear symbols on their tepees and personal items. When they died, their power went with them—it was not an inherited characteristic or honor. The bull elk—to give another illustration of animal symbolism—was considered an effective helper in love since he had shown them his ability to call females. In some tribes, marital unions between members of the same clan were forbidden, or regulated in some other manner, by clan laws. An example of this is offered by Burt (1973, 57–58). A member of the Panther Clan of the Creeks could not marry another Panther Clan member; in the Creek tribe such a union was considered incestuous and was usually punished by death.

More than any other animal, the bison dominated the strongly anthropomorphic Plains Indian society. By its death, the bison provided tribal members with shelter, clothing, food, and a diverse host of other sustenance items. In gratitude for the supreme sacrifice the bison made on their behalf, it was the custom to thank the bison spirits for this gift and offer supplication for the success of future hunts. In a somewhat similar vein, the bear was both food for the tribe and also revered as a near deity. Ceremonies involving the bear were ubiquitous, one of the more interesting being that associated with the planned bear hunt. When a bear was killed, the carcass was treated with total reverence. After the tribal hunter, or hunters, had offered appropriate words of apology to the bear and explained the urgency of the people's need, the bear was killed. The dead bear was dressed in fine clothes, as if it were a human being, and a plea was made to the bear chief to continue to send the Indians more of his children. If this ceremony was not conducted properly, it would be a serious affront to the spirit of the bear.

The bear figured prominently in a story that is told in the Hopi tribe about the origin of the *Ungwish-wungwa*, or Kachina Clan (Nequatewa 1936, 79) —a story that also mentions the cougar. As in many other Indian myths and legends, some type of quest is usually involved. In this one, a boy is sent out to discover the source of strange sounds being made at night near their camp. First he was painted with reddish clay and given a prayer plume; then he was sent on his way. Before he had gone very far, he met the old Spider Woman (a supernatural being in the Hopi culture) who gave him two charms. The first was the root of a plant; the second, a fluffy feather. The feather would go before him to show the way, and the root was to be used in order to pass four dangerous places guarded by terrible beings. The first place he reached was guarded by "a great mountain lion." He chewed on the root and spat on the lion before the crouched figure could spring on him. The second place was guarded by a bear, and the third and fourth by snakes. The boy was able to pass them by safely by using the root in the same manner that he did with the lion. Thus far, the story has focused on the appointment of a brave young man to undertake a hazardous journey in search of truth, and perhaps also to obtain tribal betterment. Constantly, there is the presence of the supernatural and the involvement of animal beings. These lead to the conclusion of the story: godlike beings, the Kachinas, teach the youth how to make Kachina masks and how to hold Kachina dances, and to make them a part of tribal religion. It's worth noting that in this story, unlike the one from California mentioned earlier, the cougar is not a benign presence but one associated more with evil.

All Indian tribes did not, and still do not, look alike or cherish the same ritualistic and religious beliefs. Although certain similarities may exist from region to region and from tribe to tribe, few cultural characteristics apply to all

Native Americans. Tribes displayed differences in language, dress, physical appearance, and social demeanor; perhaps not all would fit the mold of "the noble savage yet unspoiled by civilization"—a romantic image projected on Native Americans by some Europeans. It is therefore not surprising to find that attitudes toward the cougar were not identical across the board. Not all Native Americans admired or liked the cougar, even though some tribes and tribal members may have honored this cat for its hunting ability and strength. In fact, the cougar seems to have been something of a pariah for many, in both the Native and non–Native American societies.

Animals were considered by the Indians of the southeastern United States to belong to three general creature categories: (1) those with four feet; (2) birds—who were associated with the Upper World; and (3) reptiles and fish. Some creatures possessed special abilities and were difficult to classify: there were birds that could hunt at night, and four-footed animals that could fly (bats, and a squirrel). The cougar, because of its nocturnal talents, was one of the unclassified animals—a paradoxical status. All of the multitalented, enigmatic unclassified creatures were viewed by tribes with feelings of either wonder or dread. The seldom-seen cougar was infrequently mentioned; it was perhaps too mysterious to acquire as many tribal devotees as did animals such as the bear, the wolf, the eagle, and the raven.

The cougar did, however, become an occasional subject in tribal artistic expressions. When early English settlers met Pocahontas, daughter of Chief Powhatan, they perhaps also observed a catlike carved image that served along with three other sentinels guarding Powhatan's treasure house. The English also later secured a garment, referred to as Powhatan's Mantle, that was made from four deer skins displaying three large figures: a human, a deer, and a cougar. At Bandelier National Monument in New Mexico, the forms of two cougars, carved out of bedrock perhaps more than six hundred years ago, can be seen. The National Park Service identifies these two stone carvings as the Shrine of the Lions. Located some distance to the west in the Cochiti pueblo are two other stone carvings—the Lions of Cochiti. Unlike the Bandelier carvings, the Cochiti lions were created from two large boulders. Believed to have been created by Indians from the Keresan pueblos more than six hundred years ago, both sites are held sacred by the tribe. It is no longer permitted to take photographs, and site visitation is discouraged to all except Native Americans. The cougar formations have unfortunately been damaged by senseless vandalism, but both carvings still capture the artist's perception of crouching felines, ready to pounce.

It seems that most artifacts and legends representing the cougar in theme or subject have been produced by Indian tribes associated with the south-western and southeastern United States, Mexico, and South America. In the southeast, along Florida's western coast on the small island of San Marco, wood carvings made by former inhabitants (perhaps from the Calusa tribe or from distant relatives of the Muskogee or Creek tribes) were uncovered in 1884. Among the images was a six-inch-high cougar, which it is suggested once served as a religious idol. Works by other tribal artists—painted on ani-mal skins, sculpted as totems, fetishes, and the like—have similarly portrayed the image of a cougar, the "long tail," throughout the two American conti-nents. Examples of some of the more identifiable cougar art forms are in the southwestern United States, where soft rock walls of canyons still preserve striking petroglyphs. Occasionally, the clear likeness of a cougar, scraped and painted on the rock, can be made out.

The sharpened bone of a cougar is said to have been used by ancient Aztec physicians to "ward off human death"; they used the bone to prick the breast of an anxious patient. Cougar paws and cougar gall is also said to have been used by certain southwestern Indian tribes to treat the afflicted (Young and Goldman 1946, 7).

Cougar body parts were used in making various objects. Most tribes, prior to their owning firearms, used the bow and arrow as their primary weapon, and they usually stored arrows in a leather case (a quiver) with an attached strap, or loop, for convenience and mobility. Cougar skin, being durable and hard to tear, was favored as quiver material. It was usually taken during the win-ter months when the pelt was thick and soft. It took one complete cougar skin to make two quiver cases. To encase the bow, Indians used the cougar's tail.

Cougar claws were used to make necklaces; these generally were designed in the same manner as those made with the more common and fashionable bear claws. Indian hunters may have occasionally stumbled upon a cougar carcass, but skins and claws were usually obtained by their killing the animal themselves. That Indians actively hunted the cougar in the Southwest was noted in 1864 by Elliot Coues, a surgeon who was attached to a column of cavalry on their way to Fort Whipple, near the present-day city of Prescott, Arizona:

Of . . . the cats, first in size and general consequence, if not in point of numbers, is the cougar. With hardly the exception of the jaguar, this is the most powerful of all our digitigrade carnivores. It was formerly distributed quite across the continent, and to high latitudes; but . . . it has been gradually driven westward by the progress of civilization, till its occurrence in the East is rare, and only known in the most mountainous and unfrequented regions. . . . During a somewhat protracted residence in the Territory, I never met with one, or heard its peculiarly mournful, though terrifying cry, which has been so fancifully interpreted by different writers. . . . That the Indians pursue it successfully with only their bows and arrows I know to be a fact, as I have found skins in their possession cut in various places with the sharp stone points of their arrowheads. (qtd. in Davis 1982, 165–66)

Cougar meat was also a food item for Native Americans. It is all but impossible to identify which tribes would or would not eat cougar flesh; there are conflicting stories about this. But that cougar flesh is tasty has never been disputed and we have testimony from a great number of people, including Charles Darwin (1962, 117) and U.S. President Theodore Roosevelt (Day 1955, 207). James Capen (Grizzly) Adams despised the cougar but enjoyed its flesh; he also said that the oil from cougar fat was good for sprains and bruises (Hittell 1926, 306–10). Some suggest that cougar tastes somewhat like chicken or veal (Young and Goldman 1946, 120–21). Jack Turner (East, "Cougar in the Barn," *Danger!* 1970, 73–84), who liked both lynx and cougar meat, suggested that it tastes more like pork. In *Life in the Far West*, a fictionalized version of his actual experiences in 1846, George Frederick Ruxton states that "in delicacy of flavour, richness of meat, and other good qualities, being the flesh of panthers [cougars], which surpasses every other, and all put together" (Ruxton 1951, 98).

The Seminoles of southern Florida enjoyed cougar meat. It was common practice for these Indians, even prior to the seventeenth century, to burn the grass and weeds from their fields in the fall, and for hunters to circle the burn area and gather any animals that were fleeing from the fire, which would include cougars. Another Seminole practice when hunting large mammals such as bear, bison, and cougar was to assemble in large groups (McReynolds 1957, 7). Some of the earliest accounts of tribal use of cougar meat were recorded in Virginia prior to 1600 and in the Carolinas in the 1700s (Young and Goldman 1946, 120). According to Burt and Ferguson, the principal game animals of the

Indians of the southeastern United States were the deer and the bear. Birds, small mammals, and fish were also important food. Cougar meat was apparently insignificant as a food item for most if not all of these tribes (1973, 79).

There is no strong evidence that cougars were consistently hunted by either the Woodland, Plains, Great Basin, or Western Coastal Indian tribes; other animal species were more abundant and readily available. However, the cougar was probably eaten from time to time, and it is quite likely that it was in Indian villages that white trappers and frontiersmen first tasted cougar meat—as they also did dog meat.

Indian tribes of the Southwest perhaps manifested a level of reverence and mystery for the cougar higher than any others. They feared the cougar, but still looked upon it with respect and even veneration. The Hopi were particularly deferential in ceremonies and religious beliefs. The Apache, on the other hand, respected the cougar as perhaps they would any skilled warrior, but it is questionable if reverence was involved. There is nothing to indicate that the Apache either found cougar flesh savory or considered it taboo as a food.

Occasionally, tribal apprehensions regarding the cougar were seen by non–Native Americans as being a deity-associated fear; few people really took the time to understand what they felt was a backward culture. As an example of this, Zane Grey, famed author of Westerns, once penned a nonfiction publication entitled *Roping Lions in the Grand Canyon* that recalled his adventures capturing cougars in Arizona's Grand Canyon with Charles Jesse (Buffalo) Jones. One of the members of the hunting party was a Navajo whom Grey described as "a copper-skinned, raven-haired, beady-eyed desert savage." This Navajo, recruited because of his skill handling horses and his tracking ability if the horses should wander from their pasturage, was never addressed by his given name but was called merely "the Navvy." Grey describes the Navajo's reaction when the first cougars were roped, secured, and brought into camp:

> Presently I saw Emett [one of the members of the hunting group] coming through the woods leading and dragging the Indian. I felt sorry for the Navvy, for I felt that his fear was not so much physical as spiritual. And it seemed no wonder to me that the Navvy should hang back from this sacrilegious treatment of his god. A natural wisdom, which I had in common with all human beings who consider self-preservation the first law of life, deterred me from acquainting my august companions with my belief. At least I did not want to break up the camp.
>
> In the remorseless grasp of Emett, forced along, the Navajo dragged his

feet and held his face sidewise, though his dark eyes gleamed at the lions. Terror predominated among the expressions of his countenance. Emett drew him within fifteen feet and held him there, and with voice, and gesticulating of his free hand, tried to show the poor fellow that the lions would not hurt him. (Grey 1924, 32–33)

Perhaps fear of the cougars, even though their claws were clipped and they were chained to trees, motivated the Navajo's apprehension, but it is difficult to believe that he would have willingly partaken of cougar meat unless he were starving.

Henry W. Shoemaker, an authority on early Pennsylvania history, indicated that the Seneca Indians made pouches out of cougar skins "in which they stored their 'great medicine.' The claws were used as amulets to signify the Indian's victory over the forces of evil, panthers being supposed to have kinship to the Machtando or Evil One" (1917, 52).

It may sound rather far-fetched today, but James Adair, an Indian trader and writer who visited a number of American Indian tribes prior to 1775, suggested that there was some relationship of descent between the American Indian and the Jewish people. He noted similarities in images of cherubs involving certain animals, including members of the *panther* or *tyger* family (Williams, ed. 1930, 33). In addition, Adair noted that Indians, like Jews, consider all animals "that are either carnivorous, or live on nasty food; as hogs, wolves, panthers, foxes, cats, mice, rats," to be unclean (Williams, ed. 1930, 139).

This latter observation is somewhat compromised by Adair's universalism, which lumps together all Indians, suggesting they share some uniform belief system. Although in Native American cultures some animals may have been rejected as food in times of plenty for a number of reasons, it is doubtful that there were controlling taboos or scruples for a truly hungry tribe. Jason Betzinez tells a story that can be cited as an example. In his colorful accounting of his youth as an Apache warrior apprentice, Betzinez describes how his aunt Dilchthe and a number of women and children of her particular Apache band were captured by Mexicans and taken to a penal colony in lower California. Dilchthe and some others later escaped and traveled more than one thousand miles by foot to their home camp in Arizona. Along the way, they fed upon any dead creature that they came upon—birds, rats, rabbits, and coyotes—and were delighted to do so (Betzinez 1959, 12–13).

All tribes practiced staunch conservatism with regard to use of Earth's natural resources, but to name a single characteristic that makes Native American culture unique, I think I would say that of respect. Although tribes differed in appearance, in their religious beliefs, in their language, and even in demeanor, the one conviction they all held was that all life possessed the equivalent of an immortal soul, and because of this all plants and animals were entitled to and deserving of respect. The cougar was a part of the Indian's human world as were all animals with which they shared existence. Although, as we have seen, through its surreptitious and somewhat sinister conduct the cougar had not exactly earned the same level of tribal appreciation as did the bison, the deer, or the bear, the Indian was quite willing to accept the cougar for what it was and let it go at that. There were a few cougar totems and fetishes, and other sacred cougar memorabilia may have made it into medicine bundles, but at a level below that which would suggest icon status. However, the cougar was respected.

Over the years, the Native American has had to adjust to an imported and pervasive culture that advocated a completely different value system. Indians were expected to stop being Indians and adopt the rules and the culture of a controlling immigrant society. In spite of expanding legal and social pressures for Native Americans to conform, ancestral tribal convictions and customs have survived, including an inherent belief in the sanctity of nature and respect for the native land. Former U.S. Secretary of the Interior Stewart L. Udall (1961–1969), recognizing the current unfortunate, incongruous status of the Native American, says it is "ironical that today the conservation movement finds itself turning back to ancient Indian land ideas"—that public acceptance of the conservationist movement in fact confirms Indian land-management practices. The conservation movement is returning

> to the Indian understanding that we are not outside of nature, but of it. From this wisdom we can learn how to conserve the best parts of our continent.
>
> In recent decades we have slowly come back to some of the truths that the Indians knew from the beginning: that unborn generations have a claim on the land equal to our own; that men need to learn from nature, to keep an ear to the earth, and to replenish their spirits in frequent contacts with animals and wild land. And most important of all, we are recovering a sense of reverence for the land. (1963, 12)

When preparations were in progress for the 1976 United States Bicentennial Celebration, the event's planners, seeking advice from many sectors of society, asked for input from the Native American community. In response, the following comments were offered by Ed McGaa, an Oglala Sioux and co-chairman of the Minnesota Bicentennial Commission, in association with the Indian Week Program at the University of Arizona, Tucson (January 7–10, 1973). Under the heading "Native Americans Look at the American Revolution Bicentennial Observance," McGaa said:

> This morning at breakfast we took from Mother Earth to live as we have done every day of our lives. But did we thank our Mother Earth for giving us the means to live? The old Indian did. When he drove his horse in near to a buffalo running at full speed across the prairie, he drew his bow string back and as he did so, he said, "Forgive me brother, but my people must live." After he butchered the buffalo, he would take the skull and face it to the setting sun as a thanksgiving and acknowledgement that all things come from Mother Earth. He never took more than he needed. Today the buffalo is gone. Mother Earth is our real mother because every bit of us truly comes from her and daily she takes care of us. It is very late but still time to revive and rediscover the old American Indian value of respect for Mother Earth. (Chaudhuri 1973)

The Indian and the bison, the wolf, and the grizzly, no longer do they walk the same path or share the same natural world together. The wolf and grizzly are now nearly extinct in the United States and are endemic only to the more isolated of the northern wilderness areas of North America. The bison has been converted from the lumbering monarch of the plains to basically that of a moneymaking livestock product. But the Indian who today wishes to stroll through the wilderness may still have the cougar as a silent, secretive companion. Where the bison, wolf, and grizzly once also roamed, the cougar continues to pad, alone and aloof.

SIX The Cougar Hunters

WRITER HENRY DAVID THOREAU—he of Walden—is remembered for his simplistic beliefs and love of nature. Thoreau can be counted among those people who not only treasure the gentle unsophistication of wildlife, but also revere the naked savagery that serves to kindle the wilderness spirit:

> As I came home through the woods with my string of fish, trailing my pole, it being now quite dark, I caught a glimpse of a woodchuck stealing across my path, and felt a strange thrill of savage delight, and was strongly tempted to seize and devour him raw; not that I was hungry then, except for that wildness which he represented. Once or twice, however, while I lived at the pond, I found myself ranging the woods, like a half-starved hound, with a strange abandonment, seeking some kind of venison which I might devour, and no morsel could have been too savage for me. (1987, 127)

Something about large predators both excites and provokes the human species. Perhaps it is an innate fear that these creatures present a real or latent threat to human life, or that they offer a level of competition and even challenge to the comfortable image of human omnipotence over the animal kingdom. Whatever the reason may be, for the hunter this human awe of the beast enhances the thrill of an anticipated dangerous undertaking—a summons to greatness, the supreme test. Thus, as with the aspiring Indian warriors of yore, victory over a powerful adversary gains for the successful hunter praise, admiration, and the respect of peers.

Photo of a hunting camp in 1895 shows a typical array of animals taken at that time in the extreme northwest of Colorado. In addition to the mule deer and cougars, note the bobcat hanging from the end of the pole at the extreme right. *Photo by A. G. Wallihan. Courtesy of Denver Public Library, Western History Department.*

In the United States today there exists a strong antihunting sentiment— or sentimentality—that is driven in part by some legitimate wildlife conservation concerns, but this idea is also contaminated in part by an accompanying belief: that any taking of animal life by humans is wrong—a crime against nature. Present-day human hunters—or sportsmen, as they prefer to be called —observe and support ethical game laws; they labor in the forefront of an effort to protect wildlife habitats; and they have also been helpful in experiments designed to restore species that are threatened or endangered. But in spite of their contributions to the improvement of conditions for all wildlife (including predator), for many people the human hunter does not exude the image of the courageous and fearless champion.

However, personal challenge is not the only motivation for direct confrontation with animal predators: another one is simple economics. Although the Bible may suggest that the lion and the lamb should lie down side by side, it is more likely that the lion would prefer to lie down with the lamb in its stomach. Consequently, protection of livestock investments frequently requires the permanent removal of an offending predator.

The efforts of struggling pioneer ranchers and their occasionally tragic experiences with wolves is a good illustration of economic crisis brought about by extreme predation. Many examples could be offered, but the following incident, which occurred more than eighty years ago, perhaps describes it best. In the spring of 1913, Elliot Barker was assistant forest ranger for the Carson National Forest in New Mexico, stationed at the Cow Creek Ranger Station. It was a common practice at that time, much as it is now, for the U.S Forest Service to issue permits to livestock owners allowing them to graze their animals on Forest Service lands. Although a certain amount of predation was to be expected, the permit-holders in Barker's district were experiencing unusual and enormous stock losses from bear, cougars, and wolves. Wolves had just killed two of Barker's horses, and he was out setting traps for them when he came upon a sheepherder who was greatly perturbed:

> He said that the evening before he had lost about two hundred sheep from his herd, a cut we called it, and was unable to find them. It had snowed about four inches during the night and covered the tracks. I joined in the search.
>
> In the side of Bald Wind Mountain we found where they had been while it was snowing. We followed the tracks and soon came upon the worst bloody mess I have ever seen. An old bitch wolf and two nearly grown ones had found the sheep and killed, or mortally wounded, eighty-seven of them. A number were left alive, their flanks ripped open and entrails dragging. At the end of the killing spree, they had eaten from three carcasses, while the others had been killed for fun. (Barker 1974, 119–20)

Control measures against determined predators were, and still are, primarily conducted by governmental and contractual hunters—professional "predator control specialists." When bears, cougars, coyotes, and wolves ranged through much of America, these animals frequently presented a problem for ranchers and farmers attempting to wrest an agricultural profit from lands located on the fringe of, or within, the wilderness frontier. Initially, embattled land or livestock owners would attempt to deal with predation issues by themselves through reactive hunting efforts, carcass baiting, poisoning, and trapping. If these measures failed, they would seek out a professional hunter. Dating back to colonial times, bounties were also offered, by both public and private sources, as rewards for the destruction of predators. But for a number of reasons, including the cost involved in administering the program, many people believed that this was not the most effective or efficient way to combat the constant predation problems.

Hunting of cougars was a popular recreation in the Rocky Mountain West at the turn of the nineteenth century. Note the length of the larger cougar. Photo taken in Chico, Colorado, which is now but a ghost town, approximately fourteen miles east of Pueblo. *Courtesy of Colorado Historical Society.*

Government trappers display their catch of seven Arizona cougars in the late 1930s. *Photo from the Lowell Jett Collection. Courtesy of* High Country News, *Paonia, Colorado.*

As mentioned in chapter 3, in the latter part of the sixteenth century Jesuit missionaries in California offered cattle to local Indian tribes if they would kill cougars that were terrorizing the Jesuits' cattle herds. This was one of the first forms of bounty payment offered in what is now the United States for the repression of any predatory species. In the original thirteen colonies, cash bounties were offered for the destruction of all larger predators: bear, wolf, and cougar. When the forty-eight contiguous states came into being, all but one, Nevada, had, at one time or another, established a bounty on the cougar. It was not only because of concern for safety of domestic livestock or the potential threat to human life that bounties were offered; more frequently it was because of the widely held opinion that certain of the wild predators, such as the cougar, might ultimately kill most, if not all, desirable wildlife species such as deer, elk, and mountain sheep.

Nearly all bounty payments on cougars have now been phased out. Current public opinion does not favor payment of bounties; nor, apparently, is it believed by a voting majority that the former widespread system of bounty payments was an effective method of predation control. There are, indeed, strong arguments that the methods, and perhaps even the concept, were fallacious, and that the systems were poorly administered; but, given that the primary intention was to eliminate undesirable predator species, bounty payments were certainly helped toward the accomplishment of that objective. If we look

Photographic display of cougar heads collected by federal Animal Damage Control agents in 1989. Publicity that was subsequently given to the photo served to decrease the extent of ADC activities in Arizona. *Anonymous photographer. Photo courtesy of* High Country News, *Paonia, Colorado.*

only at the results, there is no question that bounty payments served to interest and motivate hired specialists in cougar hunting. The bounties supplemented whatever retainer salaries these hunters may have been paid with a variety of public and private funds.

Robert Grey, wildlife author and former assistant director of public relations for the San Diego Zoo, vividly recalled an incident regarding a cougar bounty that occurred in the early 1930s while he was a boy growing up in western Montana. After discovering that a female cougar with three kittens was comfortably ensconced in a canyon near his family's cabin, he spent much of his spare time tracking the mother cat and fantasizing about what she might actually look like. One day his dream came true: he spied her sleeping on a rocky outcropping. A few days after his surprising and idyllic encounter with the cougar, a bounty hunter showed up. Grey describes the ensuing events:

> Montana had a bounty on mountain lions in those times—25 dollars, an impressive sum in the years of the Great Depression. Some people made their living bounty hunting. One of them, a mountain man named Bill Smith, lived just a few miles from us. Word of my lion reached him eventually, and one morning he showed up with his dogs.
> "I heerd they's a varmint round abouts."
> My father, to whom that lion was as much a part of the canyon as its deer and trees and stream, tried to dissuade Bill Smith from killing her. But as the bounty hunter replied, "The law's the law," and off he set with his dogs.
> The following day I saw two of the cubs lying dead in Bill Smith's wagon.

A third, plus the adult, had escaped. A group of mountain people were gathered around the wagon and Bill Smith was holding forth from high in the seat.

"Them two varmints there cost me a fine dog that the female tore up when she got away. But they's fifty dollars worth of bounty laying there. Not a bad day's work."

Well all that happened many years ago. A freeway now cuts through our canyon; the cabin is gone, burned by vandals and the mine [the placer mine worked by his father] has long since caved in. My father is gone also, and I suppose that Bill Smith and the lion he hunted share the earth at last. But over the years that cat has been a living presence to me, the fascinating, beautiful experience which stays as fresh as it was on a warm springtime afternoon. (1979, 10)

The first cougar hunters in the Americas were the Paleo–Indians, who fought cougars over disputed prey animals more than they would purposely hunt the cougar. In later years, Indian tribes learned to dig deep pit traps set with carefully concealed sharpened stakes to capture larger animals, and occasionally this included predators such as the bear and cougar. In order to improve their chances for capture, the hunters would attempt to lure a predator into a trap. A small animal would be used as bait, and it was secured in such a way that its discomfort would then cause it to cry out, thereby arousing the interest of any nearby predator. When tribes acquired greater hunting proficiency through the use of stringed bows and sharpened projectiles, they became more selective with respect to the taking of predatory animals.

Prior to the coming of the Europeans, the Indian did not have guns or horses and did not possess goats, sheep, cattle, or any other domestic animal except half-wild dogs. To live comfortably, the Indian had to learn to be an accomplished hunter, resourceful not only with weapons but also with the yield from successful hunts. Great honor was accorded to the skilled hunter who provided meat for the tribe or who in battle defeated a formidable predator such as the bear or the cougar. As mighty as their hunting skills may have been, it is not plausible that, even over time, these Indian hunters would have noticeably depleted any of the then abundant wildlife species. When the European settlers arrived, however, the balance of nature substantially changed. It was, in effect, the introduction of an aggressive subspecies into an otherwise relatively benign environment. To the Europeans, there appeared to be a profound abundance of wildlife; and they, instead of hunting game animals because of actual need, often did so only for the "sport" of killing. Moreover, they had guns; they did not need to depend as much on stealth and skill with bow and arrow as did the Indians; they killed animals at great distances. The uncontrolled hunting, intensified by the later appearance of the market hunter, depleted wild game, and what was formerly wildlife habitat was eventually supplanted by a variety of agrarian and industrial activities.

Perhaps one of the more miserable examples of indulgent hunting squander was that presented in the so-called "adventures" of Count Orlando, an account of a long series of killings published in the January 1909 edition of *Outdoor Life* (Orlando, "Cougar Hunting in the Northwest," 26–29). After the count killed two bears that had been located by the count's huge pack of dogs, the pack was set to trail a cougar. The dogs quickly treed the animal. Count Orlando comments, "It was a full grown female, which fell to my bullet, and had to get a second shot to be prevented from doing mischief. I was very much surprised to see how fat she was, since I had never seen anything of the like with other members of the feline family that I had killed on other locations." The count then shot a raccoon in the foot. The dogs subsequently killed it. After the count had his lunch, the dogs shortly treed another cougar, which "came down only after my second bullet; it was again a large female rolling in fat." The following day, while traveling by boat along the coast, Orlando indicated that "a few eagles on shore at last attracted my attention and I had several shots at them, but only one fell down within sight. It was a young specimen, measuring six feet eight inches from tip to tip." After his eagle episode, the count hustled over to a tree where the dogs had trapped yet another cougar. Orlando continues:

> My first bullet struck too far back, and the wounded beast went higher in the tree. As it did so, I hit it in the leg, since it was getting nearly out of sight. Now it ran to the end of a branch, where I put another bullet through its body, the very moment it took a flying leap down. That was a picture worth seeing! From a height of about twenty-five yards, down it came, its head between its legs; its tail stretched out. My last shot must have interfered with its aim and it struck a log when it landed on the bottom. It smacked its skull to pieces, but lived, nevertheless, for about a half an hour. This puma, another female, had three embryos inside. She measured seven feet four inches.

Not having further opportunity to kill anything, the count was planning to leave "when a Chinaman drew my attention to a white-headed eagle, sitting

One of several remarkable pictures taken by A. G. Wallihan of Lay, Colorado. On a hunt with William Wells in 1895, Wallihan, observing the cougar (a rather small female) about to leap from a branch, stationed himself near the anticipated point of landing. See also the next photo. *Courtesy of Denver Public Library, Western History Department.*

near on a dead tree. I put a bullet through him and skinned him, like the other, to be sent home for mounting." The count reports that he had a "jolly time" and that he made arrangements for a hunt in the Northwest the following fall. Flushed with his success, on April 18, 1908, he boarded ship to go to Japan and complete what he said was an enjoyable trip around the world.

Along the eastern seacoast, to protect the early colonists' imported domestic animals, offending predators were gradually, and in some instances promptly, eliminated. The thorough and pitiless manner with which this removal was accomplished, through what were called animal drives, is well described by historian Colonel Henry W. Shoemaker (*The Panther and the Wolf*, part 1, 1917, 29–31). According to Shoemaker, these drives were quite common at that time, though not well documented. He describes a drive in Snyder County, Pennsylvania, about 1760, led by "Black Jack" Schwartz. Settlers in the area having found that cougars and wolves were being particularly troublesome, it

When the cougar (see preceding photo) landed, it was still out of breath. Wells's hunting hounds quickly attacked it. In such chaotic conditions, with dogs and cougar fighting, hunters often have a hard time getting a clear shot. *Photo by A. G. Wallihan, courtesy of Denver Public Library, Western History Department.*

was decided to conduct an animal drive in an area encompassed by a circle thirty miles in diameter. The center of this circle was cleared so that the drivers could dispatch all the animals gathered there. Shoemaker writes:

> In the outer edge of the circle fires were started, guns fired, bells rung, all manner of noises made. The hunters, men and boys, to the number of two hundred, gradually closed in on the centre. When they reached the point where the killing was to be made, they found it crowded with yelping, growling, bellowing animals. Then the slaughter began, not ending until the last animal had been slain. A group of Buffaloes [bison] broke through the guards at an early stage of the killing, and it is estimated that several hundred animals escaped in this way. The recapitulation is as follows, the count having been made by Black Jack himself at the close of the carnage: Forty-one panthers [cougars], 109 wolves, 112 foxes, 114 mountain cats [lynx and bobcat], 17 black bears, 1 white bear, 2 elk, 198 deer, 111 buffaloes, 3 fishers, 1 otter, 12 gluttons [wolverine] 3 beavers and upwards of 500 smaller animals.

Only the select hides were taken, as well as certain prime meat cuts such as bison tongues, and then the carcasses of the dead animals were heaped to-gether in a pile as large "as the tallest trees," and using the nearby available wood, the mound of dead animal bodies was set on fire. It was claimed that the stench was so bad that settlers up to three miles away temporarily had to vacate their cabins. Shortly afterwards, a few of the participants completely clothed themselves with cougar skins, and accordingly they received consid-erable local recognition as the Panther Boys. However, they soon disposed of their cougar apparel, discretion being the better part of valor: Indians living in the vicinity, outraged by the waste, focused their anger on the Panther Boys.

State by state, most of the large predators were eliminated. By 1850, few cougars were to be found east of the Mississippi River. Most of the cougars re-maining in the United States were located in the sparsely populated south-west and in the mountainous areas west of the Hundredth Meridian. Generally viewed as an unpopular and destructive animal, the cougar was classed as vermin, or "a varmint"; as such it could be freely dispatched without cause, need, or license. Determination of what constituted a varmint had more to do with the animal's reported conduct than its visage. In some parts of India in the early 1900s, even the beautiful leopard was classed as vermin (Corbett 1946, 79).

Over the years many methods have been employed by humans in order to kill or capture cougars. Prior to the arrival of the Europeans and their guns, Native Americans utilized pit traps, snares, spears, and bow and arrow. Since their hunting skills were highly developed, and they often used their dogs, their efforts were reasonably successful. Occasionally the Indian hunters were able to entice a cougar into the range of their weapons, or into a pit trap, by the use of live bait or calling. South American Indian tribes were reportedly proficient in the use of bolas, and it has been claimed that cougars were periodically snared in this manner. Since the bola appears not to be very effective except in open country, success must have depended upon an animal in such terrain being surprised, the wielder of the bola being reasonably close to the target. South American gauchos, mounted on horses, renowned for their skill with the bola, easily caught and disposed of cougars they encountered on the pampas.

Settlers, fur trappers, bounty hunters, and government predator-control specialists frequently employed set traps to ensnare cougars. The set trap was a relatively simple mechanism that relied upon springs, a trap pan, and two jaws that would close on the cougar's foot when the trap pan was depressed. The trap was set along a known and frequented cougar trail, perhaps near a cat's scrapes over feces or urine. The traps were not baited, but occasionally catnip oil, combined with petroleum oil, would be smeared on the trap to attract the cougar. A. F. Wallace (1912, 460–62), while acknowledging that many of the old-time hunters and trappers had maintained all along that cougars could not be trapped, suggested in a magazine article that cougar trapping was indeed a profitable and relatively simple process. He described the equipment needed, including how to construct drag hooks for attachment to the trap chain. A scent potion had to be made from valerian and musk; a piece of canvas three feet square was required, as were wool gloves and a no. 4 Newhouse double-spring trap. After washing the trap, the hooks, canvas, and gloves in hot water and wood ashes, the equipment was to be buried in the ground for thirty-six hours to "destroy the human scent." Wallace's explanation as to how the site should be selected and the trap be set was even more involved, the objective being to avoid excessive disturbance and contamination of the site.

Elmer Keith recalled springing a trap on a cougar on a deer-hunting trip on Eagle Mountain in Montana in 1934. After he and his neighbors had killed three large antlered deer, they packed two out and returned for the third to find that a cougar had helped himself to the better part of this big buck. Keith set two traps and returned the following day to find that the cougar had stepped in one of the traps and left with the traps, toggle, and chain. The trail was easy to follow and Keith soon came across the cougar. Deciding that he wanted to take a picture of the cougar before he shot him, he tried to align his camera while still keeping his six-gun trained on the cat. But in attempting to get a picture that was all cougar, he approached too close; as he took his final step,

> things happened too fast for the eye to record. I never finished that step and was conscious only of the big cat being in the air and headed for my face, as I shot from the hip by merely tipping up the muzzle of the gun and jumped as far as I could to my left and down the slope. At the shot, his big head fell down on his chest and he flashed over my right shoulder and landed plop on his big belly, up the mountain beyond where I stood. I landed down the mountain in the longest standing broad jump I ever made and with the old single action again cocked and on his shoulders. However, no second shot was needed. His tail was still held vertical and it slowly came down to the snow, just like the tail on a woodchuck when it dies. (1948, 361)

The cougar, an old male, was so heavy that Keith had a hard time getting

Northwest Washington, with its high population of deer and elk, has an abundance of cougars. The five cougars here displayed in a Tacoma hardware store were feeding on the two mule deer when they were surprised by hunters. Photo taken in Washington Hardware, Tacoma, 1946. *Courtesy of Tacoma Public Library, Tacoma, Washington.*

the dead cougar on his horse. After skinning him, he quartered the carcass and weighed the quarters. He said that "the innards and the skin with head and feet attached, and the whole works weighed exactly 200 pounds. Of course I lost the weight of the blood" (1948, 363).

A more subtle weapon used against predatory cougars was poison, such as strychnine, but it was not widely recommended for a number of reasons. The principal objection was that poison could not be designed as a selective agent. Meat that was ingested from a poisoned carcass could kill any animal—including dogs that may later be used to track a cougar. The federal government did not advocate the use of poison, and government specialists were not sanctioned to use it (although some government hunters may have done so). It was well known, however, that some sheep and cattle owners attempted to protect their flocks and herds by poisoning carcasses of cougar-slain animals.

Traps and poison were lethal, but it was the gun that triggered the demise

Cougar killed by a William Wells hunting party. Wells, who at one time had up to twenty dogs, favored foxhounds, but he used dogs of many breeds. He claimed to have had eight dogs that could, unaided, kill any cougar regardless of how large it was. *Photo by A. G. Wallihan. Courtesy of Denver Public Library, Western History Department.*

of the cougar. When cougars were still fairly abundant, and bounties were offered for their hides, most people who were armed and happened to sight a cougar shot it—or shot at it. Today this type of activity may not seem to be admirable or even desirable, but at that time it was a very efficient and effective way of disposing of cougars residing near human communities. However, unlike the later outcry at the slaughter of the bison herds, there were no public forums or organized groups sympathetic to the plight of the large predators—the grizzly, the wolf, and the cougar. That any of these species still exist is due more to the tenacity and survival instincts of the animal rather than to compassion or understanding on the part of humans.

In Robert Ruark's *Use Enough Gun*, Ruark describes his first shooting experience on safari in Africa. Using a .220 Swift on a small wart hog and then on a hyena, without any observable effect on either, he reached for his .470

Large cougar surrounded by dogs under a spreading juniper. Note how the cougar is protecting its tail. Extreme northwest Colorado. *Photo by A. G. Walliban. Courtesy of Denver Public Library, Western History Department.*

and blew the hyena's head off. Ruark's hunting guide, Harry Selby, was then said to have commented: "I cannot abide wounding things that could simply be killed if you used enough gun" (1966, 65). With regard to hunting potentially dangerous animals, and most animals qualify for this description, Selby's statement appears to be prudent. Unlike the formidable grizzly, the cougar is primarily muscle and sinew; it does not possess a massive skeletal structure. Because of this weakness in frame, the cougar has been easily killed with small caliber handguns and rifles that fire the humble .22 rimfire cartridge. Larry Kollar, in his *Treasury of Hunting,* suggests that when the animal is treed, any short-range gun will do. If the cougar is at some distance, he recommends the same caliber of rifle that would be used on a coyote, from a .243 Winchester (100 grain) to a 7mm Remington Magnum (150 grain). Several professional guides and hunters swear by the use of a .357 magnum revolver, and some have even used a shotgun with no. 4 shot or a slug.

Jerry A. Lewis, who claims to have hunted and tracked the "northern cougar" for more than twenty-five years, has stated that if he were to start hunting cougars all over again, and he had a choice of only two guns, he would select the .22 Magnum and the .357 Magnum, both with 4-inch barrels

Small cougar tracked and killed by dogs on a rocky canyon ledge in northwestern Colorado, 1895. *Photo by A. G. Wallihan. Courtesy of Denver Public Library, Western History
Department.*

(1995, 50). If he could select only one gun it would be the .357 Magnum. He
considers this "the best all-around handgun to carry on a cougar hunt"
(1995, 49). Lewis is of the belief that a rifle, although effective at short range,
is a "terrible burden in the snow-laden brush, icy bluffs and deep snow"
(1995, 46).

Jack Butler, a renowned hunting guide, over the years squired many aspiring cougar hunters through the wilds of Utah. In the spring of 1946, he guided
four archery enthusiasts in the East Fork Mountains. With five arrows, the
party killed four cougars (Maull 1947, 23, 71–72). I doubt that the best Indian
archers of nineteenth-century America could have bettered that. Hunting
cougars with bow and arrow often requires considerable patience and a lot of
arrows (Moore 1989, 29, 32–38). As is true for any method of hunting
cougars—with bow and arrow or any other weapon—it is recommended that
the hunter have a friend with a pack of trained cougar hounds go along, or
that the party hire a professional guide or outfitter with dogs. This is considered to be the most reliable way to hunt. (Kirk 1989, 19. Cooney 1990, 51,
Dougherty 1992, 28, Ray 1998, 47). Jeff Brent put it bluntly when he said:

Large Colorado cougar treed in 1897. Note the open mouth—an indication that the cat is out of breath. The cougar was shot right after the picture was taken by A. G. Wallihan. *Courtesy of Denver Public Library, Western History Department.*

"Lion hunting in the American West, simply put, is hard demanding work, often taxing to the limit of even the toughest and most seasoned big game hunters. Any bowhunter or hunter in general who has taken a cougar has good reason to be proud!" (1988, 69).

Once the United States cougar population had become noticeably reduced, and the cougar's range and habitation had become primarily that of wilderness areas in the Southwest and West, the only way a hunter had a real chance of shooting a cougar was with the use of dogs. The human hunter on foot was not generally able to keep up with an uninjured and fleeing cat. Although a horse could provide the necessary pursuit speed, the human hunter still had inadequate senses of sight and smell. To track and bring to bay the quarry, humans usually depended on the dog. The partnership of humans and dogs in hunting wild game goes back thousands of years, even to prehistoric times, and throughout the years specialized dogs and dog packs have been developed. In colonial times, the dogs used by many hunters were generally of mixed breeds. These clamorous and rowdy packs routed game animals from cover; if the animals sought to escape by climbing trees, the hunter would arrive to

Pencil drawing of Meschach Browning, created from a nineteenth-century copperplate engraving by Edward Stabler. Born in Maryland in 1781, Browning was one of several earlier writers, travelers, and hunters who, otherwise knowledgeable, suggested that panthers were not the same animal as the catamount, or cougar. *Photo of Sarah Alford drawing.*

dislodge them. Dogs are invaluable, however, to the hunter. One of the early sporting publications, *The Dead Shot; or, Sportsman's Complete Guide* (Marksman [pseud.], 1864), declared that "no good sport is to be had, or at least thoroughly enjoyed, without a good dog." The cougar hunter, however, was never considered to be a sportsman or "gentleman" hunter; the only similarity between the two was fondness for a wilderness life.

While researching my earlier publication *Of Bison and Man*, I noted that bison owners were somewhat like the animals they raised: they tended to search out and socialize only with their own kind; they disliked restraints and restrictions; and they were fiercely independent. Cougar hunters were, and some of the current ones still are, much like the animals they pursue—generally loners, marching to the beat of a different drummer, prowling the American wilderness in search of prey.

Prior to the nineteenth century, much of the land along the east coast of the United States was still wilderness. The streams and rivers were pure and clear and teeming with fish; the woods were brimming with smaller game such as turkeys, grouse, and rabbits, and the entire countryside was laden with deer, bears, wolves, bobcats, and cougars. It was a hunter's paradise, and no one rejoiced more in this abundance than did Meshach Browning.

Born in Frederick County, Maryland, in 1781, Browning did not travel great distances; he was not an explorer; he could not be called even a pathfinder. He was simply a hunter. Most, if not all, of his hunting experiences were conducted along the Alleghenies and within what is now Garrett County, Maryland. He killed his first cougar when he was seventeen, and he later said it was the largest "panther" he had ever killed. His assertion that it "measured eleven feet three inches from the end of his nose to the tip of his tail" (Browning 1942, 79) is somewhat suspect.

Another observation of Browning's that is hard for us now to comprehend was his citing the presence of "panthers, wolves, wild cats, catamounts" (1942, 20). This suggests that panthers and catamounts [cougars] were two separate species. As noted in chapter 2, a number of early writers and travelers, including Gabriel Franchere (Thwaites 1966, 323), John Russell Bartlett (1965, 555), and Col. Richard Irving Dodge (1959, 217–19), describe the panther and the catamount, or cougar, as different animals. It is interesting that such a misconception was so common—unless it actually differed in ways far more spectacular than just its cranial characteristics, as suggested by Young and Goldman (1946, 204–5).

Unlike other acclaimed cougar hunters who succeeded him, Browning sustained a healthy respect for the cougar throughout his life, although he also believed it to be "a most dastardly coward" (1942, 369). He was described as a rather large and powerful man. Reportedly, he killed several cougars by clubbing them with a broken tree bough while the cougar fought with his dogs. Considering the limited firepower of the single-shot musket of those days, he probably, after firing his single shot and wounding an animal, was glad to find a convenient club. Browning died of pneumonia, November 19, 1859. During his hunting career he claimed to have killed "eighteen hundred to two thousand deer, from three to four hundred bears, about fifty panthers and catamounts (quite as ferocious, and not much less in size than the panther), with scores of wolves and wildcats" (1942, 8).

One of the most renowned cougar hunters was Benjamin Vernon Lilly, born in Alabama on December 31, 1856, and covering territory from Mississippi to New Mexico. Ben Lilly, as he came to be popularly known, was a strange man. J. Frank Dobie, in his book *The Ben Lilly Legend* (1950), attempted to convey a few of Lilly's remarkable idiosyncrasies and strong personal values, and another writer, Frank C. Hibben, earlier said much the same thing in *Hunting American Lions* (1948). People who met Lilly said he was religious (he read the Bible and rested on Sundays), was honest to a fault, and could be, at times, remarkably expressive, but these worthy values seemed like a button onto which an overcoat of peculiarities had been sewn.

Lilly loved hunting as a youth, and throughout his life he really never enjoyed doing anything as much as he did hunting. Although other animals may have interested him from time to time (for example, alligators), it was his preoccupation with bears and cougars that fashioned his reputation as a mountain man with a spartan lifestyle. Hibben spent three days on the hunting trail with Lilly in 1934. The deeper they went into the wilderness, the quicker was Lilly's step. Although he was then approximately seventy-eight years old, he seemed to become miraculously rejuvenated by following the hunting trail. Hibben said "he swung his head from side to side as he moved among the trees, as though taking the wind. His actions seemed animal-like, and his pale blue eyes read at a glance every detail of the trail and the rocks and the earth around us. This was his element; he was indeed a part of it. Every bird that flitted past, every ground squirrel, seemed to know him and to recognize him for one of themselves. I was the outsider" (*Hunting American Lions*, 1948, 6).

Of all of the stories told about Ben Lilly, the one I enjoy the most is from J. Frank Dobie's *The Ben Lilly Legend*. As Dobie tells it, it seems that Lilly had become more impressed with his own work than that of others. Dobie met Lilly for the first time in 1928 at the annual convention of the American National Livestock Association (ANLA) in El Paso, Texas. Lilly was to give a talk there on predatory animals. After the two men were introduced, Dobie learned that Lilly planned to write a book, but had completed only two chapters, "What I Know about Bears," and "What I Know about Panthers." When Lilly learned that Dobie was a writer, he invited him to his hotel room and gave him a twenty-five-page typewritten manuscript of "What I Know about Bears"; if Dobie would read it and come back the following evening, Lilly would then let him review the panther chapter. Late the following afternoon, when Dobie returned and was duly given "What I Know about Panthers," he remembered that he had in his coat pocket a copy of the *El Paso Times* containing a short account of Lilly's address the previous day, and a recent copy of the *Saturday Evening Post*. Thinking that perhaps Lilly would like to read from these items, Dobie offered them, saying: "Mr. Lilly, perhaps you

Renowned cougar and bear hunter Benjamin (Ben) Vernon Lilly—a man who loved hunting as a youth and claimed that throughout the rest of his life he never really enjoyed anything else quite as much. Never without his knife, Lilly was also attached to his bible. *Courtesy of the Center for American History, University of Texas at Austin.*

would like to read something here while I am reading what you have written." Lilly responded in a voice of serene and settled conviction: "No, I thank you, I find this very in-ter-est-ing." When Dobie looked up at him, Lilly was deeply immersed in "What I Know about Bears" (1950, 11–12).

When he was in his prime, Lilly usually hunted with a pack of dogs that he had personally trained. Although he was one of the few humans who could successfully track animals without dogs, he enjoyed the dogs' company; he appreciated a good hunting dog. Lilly did not care much for horses or large hunting parties, preferring to travel the trail afoot and alone. In 1907 he was summoned by President Theodore Roosevelt to be his "chief huntsman" on a bear hunt in Louisiana. Although Lilly fondly remembered his acquaintance with Roosevelt, Lilly's solitary hunting methods were somewhat ineffective with the large presidential hunting party, and Roosevelt remembered Lilly as "a religious fanatic" (Dobie 1950, 96). Lilly was never without a knife, made by his own hands from any available steel item. He claimed that his best knives were "tempered in panther oil" (Dobie 1950, 59). Lilly occasionally killed cougars and bears with only a knife, but he carried a rifle, usually a .30–30, and sometimes one of slightly larger caliber, with lever action. He is said to have once claimed that he never missed anything that he shot at.

How many cougars did Ben Lilly kill in his lifetime? Probably substantially fewer than a thousand. From interviews later in his life, Lilly indicated that the total was probably closer to six hundred. What distinguishes Lilly from other cougar hunters was not the number of cougars he killed, but the skill and determination he applied. He was the perfect prototype for the American cougar hunter, an enigma having perhaps more in common with the animals he hunted than the human species to which he belonged. Ben Lilly was a car-icature for his profession, and the acknowledged virtuoso of the hunting trail.

Another cougar hunter prominent in the 1890s and early 1900s was John B. Goff, hunting guide on Roosevelt's well-publicized 1901 cougar hunt in Colorado, when Roosevelt was U.S. vice president. Born in Indiana around 1865, Goff hunted the Rocky Mountain ranges of western Colorado when much of the Colorado high country was still controlled by the Ute Indians. In 1887, when Goff was in New York selling hides, he was visited at his hotel by Roosevelt, who had been recently defeated in a New York City mayoral elec-tion. They talked for hours about hunting, and their mutual interests culmi-nated in the celebrated cougar hunt nearly fourteen years later.

Guide John (Johnny) Goff, one of Colorado's most acclaimed cougar hunters. Unlike the noted and eccentric Lilly, in the backcountry Goff preferred to ride a horse rather than walk. *Photo courtesy of White River Museum, Meeker, Colorado.*

Like Lilly, Goff surrounded himself with a pack of outstanding hunting dogs. Roosevelt was so taken by Goff's dogs that he devoted the first chapter of his book *Outdoor Pastimes of the American Hunter* to them ("With the Cougar Hounds," 1905, 1–67). After the 1901 expedition, Roosevelt continued to share hunting experiences with Goff, and as the newly elected president in 1905 hunted bear with him in Colorado's northwest. Goff was an astute outdoorsman and a keen-eyed tracker. Unlike Lilly, he preferred horses to shank's mare in the backcountry. He was also a property owner, an accomplished entrepreneur, and, although not gregarious, was congenial—devoid of the eccentricities that characterized Ben Lilly. In his most productive years, Goff functioned mainly as a guide, and consequently did not personally dispatch a great number of cougars. On the 1901 Colorado trip, he indicated to Roosevelt that he had perhaps killed more than three hundred cougars, "all but two of them . . . encountered while he was with his pack [of dogs]" (Roosevelt 1905, 1990 edition, 24).

It is perhaps not surprising that Roosevelt demonstrated his personal style of combative aggressiveness by taking on the wilderness and hunting America's

Johnny and Mattie Goff. The wife of the popular hunter and guide traveled little but she often joined her husband in his hunting excursions near home. *Photo courtesy of White River Museum, Meeker, Colorado.*

most challenging wild game—which certainly includes the cougar. Roosevelt, small and sickly as a child, boldly stormed through the pages of history in his self-assigned role as a macho leader of men. He idolized his tall and robust father and was determined to build himself into the type of man that he felt his father was, and that others admired: strong, honest, and courageous—the typical outdoorsman. Except for perhaps his early hunting experiences at his ranch in Medora, North Dakota, Roosevelt did not hunt alone. He had the money and the power and he went first class: he had the best of guides and equipment. Roosevelt wrote about his frequent hunting of antelope, bear, bighorn sheep, and bison, of bobcats, cougars, coyotes, deer, elk, mountain goat, and wolves, and he placed emphasis on acquiring trophy animals. Small wonder then that he became acquainted with America's foremost hunters and best hunting guides.

Roosevelt again took the hunting trail in search of cougars in 1913. This time, he selected as his guide James T. (Uncle Jimmy) Owens, who had been a game warden for what is now the Kaibab National Forest in Arizona. Born in San Antonio, Texas, Owens had kicked around the Southwest and the Rocky Mountain areas his whole life, cowpunching, hunting, and trapping. According to McKee (1927), Owens and his dogs accounted for fifteen hundred cougars in his career. Between 1907 and 1919, it is claimed, he killed more than six hundred cougars on the Kaibab Plateau alone. Because of his efforts, and that of other cougar hunters and trappers who worked the Kaibab, the deer population grew during this period from fewer than four thousand to an estimated one hundred thousand (Russo 1970, 126). This overpopulated deer herd consumed all available vegetation, killed trees, ruined the range, and became emaciated and ill. Many of them eventually died from disease or starvation.

Considered by many as perhaps second only to Ben Lilly in hunting skills, Owens also had nearly as colorful a career as did the renowned Lilly. In addition to his assignment as a game warden in Arizona, he worked on the famous Goodnight ranch in Texas, served as a game warden in Colorado, and, according to Roosevelt (1913, 260), was a "buffalo warden" in Yellowstone National Park, although the record is not clear on this (Monroe H. Goode reported incorrectly [1941, 70] that Owens was superintendent of the park for two years).

One of the more complicated and fascinating of cougar hunters was Charles Jesse "Buffalo" Jones. Born in January 1844 on a farm near Springfield, Illinois, when he was old enough to do so he moved to Kansas, and later pushed on to the Southwest, all the time following the bison herds. Much has been written about Jones's efforts to "save the buffalo," but comparatively little is recorded about his activities reducing the number of cougars. It is not known for sure how many cougars Jones killed in his lifetime, or was responsible for the killing of, but it could have been any number between two hundred and one thousand. With Jones, one never really knew where fact ended and fabrication began.

Jones claimed that he had a special relationship with Theodore Roosevelt, fostered by their joint interest in wildlife and the environment. There is no solid evidence of this, although Roosevelt did once refer to Jones as "my friend." (Roosevelt also wrote of his friendship with "Uncle Jimmy" Owens [Roosevelt 1913, 260].) After a lifetime of adventures and misadventures (the last being an unsuccessful effort to capture musk ox, indigenous to the Arctic Circle, and transport them to the United States), Jones learned that Yellowstone National Park was seeking bison to complement its dwindling herd. He petitioned the president for the job of managing the park's wildlife. Although there is some question as to whether President Roosevelt personally appointed Jones as game warden of the Yellowstone park or merely signed appointment papers, Jones arrived in the park on July 16, 1902.

Similar to what would occur later on the Kaibab Plateau in Arizona, Yellowstone's then predator-control policy resulted in park elk not only overgrazing their range and destroying vegetation, but also in driving many of the deer herds from the park. Although there was in effect a secretarial order prohibiting the hunting of park animals, it "was interpreted as not applying to predators because it did not name those beasts of 'fang and claw.' Thus, coyotes, wolves, cougars, wolverines and bears were shot on sight by employees and visitors, prior to the era of army management [1886–1916]" (Haines 1977, vol. 2: 80). In 1899, the army initiated a program to control cougars, and when Jones arrived he accelerated this program.

In early 1903 the park acquired a pack of eight cougar dogs, which Jones anticipated would be used during President Roosevelt's expected visit to Yellowstone. Roosevelt arrived on April 8, 1903 and, after viewing park wildlife for nearly three weeks, concluded that "the cougars were preying on nothing but elk in the Yellowstone Valley, and kept hanging about the neighborhood of the big bands. . . . As the elk were evidently rather too numerous for the feed, I do not think the cougars were doing any damage" (1905, 302–3). Despite Roosevelt's observations, reduction of cougars continued.

In the summer of 1905, three cougar hunters from Colorado entered the park with their hounds—one of them John B. Goff, who claimed that they were there to "clear the park of cougars" (Haines 1977, vol. 2: 81). They further stated that "the job came to them from the president" (2: 81). As a result of the efforts of these three hunters, and Jones, it was estimated that at least sixty-five cougars were permanently removed from the park prior to the fall of 1906. By that time the cougar was all but exterminated from Yellowstone National Park. It was not until 1908 that Roosevelt firmly ordered the park to leave the cougars alone. Roosevelt's admonishment was heeded and the park cougar hounds, purchased in 1903, were sold. Jones, however, was long gone by this time: because of personal difficulties with his supervisor, Park Superintendent Major John Pritcher, he resigned under pressure on September 15, 1905. M. P. Skinner, who conducted research in Yellowstone in the early 1920s, expressed very clearly what the early policy of Yellowstone was with respect to cougars: "They are the deer slayers, and we find we must keep their numbers down if we would preserve any of the deer. So every fall after the tourists leave, certain of our more experienced Rangers are detailed to hunt mountain lions, wolves, and coyotes, although no hunting is done in summer for fear of stray bullets" (1924, 109).

The cougar has made a rather significant recovery in the Yellowstone area since the early 1900s (Houston 1973; Despain 1986), and now that the cougar has been declared a game animal by all states surrounding Yellowstone, park management is optimistic regarding the cougar's future in the park.

In 1907, after his return to Arizona and during his "cattalo" [cattle/buffalo hybridizing] venture, Jones became acquainted with a New York City dentist who wanted to be a writer. The dentist's efforts at writing, at least to this point, had been modest at best, but at the urging of his friends, he left his practice and went West, in 1908, to share what was a unique hunting experience with "Buffalo" Jones: roping cougars on the north rim of the Grand Canyon. The aspiring writer's name was Zane Grey. After his return, Grey produced a fictionalized account of his experience in Arizona. He called it *The Young Lion Hunter*—his first successful publication. Some years later, in 1922, Grey also wrote a nonfiction version, *Roping Lions in the Grand Canyon*, in which he recounts the whole hunting episode and the cougar-roping exploits of Jones, who was at that time sixty-four years old. The ability to rope cougars out of trees was not a feat commonly practiced by cougar hunters, but there were a few others besides Jones with this skill. Steve Elkins and Scott Teague, for example, two well-known cougar hunters from Colorado, had previously roped a male and a female cougar for display at the 1893 Chicago World Fair.

Jones later took his rope and his cowpony to Africa to demonstrate that it was also possible to rope and capture African animals. Some people said the trip was a personal, sensitive demonstration of how animals could be captured

The renowned Lee brothers of Tucson may have dispatched more than a thousand cougars. Reportedly they also killed a similar number of bears and more than a hundred jaguars. Here Dale and Clell pose with a jaguar taken during one of their hunting trips to Central and South America. *Photo courtesy of Arizona Historical Society.*

without their being killed; others said it was simply Jones's intention to discredit Roosevelt because of Roosevelt's propensity to shoot and kill all of the animals he hunted; and more than a few others suggested that Jones was a promoter who enjoyed publicity and would do anything to keep his name continually in the public forum. While he was in the Congo, Jones became quite ill and he was forced to return home to Topeka, Kansas. "Buffalo" Jones was unable to lasso this final, minuscule adversary—the malarial parasite. He died on October 2, 1919.

There can be no doubt that the most renowned of all cougar-hunting families was the Lee family—seven brothers from Tucson, Arizona. The more prominent and active of the seven were Vince, Ernest, Clell, and Dale. In the 1920s, like many of their contemporaries, the Lees worked for the Biological Survey. They did this for several years, then were taken by an entrepreneurial bent and struck out on their own, guiding an international clientele on cougar hunts throughout the Southwest, Florida, Louisiana, Mexico, and South America. Their skill in training cougar hounds has never been surpassed, and many of the dogs and dog packs used by other hunters were developed by the Lee brothers (Newell 1935, 10). How many cougars the brothers accounted for in their more than sixty years of active hunting will never be known for sure. Monroe Goode, in his outstanding article "Killers of the Rimrock" (1943, 34), indicated that the Lees "have caught more than 1,000 of the beasts since they started hunting them." More than fifty years later, Chris Bolgiano mentioned that "by the mid 1960s the Lees reckoned they had bagged more than a thousand cougars and as many bears" (1995, 63).

Two other noted cougar hunters were each generally credited with killing more than a thousand cougars: Jack Butler (Schueren 1945, 21–23) in Utah and the Southwest, and George Goswick (Hibben, "The Killer of Tonto Rim," 1948, 51, 124–27) in Arizona and the Southwest. During the past eighty years, there were perhaps as many as fifty other professional predator control specialists and hunting guides who were responsible for individually eliminating hundreds of cougars.

Perhaps the most famous of all of the state-employed cougar hunters was Jay C. Bruce. Born and raised in the rugged Yosemite area of California, he began leading hunting parties into wilderness areas by 1915. Subsequently hired by the California Fish and Game Commission as a cougar hunter on January 1, 1919, he remained with the commission until 1942. Bruce, who admitted to collecting nearly seven hundred cougars throughout his career, was one of the few professionals to hold a healthy respect for the courage of the cougar. In letters he wrote toward the end of his career, Bruce expressed the following thoughts:

> I have many times seen an 80 or 90 pound female lion charge a pack of four 50-pound dogs and send them all scurrying for cover at my heels. . . .
>
> In the death battle the lion is more courageous than the black bear, although the bear averages twice the weight of the mountain lion. It is funny that no one, not even the story-book naturalists, accuses the bear of cowardice, even though a 400-pound bear will hit the timber to get away from one small dog. . . .
>
> If a person comes within reach of a cornered or mortally wounded lion, the cat will not hesitate to grab him and sell his own life dearly. In other words, all members of the cat tribe fight viciously and to the death to defend themselves. On the other hand, the black bear is a sissy and yellow when it comes to a life-and-death battle. That has been my experience with the two from start to finish. (Goode 1943, 34)

Bruce was more cerebral than many, if not all, of his contemporaries in the cougar-hunting field. A regular contributor to *California Fish and Game*, he described in one article, "The Why and How of Mountain Lion Hunting in California," the methods that he had found successful in hunting cougars with dogs. His credo was "leave camp early and travel fast" (1922, 112). Bruce may have respected the cougar as an adversary, but he had no use for the cougar as a species. In another article published by *California Fish and Game*, he stated that the cougar "is the only predatory animal in California which is apparently of no economic value to the human race. . . but is simply a liability which probably costs the state a thousand dollars a year in deer meat alone" (1925, 1–2).

Another California predator-control specialist of considerable renown was "Bee" Adkins, who started out trapping wolves when he was a sixteen-year-old boy living in southern Arizona in the mid 1920s. After hunting and trapping on his own for nearly twenty years, he was employed as a predator-control specialist in California by the U.S. Biological Service (later Fish and Wildlife Service). The primary job of predator-control specialists was to dispose of troublesome animals and unwanted species. They did not keep regular office hours, but they did have to maintain careful tallies of animals killed to provide proof of their services. Daniel Mannix, who hired Adkins to accompany him and his pet cheetah on a coyote hunt, indicated that "in a box by the back door were always a pile of coyote scalps that Bee had to send to the Fish and Wildlife Service" (1967, 170). Bee killed cougars over much of the Southwest and in California for more than fifty years. He did not keep an accurate total of the number of cougars he had personally disposed of, but it must have been a considerable number.

The first woman ever hired by the federal government to hunt cougars was Bess Kennedy. Bess was born in a small Texas town and she loved the social life. Married at sixteen to a ranchhand who later worked full time as a government hunter and trapper, she often accompanied her husband on his rounds. Although she enjoyed what little companionship this offered her, she also spent many a lonely and uncomfortable night on the open range awaiting his return. Bess Kennedy quickly learned to ride, hunt, shoot, and set traps, and when her husband became ill she was able to assist him in his work. In 1936, she was hired as a government hunter, and over the years acquitted herself well, permanently removing a number of cougars, coyotes, and bobcats from the south Texas ecosystem.

This chapter has dwelt mostly on acclaimed and colorful cougar hunters, but there are scores of others who worked without public notice. People such as Cecil J. (Cougar) Smith; Herbert H. and Andy Pidcock; Fred and John Olson of Vancouver Island, British Columbia; Don Ellis and John Lesowski, also of British Columbia; J. V. McTimmonds, of Glide, Oregon; the solitary Ute Bill, along with Cap Atwood, Jack Peters, Bill Wallace, Steve Elkins, William Wells, Bill Kent, and Scott Teague from Colorado; and Bob Bakker, Jim Whilt, and Charles Ordish from Montana, all of whom also live roped and trapped cougars. In his *Wildlife of the Southwest*, Oren Arnold claimed that Frank Colcord of Arizona "killed more than 500" (1935, 12). Some of the many other accomplished but less well known cougar hunters were Howard Bilton of Glennville, California; Carl Hert, who hunted in the San Bernardino Mountains of southern California (1955); John E. Hearn, a predator-control specialist in Texas from 1930 to 1939; the Evans brothers of Texas, George (Dub) and Joe, who were much acclaimed by J. Frank Dobie; Jim Espy and Roy McBride, both also from Texas; Orvel Fletcher, T. J. (Shorty) Lyon, L. Fisher, Nat Straw, and Frank Smith of New Mexico; Jim Caswell, John Huelsdonk, and E. Boyd Hilderbrand of Washington; Hal Mecham, Milt Holt, Roy Johnson, and Willis Butolph of Utah; Cleve Miller and Ben Black of Arizona; Allen Wilson of Idaho; and many, many others. Unlike some of us who only write about the cougar, this group of indefatigable and relentless hunters walked in the cougar's footsteps.

> Under the wide and starry sky,
> Dig the grave and let me lie.
> Glad did I live and gladly die,
>   And I laid me down with a will.
>
> This is the verse you grave for me:
> *Here he lies where he longed to be;*
> *Home is the sailor, home from sea,*
>   *And the hunter home from the hill.*
>
>   Robert Louis Stevenson, "Requiem"

SEVEN The Vanishing Wilderness

O NLY FIVE HUNDRED YEARS AGO, the North and South American continents were to white men an unexplored and uncharted wilderness empire. The arrival of the Europeans in 1492 did little to change the existing primitive and natural condition of these two continents for more than two hundred years, the newly arrived immigrants tending to restrict their settlements and movements to the coastlines.

Christopher Columbus made four voyages to the so-called New World, the last in 1502. He first landed, in 1492, on San Salvador, one of the islands in the east Bahamas, investigated the northeastern coast of Cuba and the northern coast of Hispaniola, went on to Haiti, and started a small colony there. On later trips he also explored other Caribbean Islands, Central America, and the extreme northeastern part of the South American continent. His colony in Haiti was soon wiped out, and notwithstanding the significance of these island discoveries, Columbus never really uncovered the vast continental lands located to the northwest and south of his discoveries.

John Cabot is reported to have landed on Newfoundland or Nova Scotia in 1497 (if you believe that particular historian) during his first voyage. In 1498, on his next trip across the Atlantic, it is claimed, accompanied by his son Sebastian, he sailed the east coast of North America as far south as the Carolinas, but there is little evidence to say there was shore exploration or that his ships ranged as far south as Venezuela, as suggested by certain historians. Minor jabs into the continental mainlands of the Americas were made by expeditions led by Americus Vespucius, Ponce de Leon, and Vasco Nunez de Balboa, but the more far-reaching inland campaigns were those conducted in the early 1500s by Hernando Cortez, Francisco Pizarro, Hernado De Soto, Francisco Vasquez de Coronado, and Jacques Cartier.

The Europeans, armed only with the limited information provided by the earliest explorers, believed that the discovery of 1492 was—with the exception of the islands—a single mass of land that was quite long and also very narrow. Over the next two hundred years, many shiploads of adventurers and immigrants would cross the seas, but settlements were established only in coastal areas. The cautious foreigners wanted easy access to ships and their mother countries.

The land area of the North American continent is more than nine million square miles; that of South America is nearly seven million square miles. It is not inappropriate to suggest that these two continents thus contained more than a billion acres of wilderness prior to the arrival and dispersal of European immigrants, even though on both continents, well-established Native American tribal societies occupied many delineated territories. Some of these societies were more advanced than others. Some had built permanent villages, even cities. Although no Indian tribal society possessed or used a written alphabet at that time, in Central America the Aztecs, Mayas, and others used picture symbolism. The Indians lived off the fruits of the land: some tribes were farmers, cultivating crops; others hunted and fished. Estimates vary as to the number of Native Americans living on the two continents prior to the arrival of Europeans, but a figure between 15 and 20 million is now generally accepted. Most of these native tribal people lived south of what is now the U.S.–Mexico border; no more than one million lived in the area that later became the United States. All of these peoples respected the land and the animals with which they shared it.

Animals generally reside in areas that are consistent with their species' particular environmental needs and survival requirements. The cat family, for example, will seek a habitat that offers not only an abundant supply of prey animals, but also provides opportunities suited to their unique hunting skills of stealth and ambush; that is to say, open plains and deserts are not as desirable as are forested and mountainous areas. The cougar, with no human or other enemy to fear—being but incidental prey for the Indian—its range and habitat were limited only by its own requirements and capabilities. Thus, the cougar, prior to the conversion of land from natural use to restricted human

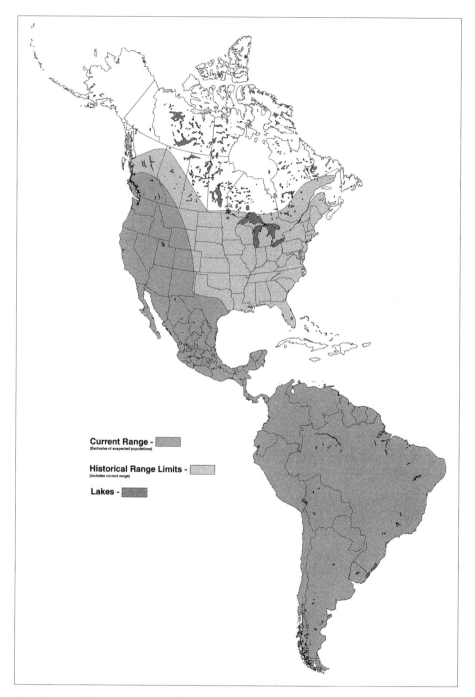

Distribution of the cougar in North, Central, and South America. (Current and Historical Range-limits Map)

use, enjoyed the most extensive range and distribution of any mammal ever found on the two American continents.

The northern limit of the cougar's historical range—reading along a hypothetical line from west to east—runs from north-central British Columbia, in Canada (near 60 degrees north latitude), southeasterly, through Alberta and the extreme southwest section of Saskatchewan, where it enters the United States approximately at the Montana–North Dakota state line. It then continues east along the Canadian-U.S. border to the shores of the Atlantic Ocean. All land on the two continents south of this line—in the United States, Mexico, Central America, and South America—to the southerly tip at Cape Horn, at one time or another has been cougar habitat.

The current known range of the cougar still begins in British Columbia, but perhaps closer now to 54 degrees north latitude, and the line turns more sharply to the southeast, passing through the extreme southwestern section of Alberta to enter the United States in Montana at approximately 110 degrees west longitude, continuing southwest to include Wyoming, western Colorado, most of New Mexico, and southwestern Texas. The suggested distribution line ends at the Gulf of Mexico, slightly to the west of Galveston. With minor exceptions, all land west and south of this line—in the United States, Mexico, Central America, and South America—is generally considered still to be active cougar habitat.

Clearly, there once were far greater numbers of cougars than there are today. Whenever it is suggested or observed that there are, or seem to be, fewer of a given species—the passenger pigeon and the American bison are prime examples—certain questions are invariably asked: How many actually were there, and how many are there now? A few intrepid individuals have suggested that the number of cougars may have once exceeded 100 million, but that is pure conjecture. Since no one actually possesses this information, most wildlife writers prefer not to attempt an estimate of their own and dislike citing insupportable totals.

Estimates of contemporary cougar populations do show a growth trend. A 1964/1965 estimate arrived at by Victor H. Cahalane, former National Park Service chief biologist who was later with the New York State Museum, indicated that there were somewhere between 7,300 and 17,500 cougars in the United States and Canada, and that approximately 4,000 to 6,500 of these were in the United States (1964, 2–3). Robert Gray (*Cougar* 1972, 140) was of the opinion that perhaps 18,000 cougars remained in North America, but he did not say how he arrived at this total or if it also included Mexico and Central America. Jim Zumbo (1983, 97), writing for *Outdoor Life*, stated that a survey conducted by the magazine in 1982 indicated that there was a growing population of cougars in the United States and Canada, of, conservatively, between 20,000 and 22,000. Based on figures recently obtained from state and province wildlife officials, it appears that there are now at least 30,000 cougars in the United States and another 5,000 in Canada.

Appendix A (following chapter 10) summarizes cougar distribution and occurrence for Canada, the United States, Mexico, Central America, and South America. In some instances, government agencies were able to provide an estimate of current cougar populations, but it must be understood that these figures are, at best, not much better than opinion. Actual population figures for noncaptive animals are extremely difficult, and perhaps impossible, to obtain. Because of the covert and transient nature of cougars, census efforts involve small samplings, factoring in results from hunting harvests, use of any and all other information available, and a whole lot of guesswork. For example, if, lacking other evidence, all we have are a few sketchy reports of possible cougar sightings in most eastern states and provinces, it is not unreasonable to assume that there may be only a few, if indeed any, cougars residing in these locations. When, on the other hand, in a given area there are continual increases in cougar sightings, incidents, accidental road kills, and hunter success reports, it is logical to accept, with some confidence, the statistical premise that there are more cougars than there were in the recent past. Recurring reports of cougar sightings in Delaware, Maine, New Hampshire, New York, Pennsylvania, Vermont, and most other northeastern states is now beginning to convince even the most obdurate of skeptics that perhaps there indeed may be some substance to claims that the cougar has returned to its former habitat. And here it will be useful to consider how patterns of human settlement have affected the North American wilderness, and with it the cougar's habitat. This involves describing the initial human intervention and its related political activity.

The erosion of North American wilderness began very gradually in the early 1600s through the establishment and later expansion of English and Spanish colonies along the Atlantic coast and in California, the, southwestern United States, and Mexico. Initially, colonists made only minor environmental adjustments, simply clearing small parcels of land in order to plant crops and remove forested areas that might serve to harbor dangerous wild beasts or Indians. As domestic livestock populations grew, colonists sought increased protection from predators by removing or reducing the amount of heavy vegetation and trees adjacent to their lands, engaging in neighborhood group hunts, and importing specialized dog species.

In the Atlantic colonies, by 1750 settlements reached as far west as the Allegheny Mountains, and predator species were slowly but firmly being dislodged from most of the coastal areas. With the exception of the Chesapeake and Delaware Bay waterway systems, there were no navigable water courses leading inland along the Atlantic coastline from Maine to Georgia. These two water courses were northerly in direction, and no navigable water courses ran in a westernly direction. Thus, the prominent Allegheny Mountain chain hindered exploration, settlement expansion, and disruption of existing wildlife patterns until the late 1760s. In addition to the problems that a major mountain belt could present to prospective settlers, some sensitive political and social issues hindered the establishment of English settlements west of the Alleghenies. Of primary concern was personal safety. The French government claimed all of the lands from the Alleghenies north to the Great Lakes and extending to the Atlantic almost to what is now the city of Hebron, in Labrador. The French claim then reached southward as far as the coastal plain and what is now the states of Florida, Alabama, Mississippi, Louisiana, and even into eastern Texas as far north as the Red River. The Spanish government claimed all of the lands south of thirty-five degrees south latitude. What was probably more significant with regard to new settlement, Indian tribes had forcefully begun to resist all efforts of European expansion beyond existing boundaries and into Indian lands.

These were times of broad human and social conflict in the Americas. The protagonists were the British, French, and Spanish governments, driven by primary interests of colonial expansion and the prospect of the extraction of riches. Caught in the middle of this political caldron were the European immigrants seeking greater social independence, economic opportunity, and freedom from governmental oppression, and the Native Americans—they who were here first and had the most to lose. The fifty-year period between 1765 and 1815 of near continuous turmoil and strife ended with one government claiming ownership rights to all land from the Atlantic coast to the Rocky

Travel across the vast plains of the West was often tiresome and occasionally dangerous. Most wagon trains employed scouts to seek game to complement their provisions
and to warn of impending dangers. This photograph, Charles Russell's *Scouts*, 1902, is
from a display at Denver Art Museum.

Mountains—territory that now is the United States. Canada achieved basic
political stability by 1840, and independence came to Mexico in 1823. But for
many of the Central and South American countries, political independence
did not lead to internal stability and the establishment of national development programs or land management.

Having started gradually, the movement of European civilization westward
quickly gained momentum. According to the U.S. Bureau of the Census, the
center of population in the United States in 1790 was located twenty-three
miles east of Baltimore, Maryland. Prior to 1790, only 110,000 Caucasians
resided west of the Appalachians and east of the Mississippi. By 1800, this
number had grown to 387,000, and by 1810 to 1,080,000. The Lewis and
Clark expedition to the Pacific began to remove the mystery of middle America, exposing many of the secrets of the previously unknown interior. Immigrants now arrived in hordes, by 1840, the population of the United States
was in excess of 17 million, and it would nearly triple within the next twenty
years. The U.S. center of population in 1880 was eight miles west by south of
Cincinnati, Ohio.

During these years of population movement, growth, and economic development on the eastern seaboard, the cougar had been completely eliminated in every state except, possibly, remote sections of Maine, Vermont, New York, Pennsylvania, Virginia, West Virginia, Georgia, and Florida. In those places, a few specimens were reported to be still holding on. By 1880, it was believed that, with the possible exception of Florida, there was not a significant cougar presence in any state east of the Mississippi River. By 1890, the Census Bureau declared the so-called frontier officially closed, and most of the land that once comprised the great United States wilderness had been forever altered.

Much of the remaining open and undeveloped lands of the public domain in the United States—apart from National Park and National Forest lands—are agriculturally, economically, and recreationally marginal. Most employees of the Bureau of Land Management and state agencies may well object to my asserting this, but the prime or choice public holdings that formerly adjoined parks or forests have long ago been transferred to the recreational agencies—Parks and Forests; such has been my observation. And, through transfer and sale, much of the remaining highly desirable land has found its way into private hands. With this in mind, with only minor exceptions, it is solely within public parks and forests and on remaining large blocks of vacant public lands that the cougar is nominally welcome and the land can be regarded as appropriate cougar habitat.

Perhaps I am cynical, but in view of the above I find it interesting that an ever proliferating number of wildlife and environmental associations and agencies express concern over commercial exploitation and growing population demands on tropical rain forests. These concerned people claim that the rain forests, being home for half of the world's species of wildlife, therefore should not be disturbed. The so-called developed nations of the world having previously converted most of their own pristine wilderness areas to "more productive human uses," now believe that the rain forests (in mainly underdeveloped nations) should not be converted to other land uses merely to accommodate growing human populations, or to achieve higher standards of living. These arguments would have been equally applicable to the developed countries at some point in time.

Nearly 80 percent of the people in the United States live in designated metropolitan areas, and more than 53 percent live in the forty-one metropolitan areas that have populations of at least one million people. Transportation of people within these expanding urban areas has become a major environmen-

The author in the Wyoming backcountry. Foothills and high rocky areas, while excellent habitat for cougars, prove to be tough going when traveling by shank's mare. Author Danz prefers a horse to walking in the high country.

tal problem. Rapid-transit systems are meeting with only limited success in their competition with private automobiles; we move ever further toward an automobile-oriented society, and private-transport-on-demand encourages urban workers with rural aspirations to live in suburban or in exurban areas and commute to city jobs. This movement of residential communities into undeveloped, natural land is when detrimental human impact on wildlife habitat most often occurs.

Where the human milieu touches upon uncultivated and wild places is an "ecotone"—a term used for transitional zones between different environmental communities. Examples of other ecotones are where grassland meets forest, where rocky slopes meet vegetative cover, and the shoreline, where water meets solid ground. It is in and near these ecotones that the cougar is most inclined to hunt. As natural history writer Barry Lopez so aptly stated with regard to the cougar, "The cat is a dweller on the edge" (1981, 113). Since deer, which are the most common cougar prey, are also an "edge" animal, it is usually in these human-invaded ecotones that unexpected contact between humans and cougars will occur.

If you have ever observed a genesis of urban sprawl, you will have likely noted that it seems to begin with just one home that is located some distance from main roads. The house will be adjacent to a forested area, perhaps, or be near a lake or stream, or be on a hill or ridge. These are often very nice homes—sometimes even showplaces. However, development often begets other development, and eventually whole communities materialize; what once was cloistered ambience is lost in the development process. Development drives out local wildlife and also encourages some people to seek residence in yet other locations—in places still undeveloped. And the cycle starts over again.

Development does not necessarily have to mean the loss of natural features when land use is changed or modified. The importance of, for example, trees as intrinsic site assets is now recognized by developers, and landscaping design that softens construction impact is usually a major consideration when raw land is to be developed. Even in the largest cities we can find a multitude of attractive greenbelts, parks, golf courses, and other open areas that harbor a variety of small mammals and birds. Thoreau captured the essence of the human craving and need for the richness of nature in his remarkable book *Walden*. He writes:

> Our village life would stagnate if it were not for the unexplored forests and meadows which surround it. We need the tonic of wilderness,—to wade sometimes in marshes where the bittern and the meadowhen lurk, and hear the booming of the snipe; to smell the whispering sedge where only some wilder and more solitary fowl builds her nest, and the mink crawls with its belly close to the ground. At the same time that we are earnest to explore and learn all things, we require that all things be mysterious and unexplorable, that land and sea be infinitely wild, unsurveyed and unfathomed by us because unfathomable. We can never have enough of nature. We must be refreshed by the sight of inexhaustible vigor, vast and titanic features, the sea-coast with its wrecks, the wilderness with its living and its decaying trees, the thunder-cloud, and the rain which lasts three weeks and produces freshets. We need to witness our own limits transgressed, and some life pasturing freely where we never wander. (1854, 317)

Most animals are amazingly adaptive to changing environmental conditions, provided that an acceptable habitat is still available. There are few metropolitan areas that have not had to deal with surprise visits from large animals that normally live in the wild. I'm continually impressed by the frequency with which some of these larger mammals suddenly appear in the most unlikely of locations—and just as mysteriously disappear. My wife Geri and I live most of the year, with the exception of some of the colder winter months, in a residential area less than three miles from the center of downtown Denver, Colorado, and only slightly more than that from Rocky Mountain foothills. Our immediate neighborhood consists of a small pond, lots of trees, some grassy neighborhood yards, a common area, and one empty field that is slightly more than an acre in size and rises to a few large cottonwoods and a fenced private golf course. Adjacent to all of this is a six-lane highway that is a constant hubbub of vehicle activity and noise. During the early evening of a recent fall day, while walking through the neighborhood, I left the road area to stroll past the pond and to see if there were any interesting nature happening that may have occurred recently within the vacant field. And there, to my surprise, in the middle of this little field, were several large piles of recent pellet droppings from deer. The regular nocturnal visits of neighborhood raccoons to our pint-sized ecotone is to be expected. But deer?

This then is the incongruity in our expectation of the living wilderness experience. The 1964 Wilderness Act (16 USC 1131 et seq.) provides a number of formal descriptions as to what wilderness areas are comprised of, and all point toward large blocks of undeveloped land, without roads or other man-made improvements, and preferably without other than an occasional human visitor. However, a wide variety of wildlife are regularly observed in areas and locations that technically do not qualify to be called wilderness areas but serve equally as well as, or perhaps better than, wilderness habitats.

Cougars are capable of making a number of behavioral adaptations in order to accommodate human trespass into cougar habitat. Normally a very secretive and cautious animal, it also has a curiosity about it that leads it to follow, observe, and learn more about humans and human presence than the human learns from the cougar. It is doubtful if the knowledge the cougar gains from its observations serves to intensify its instinctive feelings of fear for the human species. In all likelihood, continued familiarity, if not breeding contempt, at least bolsters the cougar's confidence. Three conditions are necessary for continued cougar existence in the wild: (1) suitable habitat; (2) adequate food supply; and (3) passive human behavior toward the species. If such conditions exist, occasional human intrusion should not impact cougar populations. If the habitat is destroyed, acceptable wild prey species would leave, and were

These elk have moved en masse onto winter pastures near Estes Park, Colorado.

the cougar to remain and turn to domestic animals as its source of food, the cougar in turn would be destroyed—a topic that will be covered in more depth in chapter 9, "Life in Urban America."

Wilderness is often held up as the model—the prototype habitat for the cougar and other species of wildlife. It does not, of course, fill a similar role for human beings. Human habitat requirements go beyond the needs of the lower animals, which are basic, physiological needs. Although wilderness certainly has spiritual value and substance—wilderness "invites man to adventure, refreshment, and wonder" (Howard Stagner, as quoted by Wirth 1980, 385)—it cannot fully accommodate the cultural, economic, and social needs of the human species. Wilderness, in fact, is seemingly antithetical to unconstrained human population growth patterns. In 1955, the human population of the world was estimated to be approximately 3 billion people; in the next forty years, this population nearly doubled; and by the year 2020 it is expected to total nearly 8 billion people. Although most of these people will continue to gather within large metropolitan areas, many will seek rural habitations. More and more raw land will be developed for industrial, residential, and recreational purposes.

It is instructive, however, to trace what happens to land transformations over extended periods of time. In the United States and Canada, a number of agrarian and vegetative transformations have been associated with human use (and nonuse) of land since the early 1800s. An example can be found in the New England states. When settlers cleared land for farming, they removed nearly 75 percent of all of the trees. By 1820, so much forested land had been cleared that very little wildlife habitat remained. But the soil was rocky, not particularly rich, and the growing season was short. Eventually, farming was abandoned, and forest reclaimed nearly 80 percent of its former territory. We might further note that the Green Mountains of Vermont and the White Mountains of New Hampshire are areas that have been mentioned as locations of recently reported cougar sightings.

More wilderness can also be found further to the west. In the New York Adirondacks is the six-million-acre Adirondack State Park, which was legislatively activated on May 22, 1973. All of the park land is not considered to be wilderness since it contains more than 3.7 million acres of private land, plus roads and other human "improvements." But the park is primarily natural and kept ecologically wild. Deer are plentiful, and though cougars are not now believed to be present, the park is large enough to accommodate a small population. The Catskill Mountains of southeastern New York, although still pastoral and rustically preserved, suffer somewhat from human influence. The Alleghenies and southern Appalachian Mountains, which stretch southward between the Catskill Mountains and the Blue Ridge Mountains of Virginia and the Carolinas, are a patchwork of open lands, forests, rocky outcroppings, industrial developments, and cultivated farmland. Most of the preserved areas are national and state holdings. The southern Appalachians are said to still harbor a few cougar, but, since no cougars have been killed or captured recently, their presence is still a matter of dispute.

Two other geographical areas that still possess many of the characteristics of wilderness and are suitable as cougar habitat are (1) the Ozark highlands of southern Missouri and Illinois, extreme western Kentucky and Tennessee, northern Arkansas, the northeast corner of Oklahoma, and the southeast corner of Kansas; and (2) the bayou country of Louisiana, southern Mississippi, and eastern Texas. Because of the sound conservation practices now adopted by those states embracing the Ozark Plateau, deer herds are rapidly growing, and who is to say that the cougar will not soon return, if it hasn't already? In the wildlife-management areas and inhospitable acreages located within the bayous formed by the Mississippi, Sabine, and Pearl Rivers and their numerous tributaries, wildlife abounds. Cougars have been reported, though they are officially declared to be an extirpated species by all the states hosting bayou country, with the exception of Texas. If cougars still are to be found in the Florida Everglades, why not also in the Louisiana bayous?

Another area outside of the current accepted range of the cougar that has habitat potential is the great boreal forest that once covered much of the provinces of Alberta, Saskatchewan, Manitoba, and Ontario in Canada, and northern Minnesota and upper Michigan in the United States. This forest has been somewhat reduced in size by the inroads of civilization, but a lot of land continues to exist in a primitive and wild condition. Occasionally there are even reports that a cougar had been sighted somewhere within this large area.

One of the more positive signs that points toward an ecological reformation with respect to wildlife habitat is the obvious increase in white-tail deer population—the cougar's natural prey. It was estimated—by whatever methods were used—that there were between 34 and 40 million white-tails living on the North American continent prior to sixteenth-century European immigration. By 1908, it was believed that this total was fewer than half a million. Restrictive hunting laws were then placed in effect; predators such as the bear, cougar, and wolf were made subject to a number of aggressive control measures; and as a result of these efforts, currently more than an estimated 19 million white-tails live in the United States alone.

The establishment of and continued support for governmental and private enclaves such as parks, forests, and wildlife sanctuaries, coupled with the unsuitability of certain large public tracts of western land for expanded human use, should permit the cougar to continue to thrive and its population to further increase. There is, however, always a limit as to the number of animals that can be naturally maintained within a specific land area. For example, for ungulates the limiting factor could be the grazing capacity; for carnivores such as the cougar, it could be the availability of suitable prey species. Whether or not an equilibrium between prey and predator has ever been reached, or can be reached, it is difficult to say: the amount of bureaucratic involvement in wildlife does not lend itself to such determinations and predictions.

As previously noted, three essential elements exert considerable influence over animal populations: suitable habitat, available food, and level of predation. Human involvement impacts populations when habitat is manipulated in a manner detrimental to wildlife or when the activity directly alters the populations. This is what occurred with the bison, the cougar, the wolf, and numerous other species. However, the fact that over the years the number of cougars has decreased cannot be blamed altogether on the increased human population. Determination of cause is not a simple yes-or-no question; it is a matter of degree. Although increases in human population could, potentially, initiate a cause-and-effect relationship with respect to decreases in cougar population, the fact that cougar population has not continued to decrease, and does in fact currently show an increase, suggests that these two factors are not forever causally linked.

Wilderness is more a condition than a describable entity. All natural forms change over time: mountains erode, rivers deepen and change course, forests mature, and animals evolve. All living organisms require certain conditions for them to grow, thrive, and reproduce, but some are more demanding than others. The cougar requires very little support; its geographical and climatical range was, and still is, greater than any other animal species, exclusive of humans, in the Western Hemisphere; and the cougar can even adjust to moderate human intrusion. But the cougar does require a reasonable area in which to hunt, conceal itself, and mate.

Without animals, a wilderness forest would be but trees, shrubs, vines . . . moving little except in the wind. It is because the forest shelters other life-forms that it becomes more than just a cluster of plants. By embracing the animals the forest takes on a further dimension, of flight, mobility, bones, flesh, and blood, of mystery and majesty.

EIGHT

Danger to Humans

Hushed, cruel, amber eyed,
Before the time of the danger of the day,
Or at dusk on the boulder-broken mountainside
The great cats seek their prey.

Soft-padded, heavy-limbed,
With agate talons chiselled for love or hate,
In desolate places wooded or granite-rimmed,
The great cats seek their mate.

Rippling, as water swerved,
To tangled coverts overshadowed and deep
Or secret caves where the canyon's wall is curved,
The great cats go for sleep.

Seeking the mate or prey,
Out of the darkness glow the insatiate eyes.
Man, who is made more terrible far then they,
Dreams that he is otherwise!

George Sterling. "Pumas," from *Big Cats, an Anthology*

IN COLORADO, an idyllic little mountain community, Idaho Springs, is located along Interstate 70 approximately thirty-five miles west of Denver. Established to provide service to what once was an active mining district, the town leaders placed a historical monument in the center of their town, appropriately shaped in the form of a nugget, to remember and honor George A. Jackson, who discovered gold while camped on a sandbar at the junction of Chicago and Clear Creeks in 1859.

Idaho Springs really hasn't changed since it was incorporated in 1878. Even most downtown buildings appear to be unchanged, although most have been subject to some level of historic-status preservation. These buildings and their occupants conduct business activities much as they did at the turn of the century. The people of Idaho Springs are cordial, quick to welcome strangers, and proud of their rich Colorado history. It is, however, also a close-knit community; the residents know most everyone else living in their town, and friends and family are the most treasured of assets.

Monday, January 14, 1991, did not at first appear that it would be much different than any other January day in the high country. The weather was cold, but not unpleasant. From a morning low of about ten degrees above zero, by early afternoon the temperature had warmed to nearly forty degrees. Businesses opened that morning with the usual anticipation of a steady sup-ply of customers; commuters traveling I-70 to jobs in Denver departed on schedule; and children of school age made their way to class. Life, for the people of the town, with all its hopes, dreams, and ambitions, was following its customary path.

Scott Dale Lancaster was a senior at Idaho Springs' Clear Creek High School. The youngest of three brothers—the elder of the three was an Air Force Academy graduate and military pilot—Scott longed for an opportunity to demonstrate his own special talents. He had many: a member of his high school's ski team and the track team, he was a junior member of the Colorado Velo Bike Racing Team, won second place in the state Cyclo-Cross champi-onship, and was considered by those who knew him to be a potential world-class bike racer. In fact, he enjoyed athletic competition so much that he had neglected his studies and was disqualified from participation in any further high-school athletic events until he improved his grades. Although the dis-qualification initially depressed him, he had recently made some progress on his studies; he had also embarked on a more active physical-training program.

Clear Creek High and the secondary school are located on the outskirts of Idaho Springs, adjacent to the Arapahoe National Forest. In back of the school buildings, the land rapidly rises to meet the rugged canyons and higher slopes of the mountains that almost surround the town. A cross-country footpath winds through this rough terrain, following game trails and washes. Many aspiring athletes, including Scott Lancaster, had done training runs on these harsh pathways. That January 14, with two free-class periods ahead of him, Scott decided to run some laps on this course prior to his final class of the day. Wearing a black sweatshirt, cutoff light-blue sweat pants, ski gloves, and running shoes, Scott started jogging along the trail. He felt good and was looking forward to what he hoped would be a vigorous workout.

Scott was not aware of the cougar watching the game trail, nor did he see it crouch in brushy cover in anticipation of the approach of a running animal. The cougar's attack was over in little more than a flash. Although Scott was in excellent physical condition, at five feet six inches and 136 pounds he was not large; the cougar, a reasonably healthy male, was between two and one-half to three years old and weighed 110 pounds. There was a brief struggle. Scott tried to fight back, but the cougar grasped Scott's throat in its jaws and it was quickly over.

When Scott failed to return home that evening, his mother called several of his close friends to try and locate him. The following day, when Clear Creek High School called to find out why Scott was not attending classes, his mother called the county sheriff to report him missing. An investigation led authorities to the trail that Scott had taken the previous day, and rescue teams, accompanied by three tracking dogs, searched the area without finding Scott. The following day, Wednesday, January 16, at 10:30 in the morning, members of the rescue team discovered Scott's body sparsely covered with ground debris and encircled by animal tracks visible in the light snow that had fallen sometime earlier.

So as to not disturb the scene, the rescue team did not directly approach the body. They noted drag marks and a trail of blood leading to the north. After contacting other searchers and advising them of the location of the body, the members of the rescue team began to secure the area. Then one of them observed a cougar sitting about twenty yards from the body. Its ears were up and alert—not dropped back in a flattened position, which would have indicated that an attack was eminent. As other members of the team approached, some on horseback and some with dogs, they were directed to stay where they were. Law-enforcement personnel then advanced toward the cougar, which fled. The cougar did not, however, leave the area, but began circling back toward the body. One officer who got a shot at the cougar with a 9mm pistol ap-

Ears flattened, open mouth exposing its canines, spitting and hissing its wrath, an aroused cougar gives little assurance that it is the craven and cowardly animal that it has perhaps been incorrectly reported to be. *Photo of Sarah Alford drawing.*

parently hit the animal, which was seen to jump and then fall backward over a small ledge. The cougar moved a short distance away and attempted to conceal itself in a brushy area. It was hiding in this brushy location when it was killed by an officer armed with a .308-caliber rifle.

Given the obvious human bias, there is no way that a cougar attack on a human being can be described as being anything but horrifying. Cougar attacks are not meant as warnings: the cougar's intent is simply to kill and eat its victim. In the case of Scott Lancaster, his thoracic cavity was opened, most of his internal organs were removed, his scalp was pulled back to approximately the middle of his skull, and his face was consumed. These are ugly thoughts to deal with, and although what happened to Scott is precisely what would happen to any animal killed by a cougar, when the victim is a human being, it is difficult to view the killing as a natural event.

The cougar is an opportunist in the purest and simplest definition of the term. When it is hungry, it wants to eat, and as we have seen it is willing to eat even a skunk or porcupine—and that under circumstances of less than dire hunger. So why should the cougar have scruples about human beings? There will always be those who maintain optimistic opinions regarding the behavior and intent of our larger North American carnivores—bears, cougars, and wolves—toward humans. Biologists and wolf lovers interested in returning wolves to former habitats are quick to discount the wolf as a threat to human life, but wildlife writer Barry Lopez, known for his thorough research work, seems not to agree with this assertion: "It is the fashion today to dismiss rather glibly accounts of wolves preying on human beings. However, I think it would be quite foolish to maintain that no healthy wolf ever did so, or that wolves were able to size up human beings like any other sort of domestic stock and see whether in lean times taking such a creature is worth the risk" (1978, 71).

Theodore Roosevelt often expressed his somewhat contemptuous opinion of the cougar as a proper human adversary, but in his *The Wilderness Hunter* he was cautious in his views about the possibility of a cougar attacking a human. After declaring his own lack of fear, he went on to say: "Yet it is foolish to deny that in exceptional instances attacks may occur. Cougars vary wonderfully in size, and no less in temper. Indeed I think that by nature they are as ferocious and bloodthirsty as they are cowardly; and that their habit of sometimes dogging wayfarers for miles is due to a desire for bloodshed which they lack the courage to realize" (1893, 344).

Like many mammals, cougars are curious about a lot of things. They have been known to follow and observe humans with no apparent motivation other than inquisitiveness. Notwithstanding the cougar's initial intention, if contact should later occur the cougar might attack. I find it incredible that some wildlife writers who are otherwise knowledgeable hold such quixotic views about this. Here is a sample of their statements: "Under no normal circumstances will a cougar declare war on man personally, and under no circumstances, normal or otherwise, will it turn on him the full measure of power and ferocity that it holds in reserve for other fellow brutes as may cross its will" (Seton 1929, 126); "Hunting lions very rarely and only under exceptional circumstances attack a human being. And in those circumstances where lions do attack humans, they do it half-heartedly and seldom eat human flesh" (Hibben 1948, 218); "It must be reiterated that an attack on a human by a mountain lion is extremely rare. Most stories of attacks are only yarns. Almost every mountain lion can be depended upon to mind its own business" (Cahalane 1961, 271); "If you should find a partially eaten carcass so buried, you can be sure a cougar is in the vicinity. But don't be frightened. The huge cats are timid and far more afraid of humans than humans are of them" (Ormond 1964, 417); "Most people now know that they have nothing to fear from the great cat" (Turback 1986, 29).

When I began assembling information on the recorded incidents of cougar attacks on human beings, I found myself often becoming frustrated by the lack of historical information prior to the 1900s applicable to this subject. I have to believe, given that we had a very healthy cougar population from prehistoric times through the colonial period, that there were unprovoked attacks. Perhaps they were so commonplace that they were not considered to be newsworthy happenings. In any event, it was possible to find details on only a few. A number of people who claim to be experts on cougar behavior have dismissed most historic accounts as fables, folklore, or just plain tall stories. However, if there were once far more cougars than there are now—and since, presumably, the potential for cougar/human contacts has not been exacerbated—there must also have been more attacks by cougars on human beings than there are now.

Had we the ability to transport ourselves back in time to a colonial America of the early 1700s, we would be better able to appreciate what were the true hazards that the first settlers had to deal with. Today, Native Americans are willing to accept the same laws and rules of conduct as those that regulate all other citizens, but in colonial times, most residents of eastern settlements feared the Indian, and usually with good reason. The aspirations, ambitions, and philosophy of the settler and the Indian were so diametrically dissimilar that conflict was inevitable. The wilderness was regarded by the settler as a shield for the Indian; it was impenetrable, providing comfort and succor only to the native peoples, the bear, the cougar, and the wolf. James Fenimore Cooper, in his last publication in the "Leather Stocking Tales" series, *The Deerslayer*, describes a settler's perception of the colony of New York along the Hudson, Mohawk, and Schoharie Rivers between the years 1740 and 1745: "Broad belts of the virgin wilderness not only reached the shores of the first river, but they even crossed it, stretching away into New England, and affording forest covers to the noiseless moccasin of the native warrior, as he trod the secret and bloody warpath. A bird's-eye view of the whole region east of the Mississippi must then have offered one vast expanse of woods, relieved by a comparatively narrow fringe of cultivation along the sea, dotted by the glittering surfaces of lakes, and intersected by the waving lines of rivers" (1925, 14–15).

A poignant and terrifying example of the kind of incidents recorded in the ongoing conflict between Indians and settlers occurred on May 13, 1791. Mary Kinnan was taken by Shawnee Indians after they had broken into her home, killed her husband and two of her children, and also killed a neighbor's child who was there at the time. After running from the home with a small child in her arms, she was seized and the child was killed. She was taken back to her home, and she later described the spectacle she saw: "Gracious God! what a scene presented itself to me! My child [a young girl who was also named Mary], scalped and slaughtered, smiled even then; my husband, scalped and weltering in his blood, fixed on me his dying eye, which, though languid, still expressed an appreciation for my safety, and sorrow at his inability to assist me; and accompanied the look with a groan that went through my heart. Spare me the pain of describing my feeling at this scene, this mournful scene, which racked my agonizing heart, and precipitated me to the verge of madness" (Phelps 1967, 9; Kollock 1795, 5).

The cougar, too, was perceived as adding a sense of danger to the yet untamed wilderness. To the settlers of this raw country, the cougar was felt to be a malevolent presence; it personified the essence of incarnate evil. Stories were told and retold of the cougar savaging helpless women, especially pregnant women; it was said to wait in the shadowy forest interminably for the opportunity to snatch a small child from the arms of its mother. The subject of Miriam Jones Shillingsburg's 1969 Ph.D. dissertation was the writings of William Gilmore Simms, and specifically his *The Cub of the Panther*, a novel that was published serially in 1869. Relying in part on information supplied to him from people living in the backwoods of North and South Carolina in the 1840s, Simms refers twice to incidents involving a panther and helpless women prey. The first involves a story related to him by the wife of a hunter. She advised Simms of "the appetite of the beast for women in pregnancy. . . . Horrid story of his eating one in this situation & of the discovery of her remains by her husband (Simms's 1847 journal, 112). The second incident involved a hunter who killed a "great she panther" that was circling with "catlike cunning . . . a woman, who, with one arm clasped a newly born infant to her bosom" (*The Apalachians*, second lecture, 211).

In her classic novel *The Mountain Lion*, Jean Stafford weaves a rather fascinating tale of two siblings, a boy and a girl from Covina, California, who are asked to spend part of their summer with relatives at a ranch in the Colorado

This photo, whimsically entitled *Terror of the Rockies,* attempts to demonstrate all of the purported fierceness of the cougar through the staged presentation of a stuffed animal. Photo was taken in Home, Colorado, now a ghost town approximately four miles west of Rustic, Colorado. *Photo courtesy of Colorado Historical Society.*

mountains. In addition to facing the problems of adolescence, they also dis-cover discomfort in dealing with the wilderness environment that they have become a part of. Along with their experiencing the effect of certain human social frailties, they also become part of a mutually incompatible relationship between human residents and the sole cougar surviving in the area. The alle-goric and tragic outcome is shaped by the unique conclusion of this adverse relationship. This tale, itself fictional, nevertheless highlights what are cer-tainly nonimaginary feelings of mystique and apprehension that the human species holds for the cougar.

In an article for *North Florida Living* in 1982, Davey Gnann Volkhardt por-trays life in the North Florida wilderness in the late 1800s. Volkhardt's Uncle Raleigh often told thrilling stories about encounters with wild animals—tales that in part were factual family history, but were also possibly embell-ished by Raleigh to add to the listener's enjoyment. In one story, a great-aunt of Volkhardt's who had lived in "older times" had an encounter with a cougar when she was pregnant. She and her husband lived in a one-room cabin some distance from her parents, and after sharing a good visit with her mother she had begun her long walk home only to discover that she was being closely trailed by a cougar. She had heard that cougars were fascinated by clothing carrying a human scent; so she removed her apron, discarded it and ran on. She then heard the cougar tearing and ripping her apron, so she took off her bonnet and dropped it on the trail. As she fled toward her home she continued to discard garments until she had reached the edge of the cabin clearing. With the cabin in sight, she "dropped the last stitch she was wearing—her drawers. She rushed toward the cabin, ran inside the door, and put the wooden latch down to lock it. Quickly she buil[t] a fire in the fireplace, hoping the smell of smoke would drive the panther away" (1982, 45). The determined cougar circled the house looking for an opening until it heard the approach of the husband, at which time it "slipped into the darkness."

Are all of these stories and tales true? Probably not. The temptation to embellish and fabricate increases over time. Are any of them true? Perhaps. Women and children are still, today, considered to be more vulnerable to attack than men, and there is no reason to believe that circumstances have changed. In fact, it is more likely that in the old days there would have been more attacks, for a number of reasons: (1) there were a greater number of cougars; (2) cougars' learned behavior may not by then have developed into an acquired innate fear of humans; (3) and the isolation of human habitation, often in prime cougar habitat, obviously increased the risks.

One of the earliest records of a cougar attack dates from 1751. In Lewisville, Pennsylvania, a tombstone in an old cemetery is inscribed, "Here lyeth ye body of Phillip Tanner who departed this life May 6, 1751, aged 58 years." Carved on the top of this tombstone is the image of a cougar. According to a number of accounts, including the research work of Ficcio and Gray, Tanner was reportedly killed by a cougar adjacent to a nearby forested area, and also somewhat close to the cemetery, at a location that was then named Betty Patch; the crude likeness of a cougar was chiseled on the tombstone as cause of Tanner's death (*West Chester Local Daily News*, October 8, 1956; Young and Goldman 1946, 100–101).

In a brief article published in 1885, Theodore Roosevelt expressed his belief that the cougar had formerly been far more dangerous:

When the continent was first settled, and for long afterward the cougar was quite as dangerous an antagonist as the African or Indian leopard, and would even attack men unprovoked. An instance of this occurred in the annals of my father's family. Early in the present century one of my ancestral relatives, a Georgian, moved down to the wild and almost unknown country bordering on Florida. His plantation was surrounded by jungles in which all kinds of beasts swarmed. One of his negroes had a sweetheart on another plantation, and in visiting her, instead of going by the road he took a short cut through the swamps, heedless of the wild beasts, and armed only with a long knife, for he was a man of colossal strength, and of fierce determined temper. One night he started to return late, expecting to reach the plantation in time for his daily task on the morrow. But he never reached home, and it was thought that he had run away. However, when search was made for him his body was found in the path through the swamp, all gashed and torn, and but a few steps from him the body of a cougar, stabbed and cut in many places. (Young and Goldman 1946, 101–2, quoting Roosevelt from "Hunting Trips of a Ranchman," *Review of Reviews*, 1885, 32–33)

A few years later, in *The Wilderness Hunter*, in relating a similar incident, Roosevelt wrote: "In the old days, when all wild beasts were less shy than at present, there was more danger from the cougar." Roosevelt said he had been told by General Hampton that near his Mississippi plantation, "where the man a cougar was most likely to encounter was a nearly naked and unarmed negro," such a man was waylaid and killed by a cougar late one night while he was walking alone through the swamp (1893, 344–45).

Wildlife author J. Hampden Porter stated: "There is no need to argue the question whether or not pumas can or will kill men; that has been affirmatively settled by facts" (1894, 262). Porter was the first on the scene of a cougar attack in which a rancher stumbled upon the final assault of a large cougar on a steer. The cougar left the steer and turned on the rancher, who defended himself with a knife. The cougar escaped, but the rancher was badly wounded (1894, 269). Being quite comfortable with wild animals, Porter, who should have been forewarned by this episode, later took on the responsibility of raising a young cougar, naming it Gato. After Gato had reached maturity, he became difficult to handle and had to be closely watched. One day when Gato was tethered on a chain, a strange dog appeared in the yard; the cougar broke the chain, killed the dog, and climbed a nearby tree. When a man, unaware of the circumstances, blundered into the courtyard, he was immediately attacked by the cougar. Able to reach the house before the cat did much damage to him, he seized a rifle and killed the cougar (1894, 298–99).

There are very few instances in which a captive cougar does not eventually become too dangerous to handle or end up attacking someone. Dean and Bobbi Harrison—mentioned in chapter 3 as co-owners of the Out of Africa Wildlife Park—have experienced two cougar attacks. Well aware that their animal performers—bears, wolves, tigers, lions, jaguars, and cougars—are wild animals, they avoid taking unnecessary risks. They are particularly sensitive to danger from their cougars, and with good cause. The initial attack involved an adult female they acquired as a kitten. They named her Savanna, and she was their first cougar. Although Dean and Bobbi shared the responsibilities of care, it was evident to Dean that Bobbi was Savanna's favorite. When Savanna was four years old she was given the task of raising two tiger cubs. While the two cubs and Savanna were being fed by Bobbi, Dean entered the habitat to warn Bobbi that, he thought, it was too dangerous for her to be in with the feeding cats. As Dean and Bobbi began to leave, Savanna attacked Dean. When Bobbi attempted to pull the enraged cougar off of Dean, she was also bitten. Although the Harrisons were not seriously injured, their relationship with Savanna was never again the same (*Back to Eden*, 6–14). The second attack was more serious. On October 18, 1995, Dean released Caleb, a nine-year-old male cougar, into a newly constructed natural habitat. While walking to an exit gate, Dean suddenly was gripped by a feeling of danger. Then within twenty feet of the gate, he saw Caleb crouched in a nearby ravine. Caleb leaped at Dean's throat, but Dean was able to block this initial assault. The cougar sprang again and again and eventually Caleb grasped the back of Dean's neck with his teeth. Caleb then moved toward the front of Dean's throat, trying to suffocate his prey. Biting deeply, the cougar punctured the top of Dean's right lung. Expecting that he was going to die, Dean heard wolves howling; he thought they were calling Bobbi to help him, and he himself called out with what he thought might be his last breath. Dean was relieved to hear her shout the cougar's name. Opening the gates and running through the enclosure, Bobbi picked up a thirty-gallon plastic drum. Caleb, presumably thinking that Bobbi would hit him with the drum, released Dean. Dean recovered, and in about ten days was able to resume participation in the Out of Africa performances. A brochure, "From Death to Love," describes his experience in greater depth.

Other mammals accept the possibility that an animal predator can and will kill them, but humans curiously have difficulty accepting this to be true of captive or pet predators, notwithstanding the fact that, even under the most benign of circumstances, captive cougars often demonstrate that they can be blatantly treacherous. Cougars in captivity are certainly capable of inflicting severe injury and even death on their human guardians. Tigers, lions, leopards, and other large captive felines also possess the potential and disposition to deal lethally with their keepers and other intruders into their environments. But these other large cats have also demonstrated that they can develop a tolerance for, or at least an indifferent acceptance of, their human captors. On occasion, this can develop even into an affinity or attachment. Cougars, unlike human beings, do not have a conscience. Nor does the predatory animal harbor altruistic motives. A predator will measure all other species on the basis of their being potential prey or potential threat. As Darwin suggested "the instinct of each species is good for itself, but has never, as far as we can judge, been produced for the exclusive good of others" (1929, 196). The human species has never been the sole natural prey of any carnivore, but once the fear of humans has been lost, or perhaps not yet been acquired, a human being is as susceptible to attack as would be any other species of comparable physical size and capability.

In the *Maneaters of Kumaon*, Jim Corbet described some of his experiences in hunting and dealing with predatory tigers and leopards of the Kumaon hills of northern India during the early 1900s. These fierce animal marauders were not just occasional killers; they killed and ate from more than four hundred human beings before they themselves were dispatched by Corbet. These feline hunters of human prey became contemptuous rather quickly of the simple and somewhat helpless people who lived within and adjacent to the tropical forests of India. They would freely enter the poorly defended villages and drag a victim into the jungle, where they could feed without fear of retaliation. In another gruesome account, Lieutenant Colonel Patterson tells of the infamous "man-eaters of Njombe" that killed and ate more than a thousand people in central Africa; he also describes his personal involvement with two marauding lions that in 1898 disrupted the construction of the Uganda railway near Tsavo Station *(The Man-Eaters of Tsavo)*, clearly attesting to the willingness of animal predators to feed on human flesh even if an abundance of natural prey is available. The demise of the two Tsavo lions was mentioned in the British House of Lords by Prime Minister Lord Salisbury, who stated: "The whole of the works were put a stop to for three weeks because a party of man-eating lions appeared and conceived a most unfortunate taste for our porters. At last the laborers [a work force of near three thousand people] entirely declined to go on unless they were guarded by an iron entrenchment. Of course it is difficult to work a railway under these conditions, and until we found an enthusiastic sportsman [Lt. Colonel John Henry Patterson] to get rid of these lions our enterprise was seriously hindered" (see *The Man-Eaters of Tsavo*, 1907, 20, specifically, and Peter H. Capstick, *Death in the Silent Places*, 1981, 36).

The abject fragility of the human body and the seeming incapability of even the most robust of humans to defend themselves against other than the smallest of wild animals without use of a weapon weighs heavily against the human in the event of direct conflict with an aroused animal predator. Although there really isn't any practical method to assess the true extent and depth of innate behavior or instinct, it is reasonable to presume that most wild animals have certain imbedded and logical apprehensions, if not intuitive fear, of the human species. If an animal believes that it has a choice between flight from a human or fight, it is suggested that more often the animal would typically choose flight. I believe, however, that there is an active association between innate behavior and learned behavior—that in fact conditioning can overrule genetic predisposition. Responses of an animal that are enacted without some prior conditioning or the existence of a current-life learning event can only have been acquired biologically, through genetic influence. But if a cougar raised in the wild, with a predisposition to avoid the human species whenever possible, should subsequently become more familiar with the human and the extent of actual human physical capability, it might well consider the human being as a potential, if not necessarily preferred, prey species.

Unlike with most bear attacks, nonrabid cougar attacks on humans do not occur because the cougar feels that it is threatened, or in the case of a mother that her cubs are in danger. Most, if not all, intentional cougar attacks on humans are driven by an intent to kill and then to eat. Cougar attacks on humans that do not end in human fatality do so not because of any merciful intention on the part of the cougar. Often it is simply because of a rescue intervention or because the attacked person took appropriate defensive or offensive measures. One example of effective defensive measures occurred in Southwestern Colorado in 1994. A native of upper Michigan, Susan Groves had recently moved to Colorado while still retaining a typical Midwestern belief in what the appropriate relationship should be between humans and wildlife; that is, mutual and perceptive curiosity blended with tacit deference and avoidance. An employee of the Ute Mountain Ute tribe, Susan was then a water-quality specialist working on a service contract the tribe had with the Bureau of Reclamation and the Animas-LaPlata project. Her job required her to spend lots of time out-of-doors—and she loved it, On Tuesday, December 1, Susan was taking width and flow measurements prior to gathering water samples from an icy stream that emptied into the Mancos River near Grass Canyon, a few miles south of Mesa Verde National Park.

In a conversation I had with Susan later, she recalled that the day started out rather pleasantly: the sun was shining, and the temperature was around 40 degrees. She was looking forward to completing her sampling tasks quickly and going on to other projects. Susan said that she was standing in midstream when she heard something moving along the bank above her. Looking up, her eyes met those of a cougar. The cat immediately came down the bank toward her. In the belief that the cougar was only curious, Susan stayed in the water, but when the big cat showed no interest in leaving she began to scream and to throw chunks of ice at it. The cougar continued to follow her every move, gradually closing the distance between them. The banks were quite steep, and the cougar sensed that its quarry was trapped. When Susan suddenly stumbled, and in the process of falling turned her back to the cat, the cougar attacked. The weight of the cat's body and the force of its charge carried Susan underwater. She felt the cougar sink its teeth into her head, but from then on she remembered little else until she was on the bank, where she realized she was on top of the cougar and that her arm was in the cougar's mouth.

Susan was not a typical female victim of a cougar attack. A healthy and robust individual, nearly five feet nine inches tall and 155 pounds, she had the physical ability to resist the cat, and certainly was not willing to surrender meekly; she would put up a fight. Recovering from her torpor, Susan reached in the fishing vest that fortuitously she was wearing and pulled out a pair of very sharp forceps. Susan began to jab the cougar in its eyes, at which the cougar decided to retreat. Susan was then able to make her way back to the truck and drive herself nearly seven miles to obtain medical help. Susan suffered puncture wounds to the back of her head, severe arm lacerations, a plethora of body bruises, but no broken bones. The cougar was later tracked down with dogs and killed. It was reported to be an old female with badly worn teeth, weighing sixty-three pounds.

There are a number of wildlife "experts," specialists, authors, and re-searchers who, while reluctantly acknowledging that cougar attacks on humans have occurred, still express the conviction that many of these attacks are sim-ply the result of a mistake in victim identity—that the cougar was under the impression that it was some animal other than a human being that it was stalking, or that the cougar surmised that either it or its young had been threatened by this human presence. What perhaps sustains this continuing belief is the notion that cougars fear the human species to such an extent that they would rather flee than confront, regardless of the circumstances and con-ditions. The fact of the matter is that all creatures are capable of acting in in-dividual ways—of behaving in what may appear to be an unusual manner. Human flesh may not be the cougar's most desired meal, but there is no evi-dence that they have scruples about eating all, or part of, a human carcass. Bodies of human victims that were not fed upon were spared this indignity only because of either the promptness of a recovery action or because the cougar was severely injured in struggling with its prey.

Five incidents summarized below all involve premeditated attacks by cougars on children or teenagers. These five selected examples of attacks describe most of the conditions, circumstances, and results that typically are involved in such events. The circumstances seem to suggest that cougars know just what children are, and that they have little regard for youngsters' ability to protect themselves. All of these attacks except one would probably have resulted in the death, and assuredly the later devouring, of the child were it not for the prompt intervention of an adult, and such an outcome was avoided in that one exception only because of the defensive ability of the young man involved.

The first incident occurred in March 1965 on a ranch east of Clinton, British Columbia, Canada. Fifteen-year-old John Simpkins was helping rancher Jim Baker build a fence. Simpkins was working about sixty feet downhill from Baker when Baker noticed a cougar emerging from a nearby juniper clump and moving toward the boy. Baker yelled a warning, but the cougar proceeded to leap on Simpkins's back before the boy could even turn to face his attacker. To protect his face and throat, Simpkins brought his hands up, but the cougar quickly bit through this protection and went for the boy's head. Baker ran to the site of the attack, jumped on the back of the cougar, and attempted to pull it off. The cougar, however, would not relinquish its hold. Baker then reached in his pocket and pulled out a knife. He jabbed the blade of the knife into the cougar's throat. The cougar released the boy and retreated behind a pile of brush, where Baker pursued the wounded cat with a fence hammer. The cougar fled to a nearby tree and Baker was then able to take the injured Simpkins to a hospital. The cougar was later tracked down and killed. It was an underweight seventy-pound female, approximately three years old.

An attack on December 22, 1976, involved a fourteen-year-old boy. Again the cougar was an underweight female. This boy, Thane Morgan, fortuitously had a hunting knife with him, and the outcome of the encounter was less grim than it might have been. Thane's family owned a weekend home near Rye, Colorado, adjacent to the foothills and trails of the San Isabel National Forest. Thane was on his Christmas break from school, and a snowshoe hiking trip seemed like the perfect way for him to spend this day. For no particular reason, Thane decided to take along with him a small hunting knife, placing it in his backpack. After he had gone only a short distance up the trail, a cougar suddenly sprang from its cover and bounded up to him, crouching only a few feet away. Thane and the cougar stared at one another for only a moment, and then the cougar attacked. It leaped on him, digging its claws into his body and assaulting his head with its powerful jaws and teeth. Proving not to be the expected unresisting victim, the 120-pound Thane, five feet six inches in height, fended off the initial attack while freeing the hunting knife from his backpack. Slashing at the cougar, he was able to discourage further attack. The wounded cougar bounded away. Thane was able to secure help at a neighbor's home, and after a stay of several days in the hospital, and hundreds of stitches, he was able to go home. The injured cougar was later tracked and killed.

Another attack was on August 2, 1984, in Big Bend National Park, Texas. This episode collected considerable attention in the Texas area, and thanks to Larry Mueller, editor-at-large for Outdoor Life magazine ("Cougar Attack," 1985), it also received national exposure. David Vaught, age eight, his four-year-old brother Justin, his mother Kim Brown, and his new stepfather, Chris Brown, were following a short nature trail that began and ended at the Big Bend Visitor Center. The group stopped to attend to the needs of Kim Brown who had been bitten by army ants. While Chris was still assisting Kim, David and Justin elected to walk on ahead to explore the trail. With David in the lead, they had followed the trail for only a short distance when they were surprised by the approach of a cougar. David yelled "mountain lion!," and turned to run. Within a few steps the cougar was on him, sinking its front claws into both of his shoulders and its hind claws into his thigh. Then seizing his head in its jaws but releasing its claws, the cougar continued to chew on David's head. Seeing David's limp body, Kim Brown thought her son was dead, but Chris Brown did not hesitate: he charged the cat, yelling and shouting. The cougar only snarled and continued its attempt to sink its fangs into David's skull. Chris then kicked at the cougar, slipping and falling and grabbing at the animal. Securing a grip on the cougar's neck, he was able to pull it off. Chris fought the cougar with all his strength. He was able to get his hands on a stick, brandishing it while screaming at the cougar, which fled. Only then was Chris able to pick David up and carry him to the visitor center for emergency treatment. He had severe injuries and later received a series of extensive plastic surgery operations at a Dallas hospital. Soon after the attack, the cougar was tracked down by dogs and killed. It was a male, in seemingly good health, approximately eighteen months old and weighing eighty-five pounds.

The fourth of these five attacks came in August 1985, on Vancouver Island, British Columbia, Canada—a locale that has been seen more cougar attacks than any other cougar habitat in Canada or the United States. Camp Thunderbird, near Sooke, a small logging, fishing, and farming community on the southwest corner of the island, about twenty-six miles up-island from Victoria, ten-year-old Alyson Parker and her two young female companions were hiking on a trail. Glancing up, they saw a large cougar intently staring at them. After watching the cat for several moments, the frightened girls began to scream and run. Alyson tripped and fell and the cougar immediately pounced on her. The two other girls ran back to their nearby camp for help, leaving Alyson alone to suffer the cougar's repeated assaults. The two girls alerted camp counselor Lila Lifely, who was able to drive the cougar away from Alyson. Reluctant to move the badly hurt victim without first treating her injuries, Lifely rested Alyson against a tree and ran back to camp for a medical kit. She was gone but a few moments, but on return found the cougar again attempting to kill Alyson. Using the first-aid kit as a weapon, Lifely beat the cougar over the head until it finally fled. Alyson was taken to a hospital, where she received more than two hundred stitches. The cougar was later tracked with dogs and killed. It was a healthy male cougar of near adult age.

The cougar that attacked six-year-old Sarah Fuller was a gaunt and starving female. This occurred on May 28, 1988, in the Mogollon Rim area, northwest of Payson, Arizona, a site long known as choice cougar territory. This Rim country, favored by cool summers and not too unpleasant winters, is becoming a mecca for people attempting to avoid intemperate climates and the urbanization of other parts of the Southwest. It was a bright spring morning, around 8 A.M. Sarah and her eight-year-old sister Amy had just slipped outside the family's rented cabin and they were trying to catch a lizard when they saw the big cat. The girls' mother Lisa and stepfather Greg Egnash were in the cabin. Hearing the girls' screams, Greg and Lisa dashed out as the cougar attempted to seize the smaller child with its mouth. Greg rushed to help Sarah as Lisa ran inside to get a gun. Casting the attacking cougar off Sarah, Greg grabbed both girls and headed for the cabin. Before he got there, he was met by Lisa carrying their small-caliber rifle, already loaded. Turning the girls over to his wife, Greg took the rifle and fired continuously at the cougar until the gun jammed. Sarah was taken to the Payson hospital for medical attention. The dead cougar was turned over to the Arizona Game and Fish Department.

In spite of stories like these and others that add up to an impressive assemblage of incriminating details and data, quite a few wildlife authorities, authors, and advocates persist in supporting the contention that cougars are basically harmless as far as the human species is concerned. Reports of cougar attacks on human beings continue to come in, and in growing numbers, but these "experts" discount most past attacks because of what they claim are special circumstances, for example (1) the cougar was starving; (2) the cougar was too old to catch its normal or natural wild prey; (3) the cougar was too young to hunt effectively; (4) the cougar had suffered an earlier injury, such as, perhaps being impaired by an attack on a porcupine; or (5) the human being had stumbled upon the cougar's den, or its kill, or its kittens. Based on the foregoing litany, they reason that most attacks on humans, even those on small children, are either provoked or are in some other way excusable.

Another stance taken by analytical cougar advocates is to minimize the extent of the danger from cougars present by enumerating the far larger number of attacks on humans by the family dog or other domesticated animal. These are valid observations, but they are biased: domesticated species, possessing a greater familiarity with humans, tend to act with considerable temerity in pursuit of their own interests and status, and in protecting their territorial boundaries. These attacks are usually meant to punish, perhaps even kill, but rarely with the intention of making a meal out of the human host.

The cougar is the climax wilderness predator—seemingly indolent in times of plenty, occasionally playful, but essentially always a quintessential hunter. Unlike the herbivores, or even most omnivores, the cougar does not find the food it needs for survival to be there just for the taking; it must be sought as well as fought for. In spite of possessing and skillfully using a unique complement of personal physical weapons, the cougar experiences more failures than successes in its near continuous hunting efforts. Most, if not all, of the wild animal species on which the cougar preys are equipped with superb senses of smell, sight, and hearing. Everything must be just right for the cougar in order for it to effect a kill. The cougar is willing to eat virtually anything when it is hungry, so it is not surprising that skunks, porcupines, frogs, grasshoppers, and even humans occasionally appear on its menu.

Whenever a cougar permits itself to be seen, it must be presumed that its intentions are suspect. It is not uncommon for a human to discover that a cougar has been in near proximity, perhaps even uncomfortably close. This could be merely curiosity on the part of the cat, however, since its actions and movements can be deemed to be more secretive than stealthy. The cougar's behavior after it has been seen is usually the best clue as to whether an attack is imminent. Threatening postures vary by individual cat, but if its eyes are obviously intent on a target person and most of its movements suggest that it is preparing to attack—tail quivering or moving spasmodically in anticipatory excitement; crouching, perhaps even hissing or spitting, and ears either halfway back or flat against the head—look out!

What should, or can, a person do when confronted by a cougar? A wealth of information and advice has been offered with respect to this possibility. A brochure produced by the California Department of Fish and Game, *Living with California Mountain Lions*—one widely quoted by wildlife agencies in other states—basically says that when in wilderness areas or known cougar habitat (1) *do not* hike alone; (2) *do not* let children wander—keep them close to you; (3) *do not* approach or attempt to block a cougar's passage; (4) *do not* run or avert your eyes from a cougar—make eye contact; and if you have small children, pick them up if possible so that they don't run. And don't yourself bend or turn away from the cougar when picking up the children; (5) *do not* bend over or assume a crouching position; instead, try to make yourself appear bigger than you are; for example, raise your hands in the air and if you are wearing a coat spread it out. The brochure recommends that one stare at the cougar, always keeping one's eyes on the beast; if possible, try to back away, slowly. Probably the most important point: if you are attacked—fight back!

It should be noted that these recommended human behaviors for unexpected contact with a cougar are drastically different from what most wildlife authorities endorse for if one should meet a startled bear. With bears, appear as nonthreatening as possible; avoid eye contact; and be alert for a nearby safe haven rather than spend time looking for rocks to throw or finding a stick to use as a weapon. If a bear actually attacks, be advised that the best defense is to "play dead"; assume a fetal position and hope for the best. A bear will occasionally bluff an attack, but if it attacks for real, it is not easily dissuaded by the physical defensive measures of a mere human. We are often told that in all likelihood a bear will not target a human for a meal and that the bear is interested only in removing a supposed threat, but research conducted by Steven Herrero (*Bear Attacks*, 1985, 105–6) indicated that when black bears did attack humans, in 90 percent of the incidents of human fatality examined the motive was predation. The grizzly, however, is thought to be less likely to consider a human as prey; their attacks are suggested as being primarily to remove a supposed threat or annoyance.

A cougar attack, on the other hand, is never designed or intended by the cougar as a warning; it has the sole purpose of killing and eventually eating the selected prey, be it deer, human, or whatever. Unlike most bears, a cougar can often be effectively dissuaded by an aggressive and determined defense. It is important to protect the neck and face from the initial and any following assaults; throw rocks; pick up a stick; shout; make loud noises; try not to show fear or do anything other than what will help in the process of dominating and intimidating the animal. Passivity or the application of token or feeble resistance will only make the cougar's task that much easier.

In my lengthy research for this book, I was able to verify, at least to my own satisfaction, the legitimacy of accounts of at least 33 cougar attacks, involving 36 human fatalities; and 126 incidents involving 149 people in which the attack did not result in human fatality. These attacks, with details of my sources, are listed in appendices B and C. Because of the lack of adequate information and data bases in Mexico and Central and South America, only attacks in Canada and the United States are identified. Of necessity, most of the research involved review and analysis of secondary sources. A source that provided a wealth of information was the recent work of Paul Beier, whose research addressed unprovoked fatal and nonfatal cougar attacks between 1890 and 1990.

The greatest problem I encountered in gathering information surrounding cougar attacks on humans was not the absence of a convenient and reliable data base but the general inconsistency of the incident-reporting process. In several instances, I learned of attacks that had taken place in the past twenty years that were never reported in any of the larger newspapers. Many attacks that occurred in isolated areas, or that involved Native Americans, were apparently not considered to be newsworthy except to smaller, primarily local, newspapers. I spent considerable time on Vancouver Island and elsewhere in British Columbia attempting to verify past reported attacks. In the process, I uncovered several attacks that had previously escaped mention.

The fatal and nonfatal attacks that I identify in the appendices represent only those attacks that collected more than just token media attention, thereby becoming more accessible in the public record. In the seventeenth and eighteenth centuries in the United States and Canada, cougar attacks were not really considered to be news, unless the attack was particularly heinous. Even today, when cougar attacks are again becoming more common, unless a victim is killed an attack is not usually deemed to be front-page news, unless it occurs in a national park with an aggressive public-affairs program.

The attacks identified in the two appendices do not include those involving captive animals, or attacks where the intended victim may have been the horse and not specifically the horse's rider; nor do I list attacks that were purely defensive in nature; that is, incidents where the cougar itself was being actively hunted by humans, with or without dogs.

Cougars survive by eating meat. Unless all living cougars are promptly placed in zoos or similar, secure, exhibition dwellings, there is no subsistence alternative for them except to hunt and kill. Cougars are, and should continue to be, part of the human wilderness experience. If they are left alone, they, along with all other nonhuman predator species, perform quite well toward achieving acceptable balance-of-nature controls in their part of the world.

A visitor to Yellowstone National Park who does not see a bear or any of the other marvelous predators feels deprived. Seeing these animals is a proper and necessary part of the wilderness experience. But in accepting the cougar's proper and rightful role in the overall scheme of nature, we must also insure that our role is only that of an interested observer—a nonparticipant whose right to become directly involved is granted only by license (hunting) or the implied requirements of occupational assignment. If the cougar should enter areas of human domain, it becomes subject to whatever risk that this intrusion may entail, which quite often means its immediate death. When we leave our homes and enter the cougar's domain, we should be equally alert to the rules and conditions that prevail in these wilderness areas—just as we are when we enter one of the more dangerous urban jungles that now exist in all our larger cities. Cougars, like all other wild species, have no particular reason to act benevolently toward human beings. Under certain circumstances they can, and will continue to, present real, and not only potential, threat to human life. This is not because of any implied or inherent viciousness of the cougar's, but primarily because of its unpredictability and confounding, enigmatic presence.

All predatory animals are capable of being conditioned by their perceptions about potential prey. And once a cougar has determined that humans are suitable prey, future attacks simply become a function of this learned behavior (Lorenz 1973, 294–95).

NINE

Life in Urban America

Deliver us from troubled times,
And point us toward restful places,
Where wind, trees and humanity rhymes
With God, wildlife and cordial faces.

Oh, let me be one again with nature,
Adjoined with creation and free to ponder,
If for man it is not a better future,
to forsake command and go over yonder.

Where only the lark's flight song is heard,
In consonance with the hushed sound,
Of night overtaking day with unspoken word,
And only the hunters are then to be found.

Harold P. Danz

I F WE CONSIDER all that has occurred, with respect to both the North and South American continents over the past five hundred years or more, the transformation of these two continents is even more remarkable. What was once deemed to be impenetrable and hostile wilderness has now been thoroughly plotted, charted, and developed, and is now routinely traversed by thousands, if not millions, of people in a matter of hours. And thus, one of the world's last great land frontiers no longer exists.

Although there are still a few large regions of uncultivated and uninhabited land that, even to this day, remain almost virginal in Canada, the same cannot be said for the United States of America or the United Mexican States. But even in Canada, as in each of the other two countries named, the urban population represents nearly 80 percent of the human population. However, a review of population-density statistics (Canada, 7 people per square mile of land; the United States, 68 per square mile; Mexico, 118 per square mile) makes it obvious that the extent of urban dispersion and other raw-land conversions is more important than rural/urban ratios when considering overall land-use and land-conservation practices.

As mentioned in chapter 8, the lack of detailed information about the extent and number of verifiable cougar attacks against humans in Mexico and Central and South America precluded my reporting what may be, in total, a considerable number of human/cougar incidents. I assume, however, that the interactions that did occur were generally similar in nature, and perhaps in quantity, to those listed for Canada and the United States. Attempts to improve economic conditions in Mexico and Central and South America have stimulated interest in implementing agrarian reforms and further expanding labor-intensive industrial activities. As a result, wilderness lands in Central and South America are gradually being reduced in size and differently exposed to the needs and wants of growing human populations. With population density in Central and South America now estimated at 45.6 people per square mile, and an urban population approximating 71.7 percent of total population, habitat conditions and living circumstances for remaining cougar populations can be expected to deteriorate; this will be true of Mexico, too. The deterioration will not be solely due to human-dispersal factors but also because governmental regulations for wildlife management and protection are not rigorously enforced or respected.

Prior to 1492—taken to be the beginning of European immigration to the Western Hemisphere—cougars ranged from coast to coast, except in the more northerly part of North America. As human populations grew on both American continents, wildlife species—particularly the larger animals that were incompatible with human land use—either retreated to remaining wilderness areas or were gradually eliminated. The unloved cougar consequently became, in settled areas, a fugitive, and, in primeval forests and rocky barrens, an elusive pariah. As their domain continued to shrivel, still no measure of protection was extended by the public sector to those cougars that remained.

By the late 1880s, in the United States only a few of the more persistent cougars still dwelled east of the Mississippi River. As a proclaimed "varmint," the cougar continued to be a prime target of the predator-control programs. Relentlessly pursued by bounty hunters and their dogs, cougars were all but eradicated from lands where they possibly could present a threat to domestic animals. One of the more interesting papers on the problem of predatory animals was published more than seventy years ago by Edward A. Goldman in the prestigious *Journal of Mammalogy*. Goldman, who was employed by the U.S. Biological Survey, held a narrow view of the value of America's predators (1925, 33):

> As nature lovers we are loath to contemplate the destruction of any species, but as practical conservationists we are forced by the records to decide against such predatory animals as mountain lions, wolves and coyotes. We can not consistently protect them and expect our game to be maintained in satisfactory numbers. Such a course would also alienate the livestock industry, the interests of which must be considered in connection with game administration, and would arouse opposition to such conservation projects as the establishment of game preserves, which might otherwise be favored.

Goldman went on to say that "large predatory mammals, destructive to livestock and to game, no longer have a place in our advancing civilization. To advocate their protection in areas occupied by the homes of civilized man and his domestic animals is to invite being discredited as practical conservationists and to risk through prejudice the defeat of measures which may be vital to the future welfare of the country."

Jay C. Bruce, California's nonpareil predator-control specialist, was once described as a devastating hunter of cougars. An article by Eugene B. Block in *Sunset Magazine* that said Bruce and his dogs "hunt lions [cougars] just for the sport of the game," went on: "Like a Royal Northwest Mounted Policeman pursuing a criminal, they track their lion—and they get their lion, for to Bruce every lion is a criminal—the wanton slayer of sheep and deer and other four-footed friends of man" (1927, 15). This and similar statements about the killing of deer, sheep, and other nonpredatory animals by cougars seem beside the point if we consider the facts. Of course cougars kill animals, but then so do we. Unwelcome or not, without the help of the cougar and the other larger predators, our resident deer population would soon outgrow its natural forage and we would then have more deer scavenging in the suburbs and cities or starving in the wilderness.

This would be equally applicable to elk. The elk herds of Yellowstone National Park long ago outgrew their winter food supply. Except for minor instances of predation by cougars and bears, and by coyotes on newborn elk calves, most taking of Yellowstone elk is by human hunters during designated fall/winter hunting seasons; at those times, the elk leave the park to seek better forage, such as they are accustomed to at the National Elk Refuge at Jackson, Wyoming. Even this control measure, however, has proven to be inadequate. Each year the number of elk that winter in the refuge has continued to grow. In 1997, 10,700 elk and 320 bison (from nearby Grand Teton National Park) elected to be fed at the refuge rather than accept the harsher living conditions of Yellowstone and Grand Teton National Parks. However, Wyoming wildlife experts conservatively estimate that an additional 20,000 elk are still wintering within nearby national parks and forest areas.

Bounties formerly paid for dead cougars and unrestricted hunting were effective in keeping state cougar populations at the same levels, or even somewhat lower levels. Since the cougar was, and perhaps still is, one of the more unpopular native species, killing of these animals to claim bounty payment was not considered to be distasteful; in fact, cougar hunters received consistently far better press than did cougars. A good example of this is an article that appeared in the issue of *Time* for February 21, 1944 (46). The magazine's sport editor was elated over what he declared was the "biggest cougar kill of the season (eight cats—in nine days), Jesse Stockdale and his son Url, of Twisp, Wash. this week got a $400 bounty check—$50 a carcass—from the State Game Department." The article goes on to point out that "because cougars are predatory, there are no bag or season limits."

In the United States, by the early to mid-1960s bounties either were no longer being paid or they were being phased out. Cougar hunting was permitted by license only in most cougar states, and permission to hunt was subject to a variety of fees, regulations, and seasons. California, the state reporting the largest cougar population, now prohibits hunting and identifies the cougar as a protected species. South Dakota and Florida, states with small resident cougar populations, also protect the animal: both have proscribed cougar hunting.

With the exception of California, cougar populations are now said to be subject to "controls" established by each state's fish and game or wildlife department or by a special commission. Annual harvest figures are carefully checked by these state agencies. If it appears advisable to restrict or expand hunting seasons or the number of hunting permits and tags in order to maintain acceptable population levels, these agencies say they will take whatever action is appropriate. However, when I talked to knowledgeable individuals who work for such agencies, in both the United States and western Canada, all mentioned that they have difficulty in putting together accurate estimates of current cougar populations; they believe, however, that their populations are growing.

Thus, we find ourselves faced with both a growing human and cougar population. The problems and conflicts of these two studied protagonists can become even more embroiled if the apparent and sustained increase in the U.S. coyote population continues unchecked—not that cougars and coyotes have any particular relationship to one another, except that they are both predators. The contentious issue, however, is that of species expansion, and both cougars and coyotes are now beginning to encroach flagrantly on areas occupied by an outreaching and rapidly expanding human population. The cougar is far more clandestine in its activities than is the coyote, but the mere presence of either species in human suburbia initiates considerable levels of interest and concern.

This then becomes an enigmatic and paradoxical circumstance. We hold nature in the highest esteem, and most humans defend the right of all of God's creatures to survive and propagate—but not necessarily all of them in our own immediate neighborhood. In fact, we are rather selective about this matter. We like the sounds and the sight of most small birds, but we also abhor the constant evidence of their digestive process. As to large birds—which of course offend in the same way—some may prey on the smaller birds and other animal life. Killing and eating prey is a natural phenomenon that many of us really do not want to witness. Skunks and raccoons are unwelcome visitors to suburbia and should they make too frequent appearances they are permanently removed from local ecosystems. Even deer and rabbits find that they have strong antagonists in enthusiastic backyard horticulturists. (The more knowledgeable suburban gardeners report, however, that their strategic application of cougar droppings has proven to be a most effective deer repellent.)

The protectionist perspective is not new or unique. One of the earliest

Deer fencing around trees in the backyard of a home in the foothills above Golden, Colorado, attests to intense browsing of the neighborhood by deer. Browsing dampens homeowner enthusiasm for creative landscaping and gardening.

characteristics of the urbanization process in Europe and the fledgling American colonies was to build walls around cities and to develop other natural barriers. This was done in order to protect the human inhabitants and their domestic stock and pets and permit these interior residents to "better live at their ease in wealth and plenty" (Botero, 1588, trans., 1956, 227). What we are doing now is maintaining this right to quiet enjoyment of habitat by rules, regulation, and governmental enforcement of majority will. Unfortunately, the spectacular growth of cities and their surrounding suburbs has extended this belief in the inherent public right to safety, security, and freedom from peril to protective control over areas that heretofore served exclusively as the domain of wildlife.

The current planned strategy of establishing city parks, preserving protective zones for agricultural purposes and greenbelts, and extending municipal support toward the development and continuance of recreational properties is basically an extension of some of the earliest provisions of urban law concerning the maintenance of intramural zones free from buildings. Initially, it was intended that these lands would be left undeveloped to satisfy the defensive needs of the city center, but as the aesthetic qualities that were subsequently attained by this practice served to enhance property values, the practice was continued long after the need for defense expired.

Although most people publicly support the concept of national parks, forests, wildlife refuges, and preserves, and many will also visit these areas, few would elect to live in a wilderness area unless they could take with them a lot of urban creature comforts. *Wilderness*—the word alone summons thoughts of vast distances, silence, isolation, and for some perhaps even loneliness. A Webster's dictionary definition quickly associates wilderness with wild animals, but it has little to say about the magical qualities possessed by the green wilderness that attracts people. More than thirty-five years ago, while I was assigned to one of the more beautiful areas in the United States, Yosemite National Park, California, I couldn't help but notice that numbers of people who visited the park ostensibly to become a part of the halcyon Yosemite experience elected to avoid the more isolated campgrounds. Most preferred to camp in crowded Yosemite Valley, even though in some instances their tent ropes were actually crossed with those of their neighbors.

Michael Frome, a wilderness activist and author, devoted a full chapter in his book, *Battle for the Wilderness*, to attempting to describe what a wilderness *is*—not so much as to what a wilderness may look like, but rather to describing its intrinsic qualities. Frome writes: "Wilderness is a place for men, but not for men alone. . . . Wilderness is the sanctuary of grizzly bears, mountain lions, bighorn sheep, elk, and wolves that need large areas set aside from civilization" (1974, 15). There is, of course, a big difference in the wilderness areas that Frome was describing and those undeveloped lands that may still possess a wild quality but are near urban areas or are becoming compromised by the intrusion of increased human habitation or other use. Human society, we are told, performs more efficiently when its participative activities are effectively organized, but it is also true that individuality is inherent in a democracy, and most people find pleasure in vicarious thoughts and their right to enjoy in life those things that are pure and simple—to glimpse occasionally an environment that has not been constructed by man. This need is exhibited perhaps best by the very young. Children thoroughly enjoy their out-of-doors experiences; they appreciate becoming part of something that is not confined or restrained. However, because we now entrust their maturation and to the urban

Human housing and development reaching for views and open space—an example from the West's mountain belt (Golden, Colorado, west of Denver) showing urban sprawl, from core city to suburbs to foothills.

community, nature experiences have become generally limited to that of the suburban backyard.

Although there seems to be no end to the continuous process of subjugating wild lands to the growth and demands of urban society, there will always be exquisite expanses of nature that have been set aside, either by law or philanthropy. However, unless public use of these lands is wisely managed, people who exult in wilderness areas can, through their enthusiastic visiting, erode the very values they so highly treasure. Human attachment for nature is innate, but the affinity between nature and humans cannot be better modeled than by the Native American. A statement credited to "an Indian Chief," most probably from the Delaware tribe and reportedly directed in 1796 to Thomas Mifflin, the then governor of Pennsylvania, poignantly expresses the Native American's special relationship with and respect for wilderness: "We love quiet; we suffer the mouse to play; when the woods are rustled by the wind, we fear not" (McLuhan, 1971, 5, citing Jacobs, Landau, and Pell, *To Serve the Devil*, vol. 1, "Natives and Slaves," Vintage Books, New York, 1971, xxvii).

New housing development in Estes Park, Colorado, enjoins wildlife habitat and is adjacent to Routt National Forest and Rocky Mountain National Park.

When the urban American has an urge to relocate and "become closer to nature," the move is often to an outlying suburban area or to one of the fringe areas that are now bordering undeveloped public lands. They then discover that they have thus become a part of an extrinsic neighborhood ecosystem that carries qualities that are neither pristine nor urban, and where the unexpected can and often does occur.

Land that previously was pristine wildlife habitat and is subject to only limited development is still usually considered to be acceptable habitat by many wildlife occupants. By planting and watering, the human landowners subsequently create areas of lush vegetation—forage superior to that found in the wild. This is attractive to elk, deer, rabbits, and other browsers that form the primary prey of predators such as the cougar. In addition, once cougars become familiar with the urbanized modifications to their habitat, they also become aware of the fresh presence of domestic animals and household pets. Gradually, cougars can even become thoroughly habituated to humans, showing little fear of propinquity and even eyeing children as potential meals.

If we accept the stated opinions of many declared cougar experts and behavioralists, there is a greater probability of being struck by lightning, at-

Movement of human populations into fringe and ecotone areas has changed grazing habits for deer, sheep, and other grass eaters. When feed in remote and undeveloped areas of their range becomes scarce, grazing animals find human habitat to be an attractive alternative—and predators then follow the herds into the same territory.

tacked by a deer, bitten by a black widow spider, rattlesnake, or a dog than of being attacked by a cougar. It is assumed, however, that these same experts would not infer that these imperceptible odds against a cougar attack would also hold true for the household pet. By moving into areas of human habitation, generally because of a shortage of their natural foods, cougars, or any other predatory species, are simply there to seek a new prey base. Finding household pets an easy meal, they have no reason to go elsewhere. Now conditioned to finding prey near human habitation, the probability of attack on a human becomes greater.

A multitudinous array of newspaper articles over the past decade have described in vivid detail attacks by cougars on pet dogs. For example, a recent column in a Los Angeles newspaper depicts a "brazen cougar killed in Tujunga area" that had first made a meal of two dogs and then attacked a fifteen-year-old shepherd, retreating only after the dog's owner threw a glass of water in its face. Although it is often claimed that cougars will eschew human contact and flee from the smallest barking dog, cougars have bounded onto porches and even hurdled seven-foot kennel fences to prey on canines. These attacks are not limited to only a few states and provinces; they occur wherever cougars exist in sufficient numbers to be in competition or conflict with humans for habitat. Every state or province with a recognized cougar population has noted that there has been an increase in incidents.

Accounts of these incidents may differ by location, but the circumstances and conditions are often quite similar. Note the following examples. A pair of cougars, one carrying a white rabbit or house cat in its jaws, was recently observed in an exclusive residential area near Great Falls, Montana. A cougar was also reportedly sighted near an elementary school in a dense residential area of this same general metropolitan area. The *Great Falls Tribune* claimed that, based on the number of reported incidents involving cougars, "Montana is developing a textbook case of suburban growth and wildlife in conflict" (October 9, 1995). In Nevada, where cougar population has soared since the 1980s, cougars are being frequently sighted roaming the suburban backyards of Reno; the activity has generated "a flurry of calls to animal control officers in Reno" (*Gazette-Journal*, May 6, 1994). Depredations by cougars in Texas, New Mexico, and Arizona against sheep and cattle have brought swift, and in some instances illegal, retaliation by ranchers. Cougars have also been reported to be regularly cropping up in suburban communities surrounding Tucson, Phoenix, and Flagstaff, grabbing dogs, cats, and pet goats.

California, Oregon, and Washington newspapers periodically mention the forays of cougars into heavily populated residential areas—in some instances into even older, established neighborhoods. The latter is true particularly in California. A large cougar picked off three family dogs, one by one, in a suburban Riverside, California, residential area; when finally confronted by a property owner—who threw a bottle at the cougar, and hit it—the predator nevertheless picked up a third dog victim—an eighty-pound chow-shepherd mix—before walking off (*Press-Enterprise*, April 3, 1992). In northeast and southwest Oregon, and even counties around Portland, residents have lost pets and livestock to what is perceived to be a burgeoning cougar population. The Oregon state biologist noted that most of the problem "happens on the edge of wild country where humans are building homes" (*Oregonian*, September 15, 1996).

Reports of the incursions of cougars in Colorado residential areas has become so commonplace that unless a human is attacked these incidents are not considered particularly newsworthy. The loss of dogs, cats, sheep, chickens, and even llamas is now accepted as being one of the risks of living near the foothills of the Rocky Mountains. According to Jim Halfpenny, a research associate at the University of Colorado, a study completed in 1991 of 398 cougar/human encounters between 1964 and 1991 revealed that "the number of incidents is "on the rise; they are being reported closer to towns and cities; occur year-round rather than just during the winter; and more are coming during daylight hours." Halfpenny also stated that he has been often asked whether dogs would prevent attacks on humans, and goes on to say: "In 37 interactions [that the study reviewed], we found that 68 percent of the time, the lion remained the dominant animal; in 59 percent, the lion attacked the dog, and 41 percent of the attacks were fatal to the dog; only 11 percent of the time were dogs dominant" (Gary Gerhardt, *Rocky Mountain News*, April 25, 1991).

Apparently the size of the dog usually makes little difference to the outcome. In one incident, a resident living in Denver's Coal Creek Canyon suburban area heard a disturbance in the kennel near his back door. He grabbed a flashlight and went out to look and saw his Great Dane "pulling back against the fence in the kennel." He then heard a low growl and "his light caught the lion in the kennel with the [owner's] dead terrier in its mouth. The cat suddenly dropped the dog and leapt over a 7-foot fence." This cougar had previously killed or wounded, in addition to the terrier, a German shepherd, a Labrador, and a Doberman pinscher (Gary Gerhardt, *Rocky Mountain News*, January 30, 1990).

Similar incidents have been reported from Canadian provinces with cougar populations. In one case, a cougar chased a dachshund through an open front door and into a living room before the cat was shot by the homeowner. Dennis W. Pemble, a wildlife-control officer for the British Columbia Ministry of Environment indicated that he would rather relocate cougars than have to shoot them, but that he would "trap them or shoot them, whatever I have to do. When they are walking though a subdivision, you know they are looking for something to kill" (Carol McGraw and S. L. Sanger, *Los Angeles Times*, March 1, 1992).

There are reports of cougars being sighted again in Eastern states, from which they were presumed to have been extirpated many years ago. The sightings have elicited both enthralled statements and apprehensive and concerned journalistic comments. The Maine Department of Inland Fisheries and Wildlife does not admit that there are cougars in Maine, but Nancy Davis, of Stetson, Maine, is convinced it was a cougar that killed her chow chow dog, A. J.'s Grizzly Bear. A wall-mounted metal cable attached to the dog's collar was torn out, and the mortally wounded dog was found in a ditch. There were deep claw marks on its body. The only tracks in the snow other than the dog's were four-inch-wide cat footprints (*Boston Globe*, April 23, 1996). Throughout the tri-state area of southeastern Pennsylvania, Delaware, and Maryland, residents have reported many cougar sightings. Cougars were said to have taken chickens and other domestic animals (*Wilmington (Delaware) News-Journal*, October 18, 1996).

Three solid reasons for the increase in incidents between cougars, humans, and domestic animals, already mentioned in earlier chapters, are (1) the extrusion of a growing urban population into outlying areas and the intrusion of this population into cougar habitat; (2) the obvious change in cougar demeanor as a result of this closer exposure; cougars are becoming accustomed to the human presence; and (3) the presumed increase in the number of cougars.

When we have more cougars, more heavily traveled roads into and adjacent to cougar habitat, more homes being built in areas that are still subject to considerable wildlife use, there also will be an increase in the number of human/cougar conflict-of-interest incidents. More cougars will also end up as roadkill victims. Currently, fewer than fifty specimens of the endangered Florida panther (*F. concolor coryi*) remain, and road accidents, not poaching or illness, are reported to be the number one cause of death. To mitigate this problem, where roads cross known panther [cougar] habitat, the state has constructed tunnels to permit the cats, who are in pursuit of game, to cross the road without risk of injury. Elsewhere in the United States and Canada, no special efforts have been extended to accommodate road crossing for the hunting cougar, with the exception of occasional placement of a nonspecific "animal crossing" sign.

In citing the habits and characteristics of the cougar, Goldman and Young indicated that "it is rarely seen by man" (1946, 51). However, now that humans and cougars often share the same habitat, Goldman and Young's "mysterious cat" is seen with greater regularity. In years past, rarely was a cougar

Shared territory. At Boulder Mountain Parks, Colorado, and in particular on the Mesa Trail, ever-increasing human recreational use extends into the foothills—an area where cougar and human may unintentionally cross paths.

seen except in a zoo or by someone hunting with dogs. One could drive along some of the few isolated roads that were in prime cougar habitat and never see a cougar. One could walk game trails in the mountains and foothills and, although one might find some sign, would be unlikely to see a cougar. I have walked quite a few game trails in Utah, Wyoming, Arizona, and California, and driven over a lot of roads, and seen only one cougar. What an exciting experience that was for me!

It was in 1961, while I was stationed in Utah's Zion National Park. We were traveling during the late night hours along one of the more scenic drives in the park, the Mount Carmel Highway. Construction of this beautiful road with its mile-long tunnel began in 1927, and when the sun is shining brightly what magnificent views the park visitor is privileged to enjoy while driving this road! The scenery is hard to surpass. However, while driving this road at night it is important to keep a sharp outlook for cars approaching from the other direction and for the deer that often cross the road. Mindful of the need for caution, we were traveling rather slowly and were startled to see a tawny form with long tail shoot across the road in front of our car. My passenger and I both shouted in unison, "Cougar!" And just as quickly as it had appeared, it was gone.

While most cougars are still secretive and elusive, there are now a few intrepid, nonconformist cougars that show little fear of humans and not only permit themselves to be seen, but are also willing to argue over right of habitat. These far from unusual circumstances suggest that remarkable changes in cougar behavior are taking place, and that these changes have been influenced, at least in part, by the environment the cougars have been exposed to. Cougars are in the process of learning and adapting to conditions engendered by an encroaching urban society. One example of this very noticeable behavioral shift was an incident that happened to a sixteen-year-old boy in the spring of 1990, while he was hunting rabbits about fifty miles southwest of Denver, near Tarryall Reservoir in Pike National Forest. His destination was an area where he had previously experienced a measure of success hunting rabbits and coyotes, Packard Gulch. Reaching the gulch, he happened to glance upward and was startled to see a large cougar out on the edge of a rocky crevice, not too far above, obviously watching him. He thought to discourage the cat by firing his little rimfire rifle at the rocks near the cougar. As the boy saw his shot harmlessly ricochet away, the cougar, now crouching ever so slightly, evidenced no fear of the gun, or the boy, and began to hiss and growl. The young hunter then decided, astutely, to back away.

I know of several knowledgeable wildlife staff writers who are doing a fantastic job for their newspapers and their readers in providing factual and unique environmental information. These writers do not attempt to gloss over some of the risks that are inherent in nature. Any number of excellent articles urge hikers and backcountry users to remain alert, to exercise good judgment, and to be extremely cautious when they are in remote wilderness areas or when they know they are in the habitat of large predators. However, there are also writers who, unfortunately, repeat familiar dogma that has been produced over the years by certain biologists, ecologists, naturalists, and preservationists: that cougars are basically shy, secretive creatures, afraid of human contact and ready to flee if a human being should attempt to approach them. Frank C. Hibben, who was conducting research in 1937 under the auspices of the University of New Mexico, once wrote: "Perhaps in the next few years a little of the energy which has been expended in the hunting of the lion will be spent on the study of this interesting animal. If such were the case, there is no doubt that we should find a curious, gentle, and very likeable disposition supplanting the vicious side. It is well known that the cougar tames easily and makes a very lovable pet when a kitten. It has been said of the lion by those that have raised them that they have the heart of a kitten even when full grown, and are very mild mannered" (1937, 14–15).

However, it is also interesting to note that Hibben, some eleven years later, authored a nonscholarly but thoroughly entertaining book, *Hunting the American Lions.* This book described his personal experiences and feelings while satisfying his "urge to hunt" (1948, 19). But while he thoroughly enjoyed hunting them, he still held fast to the belief that cougars "only rarely and only under exceptional circumstances attack a human being. And in those instances where lions do attack humans, they apparently do it half-heartedly and seldom eat human flesh" (1948, 218)—a statement we have since learned is, unfortunately, definitely not correct.

Whenever a cougar attack on a human does occur, one can usually count on the cougar partisans to offer the rationalization that the cougar "is only doing what is normal for a cougar." Or, more recently, when a mother of two was killed by a cougar while she was jogging, "mistakenly believed she was a deer. She was running by at a fast speed and it attacked. It was instinctual." One biologist, testifying at a court trial concerning the claim of the family of a four-year-old girl who was horribly mutilated by a cougar in a county park, stated that, statistically, cougar attacks "are trivial things, like pianos falling out of the sky."

Cougars and human families cannot reside comfortably in the same locale unless there is provision for, and the existence of, varied habitats and abundant space for the cougar to roam. There just is no convenient way in which they both can share the same closed habitat. Cougar and human needs are somewhat similar, but the means and methods they use to satisfy these needs are totally disparate. When humans become hungry, food is usually readily or reasonably available to satisfy their physiological needs. Even under the worst of circumstances, such as national famine or enforced starvation, their behavior is more that of forbearance and supplication than frenzy. If a cougar has not eaten for some time, its feeding drive becomes enormous and essentially overwhelming; it has no intention of dying quietly of starvation. A cougar has no refrigerator or cupboard; its larder consists of whatever it can catch and eat. Although its favorite prey may be deer, when it is famished it will attempt to kill and eat whatever prey it can overpower and is immediately available—and this could be an unwary or physically susceptible human.

One way of mitigating this conflict was advanced by noted biologist and cougar aficionado Maurice G. Hornocker. Writing of the possibility of curbing cougar aggression toward humans, Hornocker said he believes "certain behaviors, such as aggression, are genetic. If so, we could change the behavior of wild populations by replacing more aggressive individuals with less aggressive ones, much as humans have done with domesticated animals" (1992, 64). It seems, however, that this singular act of human intrusiveness in species genetics would provide us with an animal that looks like a cougar but that would behave in a pusillanimous manner. From a purist standpoint, that is undesirable.

Cougars are certainly not the only, nor even the most prevalent, wild species impacted by urbanization; whole ecosystems are affected. Ecosystems exist virtually everywhere and all living and nonliving elements within these systems are interlinked. When newly urbanized areas are created, subtle, and not so subtle, environmental alterations are effected. In addition to those obvious changes occasioned by construction of physical facilities, increases in human population presents direct and adverse implications for other animal species; for example, increase in traffic; loss of habitat and familiar food sources. There are also the indirect, but equally disastrous, consequences of human population increases: the circumfluent pollution of environmental quality. One of the more insidious, but potentially pernicious, consequences of life in urban America for indigenous wild species is that of pollution. This is not only the well-known anthropogenic degradation of quality of urban air, but also a resultant impurity of water supply and a multiplicity of human activities that precipitate the contamination of soil.

When mammals and birds are obliged to breathe polluted urban air tainted with sulfur dioxide, nitrogen oxides, carbon monoxide, and perhaps also heavy with suspended particulate matter, their lungs are just as apt to develop blotchy patterns of stiff dark spots and other respiratory ills as are human urbanites. This accumulation of fugitive dust and soot in the air serves to stunt the growth of plants that deer and other prey animals feed upon. Chemical additives used for fertilization and pesticides also have deleterious effect on wild species when delivered as waterborne residues. This form of source pollution (polluted runoff) can contaminate not only lakes, rivers, streams, creeks, ponds, and even ground water, but, through atmospheric distribution, even distant waters and soils. Since it is now generally accepted that urban pollution contributes to human cardiovascular and neurobehavioral difficulties, it follows that other animal species are at least at equal risk.

It is possible that the urbanization of America may eventually become the concluding chapter, ending for all time the contentious, sometimes enigmatic, but always dichotomous relationship between cougars and humans. History reveals to us that if two different species of animals compete on a daily basis for the same territory, each pursuing their own existence, one species will be totally annihilated. There can be no coexistence between competing species. Humans have demonstrated very clearly their ability to regulate and, if they deem it necessary or desirable, effectively repress the existence of another species. From all reports it would appear that the cougar population is now not only stable but may even be growing. Occasionally there are conflicts between humans and cougars—usually resolved by the permanent removal of the miscreant cougar from the ecosystem. As more people move into cougar habitat, the potential for conflict accordingly increases, as does the prospect for establishing broader and more definitive cougar-control measures.

With the exception of the People's Republic of China, there does not appear to be genuine effort toward reducing human population growth. Nations in our Western Hemisphere face serious and exceedingly perplexing population problems—problems that are exacerbated by (1) high birthrates in the undeveloped and generally poorer nations, and (2) the seeming inability or lack of desire on the part of these underdeveloped countries to control immigration to the richer and more developed nations. Consequently, as the habitat needs and numbers of humans inevitably increase, the numbers of larger wild mammals must correspondingly decrease.

For the cougar to continue to survive near an urban and geographically expanding human society, it will have to be in smaller population numbers than there are at present, or we will have to adopt far more restrictive land-use policies. The erosion of cougar habitat will continue unless measures are taken promptly to effect control over human population and human movement into all but the most rugged and inaccessible of locations. For thousands of years, the cougar thrived in lands that were teeming with a variety of prey animals, and with few humans. Today we have the opposite situation: there are more people than there are prey animals for the cougar—a circumstance that seems unlikely to change.

Threatened, endangered, and extinct species all have or had one thing in common: the inability to adapt to changing conditions. In order for the cougar to continue to endure as a viable species, not necessarily within its existing range but anywhere in the wild, the cougar must learn to adapt gently to an increasingly urban America. By continuing to behave in a secretive, stealthy, mysterious manner, the cougar's chances of survival may still be good. However, the bold and the belligerent cougars may well be the ones that orchestrate what future human reaction will be to the cougar's continued presence.

TEN The Future of the Cougar

FOR ALL SPECIES there had to be a beginning, and there will also be an
end. Given enough time, most species evolve through natural selection
and eventually achieve the form that is best suited to whatever changes
in environmental conditions the species may be obliged to face. The most essential requirement, however, is that they are able to protect themselves from
enemies and find food. If they cannot do so, they do not survive.

In its present form, the cougar has been around for more than ten thousand years. In general appearance it has changed very little. There have been
minor adjustments in size or form—although perhaps nothing more dramatic
than simple species adaptation to local conditions—whereby taxonomists
identify thirty-five subspecies. One can speculate that, because of the omni-
present need to adjust to and accommodate a habitat that is becoming increasingly saturated with human beings, there is now perhaps greater potential for
the evolution of anatomical and behavioral differences among *Felis concolor*
subspecies than at any previous time. Through the processes of mutation and
selection, existential behavioral and morphological changes may develop in
response to the obvious environmental exigencies.

Paul Colinvaux once said that "people are animals that have learned to
change their niches without changing their breeding strategy" (1978, 212).
In his *Why Big Fierce Animals are Rare*, Colinvaux argues that it is a simple
matter of energy supply; that is, there is only so much energy to go around,
and therefore without viable restrictions on growth of human populations

there will be logical limits to sustainable populations of other large carnivores. When a cougar intrudes on, injures, or threatens the human properties of home, possessions, or human life itself, that cougar, usually, is promptly and permanently removed from that ecosystem. Thus, in order for them to coexist successfully in a habitat with humans, cougars must exhibit deference, studiously avoid human contact, and not attack any creature or object with domestic human association.

History suggests that when cougar populations increase to the point that these cats become a more noticeable species, human problems with the animal accordingly increase. Years ago cougars were a nuisance to settlers and homesteaders occupying land within or near cougar habitat simply because of the number of cougars. When the number of cougars was reduced, incidents and conflicts became fewer. Some of these incidents were rather unusual. Herndon Smith, who compiled a chronology of notable events that occurred in Centralia, Washington, from 1845 to 1900, describes an incident involving the Ready family, who homesteaded in the area in the early 1870s:

> Mr. Ready once had an exciting experience while driving through the woods at night. He had done a service for a neighbor for which he received a quarter of beef. He had the meat in the rear of the wagon, and, en route home, a large cougar attempted to drag it away. The oxen became frightened and in order to control them, Mr. Ready jumped on one of the cattle and kept beating them in the face with the goad stick to keep them from running away, all the while shouting at the cougar which would jump off the wagon and slink away at each shout, then return. Mrs. Ready and the children heard Mr. Ready coming a half mile away and ran out to see what the trouble was, taking a lantern with them. The light frightened the cougar away, but not until it had followed the wagon to the barnyard gate. (1942, 281–82)

As the number of cougars was reduced, eventually to the point of near extinction in the United States east of meridian 105 longitude (except for Texas), those that remained were so rarely seen that they were more of an enigma than a threat, or potential threat. Now that the cougar population is again growing, cougar and human encounters are becoming correspondingly more frequent, and this familiarity does not bode well for either species. The cougar learns quickly, and eventually may demonstrate little fear for the two-legged animal whose defense appears to be mainly noise and bluff.

There is no evidence that there has been significant anatomical modification of the cougar for more than ten thousand years. However, there now seem to be a number of reasons for the species gradually to evolve toward being a smaller animal. In those states and provinces where cougar hunting is permitted, it is the larger animals that are sought, and as was the case earlier with the bison, the functions of natural selection favor the larger, stronger progenitor only as long as its potential for a normal lifespan is not inhibited. The hunting prohibition in California may palliate processes of genetic change for cougars in California, but it is my expectation that public opinion in all states and provinces with cougar populations will eventually compel effective management—involving responsive control—of these animals. Without human intervention in the species process, the larger and more belligerent of male cougars will continue to be the dominant ones in territorial possession (i.e., home-range tenure, the mating process, and the siring of offspring). However, if the more aggressive specimens are prematurely removed from the gene pool by human intervention, there would be greater opportunity for the sexual success of smaller, but perhaps more prudent and wary, cougars.

It is my belief that the cougar population has already reached the apex of its population recovery. While it was on the decline, public opinion advocated a policy of benign management and control, almost to the point where the cougar was mistakenly considered by many to be a threatened or endangered species deserving of special protection. As the number of cougars grew again, and their presence became obvious, in some instances even blatant, more hunting permits were issued by state and provincial game and fish authorities, and the taking of cougars by the U.S. Animal Damage Control agency (ADC) for real as well as suggested threats or actions similarly increased. Yet there is no evidence that these actions have had a significant effect as yet on the numbers of cougars within the affected states and provinces.

For a moment, let us consider the history of the grizzly bear, *Ursus arctos horribilis*. The grizzly, like the cougar, once enjoyed a much greater geographical range than they do at present. Not believed to have ever been common to eastern sections of North America, the grizzly now is found only in Alaska, a few isolated locations in Wyoming, Montana, Idaho, and Washington, and in the far western provinces of Canada. In the contiguous United States, one of the best-known grizzly habitats is that of Yellowstone National Park. In a somewhat similar, but perhaps microcosm circumstance of the cougar's environmental situation, the grizzly of Yellowstone was simply incompatible with the hordes of people that began to visit Yellowstone after 1946 and the subsequent 1950s and 1960s expansion of visitor facilities. The decline of the grizzly population in Yellowstone, over the numbers believed to have existed in the park prior to the mid-1940s, was caused primarily, according to a number of wildlife aficionados, by faulty bear-management policies of the National Park Service. What particularly disturbed these individuals was the service's decision abruptly to eliminate garbage dumps frequented by park bears. The position of the National Park Service was that the presence of bears at these dumps introduced an unwanted visitor-safety problem; that the practice was not consistent with the service's charge of maintaining park wildlife in natural surroundings and conditions; did not provide a healthy diet for the bears; and through the bears' resultant familiarity with humans and human food, it exacerbated existing problems of aggressive bear behavior; the practice promoted an anomalous food-gathering routine.

The bison and the grizzly of Yellowstone have become two of the more obvious losers in a basically noncontentious struggle to occupy and use the lands that immediately surround Yellowstone National Park. Yellowstone's popularity as a vacation destination has compounded the environmental dilemma for park animals. The park habitat now requires an extensive infrastructure to accommodate human needs. As much as we may regret that this metamorphosis of wild America is taking place, it is an inescapable outcome of those processes related to the force and balance of nature. Without any check on human population and movement, all other competitive species must decline in number. It is inevitable. This observation in itself is not particularly controversial; we have been warned continuously by legions of wildlife writers and advocates that we are relentlessly moving toward a time when many of our native wild species will no longer be with us or will be found only in zoos.

In *Fathers and Sons*, Ivan Turgenev has the revolutionary character Bazarov haughtily exclaim: "I agree with no man's opinion. I have some of my own" (1862, ch. 13). That seems to be the case, too, with the diversity of opinion with respect to America's wildlife—especially that of the larger mammals. Everyone seems to have an opinion as to how certain extant wildlife species should be managed, and with North America's former large expanses of conifer and hardwood forests now reduced to that of but limited stretches within public lands, the range of large carnivores has been similarly condensed.

The open spaces that are now ecologically and aesthetically part of nearly all urban areas provides harbor for birds and some of the smaller mammals. Even New York's Central Park is home to more than two hundred bird species, plus an interesting assortment of rabbits, squirrels, bats, and rats. Human residents of urban America accept with delight, and occasionally with bemusement, the visits of deer, raccoons, foxes, and other small wildlife species. However, the appearance of bears, coyotes, or cougars within urban neighborhoods is met with suspicion and apprehension. It is not that these creatures are viewed with antipathy by humans when they are in a wilderness habitat; it is simply that in an urban setting, the nature and habits of medium-to-large carnivores are basically incompatible with the human needs and requirements.

The cougar can and should inhabit only locations that are not used as everyday living space by humans. These areas need to be large enough to accommodate the cougar's territorial and dietary needs. However, when people move into, or adjacent to, areas of known cougar habitat, the number of cougars that this area can support will decline. For a number of other species, in addition to the so-called "panther" of the eastern United States, this condition of incompatibility has already occurred in the North and South American continents. As people continue their seemingly endless course of population growth and the occupation of yet undeveloped land, the remaining cougar population of western North America and of South America will undoubtedly be adversely affected.

If they would have somehow been able to survive the cataclysmic disaster that occurred some 65 million years ago, it is obvious that there is now no place in this world for animals such as the dinosaurs. Similarly, it is not possible to maintain continuing levels of bear, cougar, or wolf populations when humans are claiming increasing amounts of wildlife habitat. It is interesting to note that even today, myopically challenged researchers are suggesting that "Yellowstone National Park's grizzly bears need more room, they need it soon and people need to change how they behave there" (*Rocky Mountain News*, June 19, 1997). Although some people may consider land and all other natural resources to be "free gifts of nature," social and economic considerations will always limit the marginal utility of aesthetic or esoteric scientific values, regardless of their merit.

The cougar adds a flavor of mystique and uncertainty to the human wilderness experience. When walking on forest or mountain trail, it is exciting to conceive the thought that a hidden peril still may lurk nearby. Do we extend this need for a vicarious sensation to our backyard? Probably not. In our interminable search for order as well as meaning in life, everything must have its place; and the cougar's place is not in or near human residencies. If one must be dislodged for the benefit of the other, the cougar has to go.

Economically, the cougar adds little to human society. Whatever funds are gathered in hunting permits and licenses are more than expended on depredations and lawsuits. By way of example, more than $2 million was awarded to little Laura Small for injuries suffered in a 1986 cougar attack in Orange County, California. Although redemptive payment for loss of livestock is generally an agreeable practice for the recipient, the actual payee is not a faceless bureaucracy but the taxpaying public. Notwithstanding its unique, and perhaps even wicked, contribution to the wilderness experience, the primary value of the cougar, with respect to its relative benefit to humankind, is its role in the ecological pattern of nature; that is, its control over excessive deer populations. Unlike the jaguar, the cougar continues to be relatively unimportant to the fur industry. Although its meat is considered to be quite tasty by those who have tried it, most humans have scruples over dining on members of the cat and dog families. Outside of its mystical and aesthetic qualities, the cougar's only fundamental economic value is its worth and esteem as a game animal.

Sport hunting of cougars has proven to be a greater recreational diversion and physical challenge than the hunting of any of the other game species in midcontinent America. It requires a competent hunter or guide, trained dogs, stamina and endurance, patience, and determination. For the most successful method, it also requires skill in handling a horse. Hunting deer, birds, or even elk can become an annual activity for those with even the most limited of budgets. On the other hand, controlled and legal (licensed) trophy or head hunting of cougars is a very specialized and costly event—one that is not likely to be repeated year after year or promote decimation of the cougar species. The cougar is not hunted for its meat; it is hunted because, like the grizzly, it is considered to be a dangerous animal. The larger specimens are the ones sought; thus, it becomes a trophy hunt, and the cougar is subsequently mounted, with its head usually assuming, in death, a fierce and snarling appearance.

Texas alone, among the states and provinces mentioned, permits hunting of the cougar at any time of the year by anyone with a hunting license. There is no closed season and no bag limit. Yet the Texas Parks and Wildlife Department indicates that instead of the numbers of cougars declining, there may be more cougars in Texas today than at any time in recent history. California, which changed the status of the cougar to that of "game mammal" in 1969 and to "special protected mammal" in 1990, believes that its cougar population has increased by more than 300 percent since the 1970s. Colorado has also seen an increase in its number of cougars. As in California, the expanded population in Colorado has been accompanied by an undesired number of human/cougar incidents. When a ten-year-old boy died in 1997 as the result of an attack by a cougar in Rocky Mountain National Park, it was the ninth cougar attack in Colorado in seven years, two of which resulted in human fatalities.

Recent attacks have been the catalyst for a considerable number of letters to the editors of metropolitan newspapers in both California and Colorado. The correspondents have either appealed for the government to initiate controls over the growth of the cougar population or in the name of animal rights have asked that the public exercise restraint in adopting retaliatory legislation. California is still agonizing over its policy of protective status for cougars. When Proposition 197, a bill that would have eliminated the protected status for cougars and permitted hunting, was first introduced, opponents, such as the Mountain Lion Foundation and California Wildlife Protection Coalition, assailed the bill as being "cruel and unnecessary." Voter defeat of the bill in March 1996 left the California Fish and Game Department still powerless to control the state's growing cougar population.

Although Colorado, like most other cougar states, permits hunting with a license, the Colorado Wildlife Commission in 1994 directed that the cougar season be closed between March 31 and mid-November to protect females at the time of having kittens. This action undoubtedly enhanced the life expectancy of the kittens and growth of the state cougar population. Colorado public sentiment on the issue is split, but perhaps not in equal proportions, between those who favor increased hunting and those who are sympathetic to the plight of the cougar. When the cougar responsible for the recent fatal attack on the ten-year-old boy was shot by park rangers, several reactive letters were written to the newspapers. One stated: "With all due respect to the family, I have to question the authorities' response. The lion had no previous incidences or contacts with humans. More than likely, it was merely protecting its domain or its young." The writer did not consider the fact that the destroyed cougar was carrying two fetuses; that she was in apparent good health; and that she was not being threatened by anyone or anything. She was simply looking for an easy meal, and it happened to be human. If she had not been killed, who is to say that she would not have again attacked a human? Or worse, after her young were born, pass on to her offspring, by example, this aberrant and unacceptable behavior?

In response to the attack in Rocky Mountain National Park, and the specter of a possible similar such attack occurring along the populous Wasatch front, the Utah Division of Wildlife Resources planned to issue more than five hundred cougar-hunting permits. This proposal angered Utah preservationists, who were of the belief that any increase in cougar hunting was unjustified and unnecessary. And thus the battle goes on.

Every species has its own requirements, customs, and ways, but—in my opinion—the issue of natural rights and intellectual ascendancy places the needs of the human being paramount to that of any other species. Certain environmentalists and animal-rights activists contend to the contrary. The course of human affairs and the quality of human life expectations will not, and cannot, be suppressed even if it means discomfort or demise of another species. Humans are essentially selfish, but in this regard we are actually no different than any other animal, except insofar as it is human society, rather than the individual, that is the principal protagonist in the struggle for existence.

We are not going to change human nature and its notions. People will always be on the move—seeking new jobs, new homes, better living conditions. Undeveloped land will become exceedingly precious. When the future needs of wildlife and humans are assessed, we should not anticipate there being any more large sections of land, public or private, set aside as wildlife or wilderness reserves. We are a human consumptive society, and consequently it is logical to assume that land utilization and distribution will be likely directed toward society's plebeian needs rather than preservation and wildlife havens.

By the turn of the nineteenth century, the American bison had been nearly exterminated. The vast herds had been decimated by hunters, ranchers, and homesteaders, until no wild bison remained on the plains where they once ranged in countless millions. Unlike the passenger pigeon, whose numbers once reached the billions, the bison were spared extinction, because a few people cared enough to take the necessary actions to save the species. The grizzly bear of Yellowstone also had its champions, not the least of whom was former Yellowstone National Park superintendent John A. Townsley. This fighter, despite a seemingly constant barrage of criticism over his management style from resentful detractors, worked diligently for a greater geographical protective area for the Yellowstone grizzly, even to the point of exclaiming in testimony during a congressional subcommittee hearing, "Who speaks for the bear?"

Outside of the occasionally irritating but still clamorously effective animal-rights activists, the most quoted of the spokespeople for cougars are usually scientists and researchers—people who are interested in studying, investigating, and reporting in scholarly fashion on the surreptitious doings of the cougar. Whenever a human being is attacked by a cougar, these spokespeople typically point out the rarity of these incidents, plead for public calm and reason, and then call for more research.

The Mountain Lion Foundation (MLF), a not-for-profit corporation headquartered in Sacramento, California, declares itself to be "dedicated to protecting the mountain lion, its wild habitat, and the wildlife that shares that habitat—for present and future generations throughout California and the west." The MLF further states that it is interested in preserving "the cougar" as a viable species, and plans to accomplish this objective through habitat conservation, research, livestock protection, management, and education. The organization even offers an "adopt a lion" program that is bolstered by $25 contributions. Although there are those who hold the opinion that the MLF is actually simply another antihunting group, the foundation seems to be quite well focused. It rightfully points out that it was instrumental in defeating Proposition 197—the proposition suggesting that the state should eliminate the protected status of cougars in California. The proposition would have given the California Fish and Game Department the authority to allow hunting of cougars if the department determined that this was a viable option in controlling the growing cougar population.

Although animal activist and conservationist organizations are generally well intentioned and espouse only the most honorable and lofty of objectives, they are in fact nothing more than special-interest groups with single-minded concerns; they seem to be more efficient when blocking actions rather than mitigating problems. Who then speaks for the people? In a representative bureaucracy sometimes the people's will gets lost in the shuffle of balancing that which is expedient with that which is correct.

All large carnivorous animals are extremely powerful and they should be considered potentially dangerous. There is nothing sacrosanct about the human body that would stop its being prey should a predator be so inclined. The harsh, sometimes fatal, experiences of people who have been assaulted by cougars over the years unequivocally answers the question as to whether or not, under the right circumstances and conditions, cougars will attack humans and consider them prey. Of course they will! What we need to do now is accept this as a fact of nature, and move on.

I mention below a few rather simple actions that we can take to mitigate current human/cougar problems and still provide reasonable assurance that the cougar will continue to exist as a viable species. No doubt other suggestions could be offered by people more experienced in wildlife management than I:

1. There already is sufficient habitat to maintain a healthy and vigorous cougar population. We do not need more habitat. What we need to do is insure that the population does not exceed viable levels so that they do not become any more of a problem for themselves or humans. The best way to do this is to continue to support wildlife agencies in their efforts to safeguard the animal and the public. Sport hunting has proven to be an acceptable and effective method of control; provincial and state agencies need to have the option of introducing, limiting, or expanding the season as circumstances warrant.

2. The use of public funds to pay for depredation by cougars on livestock is neither fair nor equitable to taxpayers. Cougars are not wards of the government, and if ranches are located in or near areas that are known to be cougar habitat, any resultant livestock loss or damage from cougars should be considered part of that rancher's cost of doing business. A livestock owner does, however, have a right to protect property, and should be permitted, when necessary, to remove a depredating cougar, but without cost to the government.

My suggestion may be perceived as penurious. But currently, more than enough agricultural goods to satisfy market needs are being produced, through farming and ranching, in areas that are not within, or even near to cougar habitat. To argue a need to raise crops or farm animals in incongruent or risky environments does not make sense, unless the operations can become economically successful without governmental intervention or support. In addition, it would be inappropriate to take predator-control action with respect to livestock losses that occur on public lands where grazing permits have been issued. Permittees must assume responsibility for loss as they would in the event of natural disaster or accident.

3. Where there are more than a token number of human residential developments (nonagricultural) existing near, or close to, cougar habitat, intru-

sion by cougars into these rural communities should lead to the permanent removal from the ecosystem of that animal. Live trapping and relocation provide no assurance that the cougar will not return to its former range.

The cougar is not endangered. The loss of these presumptuous animals will have little overall effect on the species. Zoological gardens and private animal preserves are already overstocked with cougars. In fact, there are so many cougars in private hands now that, for the lack of an acceptable, humane alternative, some of the less-qualified owners elect to release difficult-to-manage or overlarge cougars into the wild. This is an extremely dangerous, potentially lethal, practice. It needs to be promptly discontinued.

4. We continue to be in dire need of research into cougar behavior. But my concern is primarily with its behavior toward the human species. Already, a wealth of information has been gathered about the animal, but most of this has been devoted to its day-to-day existential activities and processes. Research conducted by or under the auspices of wildlife-advocate organizations is suspect for obvious reasons. State and provincial wildlife agencies have only limited information about the numbers of cougars now existing. They have fairly good numbers on how many are taken from the population, but they lack the capability to develop accurate estimates of the numbers remaining, or of what number is needed to assure perpetuation of the cougar as a viable and healthy species. The use of revenues from sport-hunting permits could greatly assist state support of research programs.

5. Public information about the cougar is limited, and on cougar/human relationships is in some instances faulty. Public parks, forests, and recreational areas that have, or occasionally support, a cougar population are now attempting to improve visitor-information procedures to better insure that recreational users are aware that cougars can be dangerous. They advise visitors of precautions they should take. Media sources should do so as well. Hopefully, earlier dogmatic conclusions that cougars are cowardly, present no threat, or that they "are as afraid of you as you are of them" will be quickly forgotten.

Although human life may be paramount, all life has importance. More than one and a half million species of animals inhabit the earth. Many of them we may not even know exist. However, were one of these unknown species to perish, would we, if we should become aware of the event, find this to be an appalling tragedy or would it simply be ignored? Unfortunately it would probably be the latter.

In that most compelling of works *Silent Spring*, Rachel Carson describes a world where birds may not again exist: "Spring now comes unheralded by the return of the birds, and the early mornings are strangely silent where they once were filled with the beauty of bird song" (1962, 103). This possibly touches us very deeply because birds are so much a part of our culture. Although we may not share the same feeling of warmth and need for the cougar as we do for the presence of songbirds, from the standpoint of control over egregious growth of deer herds, the cougar fulfills an important role. Its loss we might soon discover to be one of equal, or perhaps even greater, significance than that of the loss of birds.

We wish the cougar well as it continues its battle for survival into the twenty-first century. It faces formidable obstacles in its struggle. Although the cougar is an enigma and pariah to humans, it is habitat loss, rather than direct harassment, that is unquestionably its most serious predicament. Habitat loss is the primary cause of the cougar's uncertain future. Within this shrinking habitat, there still remain considerable numbers of prey animals, sufficient to support even moderate cougar population levels. Unfortunately, the cougar, like most cats, is a wanderer; its home range can sometimes be as small an area as ten square miles, but occasionally can encompass an area as large as five hundred square miles. While the availability of food most often is the determining factor in range size, the intolerance of resident adult cougars for the presence of other cougars in their home range also plays a definite part. Fledgling cougars must often travel considerable distances in search of their own home range. Throughout the process of wandering and search they may stray into the milieu of humans, and their life may then come to a sudden end.

Francis Bacon once claimed that "nature is often hidden; sometimes overcome; seldom extinguished" (Essays, "Of Nature in Men," 1974, 152). This observation seems particularly applicable to the cougar, with its uncanny but remarkable elusiveness, its marked frailties if tracked by dogs, and its tenacious ability to survive as a species.

The cougar may never again exist in the same numbers it once did, or reside in the same locations, but as long as there are wilderness areas that are large enough to support viable and genetically healthy animal communities, the cry of the cougar will be heard.

APPENDIX A Distribution and Occurrence

UNITED STATES

Alabama

Cougars were once generally distributed over much of the state, but by 1921 they were considered to be extinct. Bruce Wright (1972, 111) indicated that a cougar was reportedly killed near Ashville in northern Alabama on March 16, 1948. Nowak (1976, 130) indicated that Ralph Allen, Alabama Division of Fish and Game, expressed the thought to him that "there is no doubt that a few cougar are still to be found in Alabama. In my opinion, however, their numbers would not exceed 25." Although there have been a number of confirmed sightings since that time, Fish and Game is not at present willing to confirm that Alabama has a resident population of cougars.

Alaska

Alaska and the Yukon have never had even a modest resident population of cougars —Charles Sheldon, an expert on Alaskan and Yukon wildlife (1912, 257). The Alaska Department of Fish and Game indicates that they have had only one confirmed report of a cougar in Alaska—an animal killed near Wrangell, in extreme southeastern Alaska, in 1991. State game officials indicate that transients may move in from time to time, but there is no established resident population.

Arizona

This southwestern state has always been able to maintain a vigorous cougar population. The state has a large deer population and much wilderness. Cougars also freely migrate between Arizona and Mexico and Arizona, California, and New Mexico. Prior to 1947, the cougar was considered to be an undesirable species. It was not protected. Government hunters and trappers killed at least 2,400 cougars in Arizona prior to 1947. After 1947 the state established a bounty that was funded until 1968. Between 1947 and 1969, more than 5,400 cougars were killed. In 1970, the cougar was declared a big-game species and hunting permits were required. Since that time, an average of 376 cougars have been harvested each year. The Department of Fish and Wildlife estimated in 1997 that Arizona's resident cougar population now exceeds three thousand animals.

Arkansas

Cougars were once fairly well distributed over much of the state, but by 1920 the cougar was no longer considered to be active. Wright (1972, 111) suggested that the cougar's presence was still regularly reported within the state. Sealander (1951, 364), Tinsley (1987, 73), and Nowak (1976, 125–26) say two cougars were reportedly killed in Arkansas as late as 1949. East (1979, 57) stated that cougar scat was regularly found and that forest service officials "think the cats are present and slowly increasing there."

California

The state has some of the best cougar habitat in the United States because of extensive state holdings in forested land, drainages, and mountains. It also has a high deer population. Cougars currently are found in locations ranging from deserts to humid coast-range forests, and from sea level to elevations in excess of ten thousand feet. Through hunting and aggressive control measures, by 1920 the state's population of cougars had dropped to approximately six hundred. Cougar hunting was banned in 1972. The population estimate at that time was approximately two thousand. In 1997 the state's Department of Fish and Game indicated there may be more than six thousand resident cougars in California.

Colorado

The state has been well known for its large and healthy cougar population for many years in areas from the Utah border on the west to the plains east of Denver. Colorado's wide variety of suitable prey animals encouraged the cougar to extend into the plains along river bottoms and into brushy hills where adequate hunting cover was available. Earlier classed as a varmint, a $50 bounty was offered from 1929 to 1965, when the cougar was designated as big game. The Colorado Division of Wildlife estimates that the state now has perhaps more than three thousand resident cougars. Colorado Agricultural Statistics Service numbers on sheep and lamb deaths from predators support this estimate. Sheep and lamb growers incurred a loss increase of more than 100 percent through cougar activity from 1990 (2,500) to 1994 (5,100). It is interesting to note that sheep and lamb deaths due to coyotes dropped 41 percent from 1990 (32,200) to 1994 (18,900).

Connecticut

Cougars were once quite common here, particularly in northern sections. Although they rapidly gave way to the press of civilization, a few still were found in the northwestern high country as late as 1935. Wright (1972, 106) reports two unconfirmed cougar sightings in 1967.

Delaware

Cougars probably once resided in Delaware because of its healthy deer population, but not in any great number. There have been no recent reported sightings.

Florida

Cougars, or panthers, as Floridians call them, were once quite common over most of the state. Now they are seldom seen, and then only in the southern and unpopulated areas. By 1900 it was believed that the cougar had been eliminated from most of the northern sections of the state. In 1988, Texas cougars were released in northern Florida to evaluate the area's potential as a cougar habitat. A captive breeding program was also initiated in 1991, and in 1994 the U.S. Fish and Wildlife Service approved the Florida Interagency Committee plans to restore gene flow between Florida "panthers" and other cougar populations by releasing nonnative cougars in southern Florida. The Bureau of Wildlife Research, Florida Game and Fresh Water Fish Commission, estimates that there are now between thirty and fifty cougars in all of Florida.

Georgia

Although never found in great numbers, cougars were once reasonably distributed over most of the state, but perhaps more common along the water courses, swamps, and hill country. By the 1920s, cougars were considered to be extirpated. There have been a few reported sightings, but fewer than a dozen a year. East (1979, 55)says a Forest Service wildlife specialist told him of his belief that "the cougar is established in the southern Appalachians, including Georgia—not many, but in sufficient numbers to be seen occasionally." There was an unconfirmed report of a kill in 1975 (Nowak 1976, 131).

Hawaii

Cougars were never endemic in Hawaii.

Idaho

Once rather common to most of the mountainous, forested, and rolling hilly areas of Idaho and its river courses, the cougar still maintains a healthy population in the mountains in the north and west. Idaho Fish and Game report that the annual harvest of cougars averages more than 350 animals; in 1993 it was 410. Based on the number of sightings, Bureau of Wildlife officials suggest that the state population of cougars is rapidly increasing. They now estimate the resident population at more than 2,500.

Illinois

Cougars formerly frequented the forested sections of Illinois, but never in any great number. It is believed that most, if not all, resident cougars disappeared from the state prior to 1860.

Indiana

In the forested areas of the central and southeastern sections of Indiana, cougars preyed on elk and deer, and they also frequented the northern lake dunes area. But by the early 1800s cougars were rarely seen. By 1850, it is believed, cougars were eliminated entirely.

Iowa

Although numbers of deer were once found on the plains, in forests, and along the rivers, Iowa never attracted a large number of cougars, By 1870 the cougar was presumed to be extinct.

Kansas

The cougar was never common throughout the state, but it was once found along the western and southern borders and the timbered areas along eastern streams and rivers. It is likely that by 1905 there were no longer any resident cougars, although occasional sightings have been reported (Nowak 1976, 119).

Kentucky

Once widespread, and particularly plentiful in the mountainous east and the wooded, rocky hillsides of the Pennyroyal, the cougar fell upon bad times in a state that should provide good habitat. Although there have been occasional reports of sightings in recent years, the cougar is no longer included in the fauna inventory of Kentucky. It is believed to have been extinct within the state since approximately 1886.

Louisiana

With its climate and varied wildlife, Louisiana offered ideal habitat for the cougar. It thrived along the rivers and marshes and in dense growths of cane. Cahalane (1946, 4) suggested that if the cougar had not already been extirpated in Louisiana by 1946, there were fewer than ten left. Any cougars left in the state at the present time would be found in the swamps of the eastern and southeastern parts of the state. A 116-pound cougar was reportedly killed on November 30, 1965, near Keithville in western Louisiana in bayou country (Tinsley 1987, 73). State Game and Fish officials have received reports of cougar sightings from time to time, but nothing that could be confirmed after the 1965 kill.

Maine

Cougars, by all reports, were completely eliminated in Maine by 1900. However, there have been numerous sightings since 1900 (Wright 1972, 100). One cougar was killed in 1938 near the Quebec border; a paw print discovered near Levant was confirmed to be that of a cougar; and there was a sighting in 1966. A dog was killed near Stetson by a large animal that could have been a cougar or large bobcat. Cougars were reported to have been sighted in Holden and Bucksport in May 1996, and in Pittsfield in January 1997. According to the *Bangor Daily News* (January 27, 1997), more than two thousand sightings have been reported since 1938.

Maryland

The cougar was once fairly common throughout the state, but it was most likely seen in northwestern sections, the Alleghenies, and the Pennsylvania border areas —the former hunting grounds of Meschach Browning. Presumably none were left by 1840. Wright (1972, 106) mentions that a cougar was reportedly seen on August 26, 1971. The Eastern Puma Research Network say they received reports of twenty-three alleged sightings of cougars in Maryland in 1995 (Boyle 1996, 42).

Massachusetts

The cougar is believed to have been somewhat common here until the early 1800s, but by the early 1840s it apparently was not to be seen. There have been a number of reports of sightings in recent years, but nothing that could be positively confirmed. Wright (1970, 104–5) commented on some reports of several sightings as late as 1960 and one possible sighting in 1968. Disclaimers suggest that these animals could not be true "eastern panthers" but were perhaps merely *Felis concolor* subspecies from out of state or released captive cougars.

Michigan

The low, rolling, forested hills of Michigan were once home to vast herds of elk, deer, and moose. The cougar may have been common to much of the state, but reportedly all were eliminated by 1870. Some cougar tracks were noted in the Porcupine Mountains of the Upper Peninsula in the early 1970s (East 1979, 57). According to Boyle (1996, 42), the Eastern Puma Research Network run by John and Linda Lutz received reports of thirty-three alleged sightings in Michigan in 1995.

Minnesota

The lake regions of Minnesota were never prime cougar habitat, although deer were quite common. By 1885 it was doubted that any resident cougars remained in the state. The track of a cougar was found in deep snow in the southwestern part of the state in March 1951 (East 1979, 58). According to Bill Berg, Minnesota

Division of Wildlife, there are an average of sixty sightings a year, primarily in the northern parts of the state, but these may be transient cougars or released captive animals rather than residents.

Mississippi

The piney woods and marshlands of Mississippi offered cover for the limited number of cougars that this state once supported. Cougars were still found along the Mississippi River until perhaps the late 1880s. There have been a few sightings in the past twenty-five years, two of the most recent occurring in 1973 (Nowak 1976, 129) and 1978 (East 1979, 57).

Missouri

The cougar frequented Missouri in years past, but not in any great number. It was believed that any resident cougars were eliminated by 1890. Since then there have been a few sightings, the most recent in 1972 (Nowak 1976, 124).

Montana

The cougar formerly was quite common throughout much of the state, even within the plains area where it gained access by way of forested water courses. Although its range has been significantly reduced, the cougar is still routinely observed. Montana Department of Fish, Wildlife and Parks indicate that their harvest records, sightings, depredations, and human/cougar encounters point to an expanding population. Although they do not have any way of estimating the number of resident cougars in Montana, the department suggests that the numbers are quite high.

Nebraska

This dry, flat, plains state never had a large cougar population. The last confirmed sightings were in the north, along the wooded and brushy sides of river beds. No confirmed sightings have been reported since 1884, when an adult female was shot near Hays Springs (Jones 1949, 313), except for one "almost positive" sighting in 1966 in a timbered area along the Little Blue River in southeastern Nebraska (Tinsley 1987, 73).

Nevada

This state has substantial acreage in arid, bleak desert, and most of the cougars that reside in Nevada are, as they have always been, located in the mountainous eastern, northeastern, and central parts. More than a modest number still inhabitat these sections. The state Division of Wildlife indicates that, based on their known annual cougar-population losses, in 1994 more than 1,500 cougars resided within Nevada. According to a recent article in the *Reno Gazette-Journal* (January 16, 1996), the number may be as high as 3,189.

New Hampshire
Never present in more than limited numbers, the cougar was fairly well killed off by 1850. Bruce Wright (1972, 100), however, provided several accounts of cougar sightings in 1948. Reports still come in from time to time of even more recent, but unconfirmed, sightings.

New Jersey
Prior to the settlement of New Jersey, the cougar was well represented in most sections of the state. It was gradually eliminated until the few that remained were restricted to the Appalachian Highlands. By 1840 it was considered quite probable that all cougars had been eliminated. Wright (1972, 105–6) reports a cougar sighting along the Garden State Parkway in 1958.

New Mexico
At one time the cougar was fairly well distributed throughout much of New Mexico. Now, although there still is widespread good cougar habitat, most cougars are located in the mountainous areas of the west and north. The state Department of Game and Fish indicates that on average a hundred cougars are harvested annually. In addition, their predator-control specialists permanently remove from the state ecosystem an average of twenty-four cougars a year in response to depredation complaints and special control needs. State agencies were reluctant to provide an estimate of the resident cougar population, but they agree that, in all probability, the state has in excess of 1,500 resident cougars.

New York
The cougar was once reportedly common throughout much of the state, but perhaps more commonplace to the Adirondack and Catskill Mountains. By 1900, it is believed, the cougar was extirpated. A few reports of cougar sightings in the Catskills were filed in the 1950s. The Baltimore-based Eastern Puma Research Network received reports of ninety-two alleged cougar sightings in 1995 (Boyle 1996, 42).

North Carolina
At one time a familiar sight in Carolina wilderness areas, the cougar still existed throughout the state, but in more limited numbers, until perhaps the mid-1840s. It was presumed to have been totally removed from the state by 1890. The Great Smokey Mountains, part of the Appalachians, were once a favored haunt of the

cougar, but cougars have not been confirmed in these mountains for sixty years. Nevertheless, reports are regularly filed (e.g., of cougar screams and some sightings—Frome 1979, 82). There was a sighting in 1975 of a female cougar and two kittens along the Blue Ridge Parkway (East 1979, 56), but a cougar presence in North Carolina is still subject to considerable doubt.

North Dakota

The cougar was present in North Dakota in years past, but it has not been seen for more than fifty years. Never found in great numbers, its range was primarily the extreme western part of the state and the Missouri River valley. Unverified reports of a cougar presence were filed in the 1950s and 1960s.

Ohio

Forested lands, gently rolling plains, and the Allegheny plateau once offered at least minimal habitat for the cougar. Its probable last haunts were the lakeshores, river courses, and swamps of east central Ohio. It was doubtful if there were any cougars left in the state by 1820, but a small cougar was killed by a car in the 1960s near the West Virginia border (East 1979, 57). The Eastern Puma Research Network reported twenty-six alleged cougar sightings in Ohio during 1995 (Boyle 1996, 42).

Oklahoma

As long as Oklahoma remained "Indian Territory," which it did until approximately 1889, the cougar had a home in the numerous hills and small mountains and along the rivers of eastern Oklahoma. Cougars were not found in any great number, however. Most resident cougars probably passed from the Oklahoma scene prior to 1900. The state Department of Wildlife Conservation does not believe that Oklahoma today has a resident population, but they are aware that about fifty transient individual cougars regularly wander into the state from Colorado, New Mexico, and Texas. They believe that most of the cougar sightings reported to them are, if factual, of escaped or released captive-bred cougars.

Oregon

From the time of earliest explorations of Oregon, a cougar presence was continually noted, primarily in the Coast and Cascade Mountains and the heavily forested river valleys, preying on the large deer and elk herds. Oregon timber and agricultural industries petitioned for more aggressive government cougar control, and bounties began in 1843. The state Department of Fish and Wildlife says that between 1900 and 1930 bounties were commonly paid on two hundred or more cougars annually. In 1961, the final bounty year, only thirteen cougars were killed for the bounty payment. In 1970, a controlled-hunt season for cougar was authorized; the harvest has steadily increased from a total of 10 in 1970 to 187 in 1992. Big-game biologists for the state estimate that there were more than three thousand cougars residing in the state in 1994.

Pennsylvania
The sheer number of historical accounts of cougars in Pennsylvania leads to the conclusion that there were immense numbers of resident cougars in the state. By 1895, however, most knowledgeable wildlife experts doubted the continued existence of cougars there. Noted Pennsylvania cougar expert Henry W. Shoemaker (1943) prepared a fairly lengthy list of cougar sightings up to 1942. Wright (1972, 109) mentions that an immature female cougar was reportedly killed in northwestern Pennsylvania on October 28, 1967. Frequent sightings of a cougar apparently traveling between southwestern Philadelphia and Delaware from April 1995 through the spring of 1996 add fuel to the fiery contention cougars still live in the wilds of Pennsylvania. According to Robert H. Boyle (1996, 42) the Eastern Puma Research Network received reports of ninety-eight alleged cougar sightings in 1995.

Rhode Island
Since 1840, records of sightings and killings of cougars in this small state have been rare. Many of these reports could well have been of transient animals.

South Carolina
Prior to settlement, South Carolina is reported to have held a large resident cougar population. These animals were probably concentrated in the coastal plain area. By 1850, it is believed, few if any cougars remained. Bruce Wright (1972, 110–11) mentions two cougar sightings in the Santee area—one in 1948 and another in 1951. Sass (1954, 133) mentions two in 1953. Nowak (1976, 131) indicated that there were reliable sightings in 1973. East says a Forest Service biologist told him there have been no sightings in national forests in recent years (1979, 55).

South Dakota
More common to the Black Hills area, the cougar was also found along rivers and streams where timber provided protective cover. South Dakota's modest cougar population gradually dwindled; few sightings were reported after 1920. The state Department of Game, Fish and Parks says there is currently an increase in cougar population, but they are unsure as to what this number may be.

Tennessee
The cougar was common in years past in most locations in Tennessee. Cougars could be found in decent numbers along the Cumberland, Chilhowee, and Great

Smoky Mountains. Sightings became fewer, but cougars were still reported along the western border of the state. The last sighting occurred in 1973. Nowak (1976, 133) indicated that a specimen was collected near Pikesville, Bledsoe County, in 1971.

Texas

Cougars have always been rather common in Texas. The Trans-Pecos, the Chisos, other low mountain groups, and the southern two-thirds of the hill country in southern Texas offer reasonable levels of protection, as do the forested and shrubbery covered river and streams throughout the state. It is believed that quite a few cougars still migrate into Texas from Mexico, but even without these immigrants, the resident cougar populations are believed to be holding their own, or even increasing in the southern, central, and western portions of the state. During the ten-year span of 1984–1993, reported cougar mortalities averaged 134 animals per year. The kill in 1993 was 182, most of them in the Trans-Pecos Mountains and the Basins. In spite of the harvesting, it is now believed that there may be more cougars in Texas today than at any time in recent history.

Utah

In addition to Utah areas now designated as national parks, the cougar still frequents the rugged high country of the Rockies and Wasatch ranges. Primarily found in central Utah, cougars also occasionally visited the extreme southern and eastern boundaries adjoining Arizona and Colorado. The state Division of Wildlife Resources estimates that there are now approximately three thousand resident cougars in Utah.

Vermont

Historically present only in limited numbers within the state, the cougar reportedly was extinct by the early 1880s. Bruce Wright (1972, 101) provided accounts of some more recent reported sightings, prior to 1963. In April 1994 three cougars were seen by a number of people. It was confirmed that these three animals were cougars and that they were indeed passing through the woods of northwestern Vermont's Green Mountains. Other credible reports indicate that in October of the same year a cougar was seen approximately seventy miles further south but still in the Green Mountain area. A month later, an adult cougar was seen approximately fifteen miles east of the April sighting.

Virginia

With its unusually large deer population, Virginia at one time had a major concentration of cougars, particularly in the Blue Ridge and Allegheny Mountain area. The cougar was fiercely hunted and was considered to be extinct in the state by 1900. In recent times, Russ (1973, 310–11) noted the collection of "about 20 sightings for the previous 12 months" (1970) on the Jefferson Forest and on the Blue Ridge Parkway. East (1979, 56–57) advises of a confirmed sighting in the fall of 1978 in the Jefferson Forest. Wildlife officials acknowledge that there have been numerous reported sightings but are unwilling to confirm that there is currently a cougar presence in the state. According to the Eastern Puma Research Network, there were a total of twenty-seven alleged sightings in Virginia in 1995 (Boyle 1996, 42).

Washington
In earlier years cougars were relatively common throughout much of Washington, but were more typically found in the Olympics, Cascades, and Blue Mountains. With the number of national forests and parks in the state, the cougar has been able to maintain a solid and growing population here. The state Department of Fish and Game estimated that as of October 1994, there were between 1,500 and 2,300 resident cougars.

West Virginia
Prior to the expansion of colonial settlements, the cougar was common in the forests, mountains, and river valleys throughout the state. Industrial mining, agriculture, and lumber production into the mid-1880s depleted the land and the forests, and by the early 1900s it was believed that the cougar no longer existed in West Virginia. Wilderness rehabilitation has brought many wildlife species back, but there has been only one recent report of a cougar being taken, in 1976 (Frome 1979, 86). Many sightings have been alleged. The Eastern Puma Research Network received a total of twenty-nine sightings for West Virginia in 1995 (Boyle 1996, 42).

Wisconsin
Prior to the mid-1850s, the cougar was common to the entire state, particularly the valleys of the Mississippi and Fox Rivers and their tributaries. Cougars preferred forested areas and rough, hilly, rocky terrain, but also sought out the headwaters of rivers. The cougar is generally believed to have become extinct in Wisconsin by 1870. A few cougar sightings have been reported in recent years (East 1979, 57).

Wyoming
Although only limited numbers of cougars have been obtained from outside the rugged western sections of Wyoming, the brushy and timbered water courses of Wyoming's rivers and streams were additional prime habitat for the cougar. In years past even national parks in Wyoming could not provide sanctuary for the cougar: it was trapped and hunted with dogs until only a few were left. With more restrictive game laws and an assured sanctity from illegal poaching or the adoption

of predator-control measures in national park areas, the cougar population has significantly grown.

CANADA

Canada is the largest country in land size in the Western Hemisphere. Much of its land is located in a climatic zone considered to be less than temperate, between fifty-five and sixty-five degrees north latitude. Most of this northern land is rather barren. Of Canada's ten provinces and two territories, cougars are known to have resided in Alberta, British Columbia, New Brunswick, Ontario, Quebec, and Saskatchewan.

Alberta
Situated directly north of Montana, Alberta's southwestern border with British Columbia straddles the Continental Divide and the Jasper and Banff National Parks. The water courses, woods, and mountains of southwestern Alberta are prime habitat for the cougar. The cougar of Alberta, like most of its Rocky Mountain brethren, is a big cat. Boone and Crockett Club big-game records, which are based on the greatest length of skull without the lower jaw, place two Alberta cougars in the archive's top six. Bounties are no longer paid, and permits and tags are issued only during designated hunting seasons. Landowners, however, are authorized to permanently remove cougars that cause damage to livestock. The average harvest of cougar each year is approximately sixty animals from an estimated population of eight hundred.

British Columbia
The westernmost province of Canada, British Columbia even today still has an extremely large cougar population, estimated currently to be between 3,450 and 4,050 animals. Vancouver Island has an extremely high concentration of cougars in its limited boundaries. Current estimates count between seven and eight hundred cougars on the island. No region in either North or South America has acquired as extensive a record of human/cougar contact and confrontation as has Vancouver Island. Bounties are no longer paid. Hunting licenses are issued, and the average annual harvest of cougars from 1992 to 1995 was 299 animals; 61 of these were from Vancouver Island.

New Brunswick
Located adjacent to Maine, New Brunswick has a rich history of cougar experiences. Its southwestern lake country is similar to Maine's—prime cougar habitat. Bruce Wright (1948, 54, 118–19), (1972, 22–79) provides many accounts of

cougar sightings and encounters, even of so-called "black panthers," in the province through 1970. There is an abundant deer population in the province, water courses that provide excellent cover for the stealthy cougar, and a rural setting with minimal human developments. Reports of cougar sightings even in the northernmost regions touching forty-eight degrees north latitude are common.

Ontario
Few cougars ever chose the province of Ontario as their home. Bounded by the Lakes Superior, Huron, Erie, and Ontario to the south, Hudson Bay to the north, Manitoba to the west, and Quebec to the east, there are not now, and were not in the past, many opportunities for a wandering cougar to enter the province except along Ontario's southern border with Minnesota and the northeastern border with Quebec. It is claimed that the so-called eastern cougar was somewhat common to the southern sections of Ontario prior to the land becoming settled, and sightings were reported in the 1950s, 1960s, and 1970s. The cougar is not now considered to be a resident of the province. It is either extinct or extremely rare.

Quebec
The cougar is still an occasional visitor to Quebec. Reports of cougar sightings in the northern suburbs of Montreal caused a furor in 1959 (Wright 1972, 92–94) and sightings in areas south of the St. Lawrence River are common. It is quite probable that in years past the cougar inhabited some of the more northerly sections of Quebec, but the winter season is long and very cold above fifty-two degrees north latitude, and few grazing animals, possibly the caribou, can survive this climate. Without the grazing animals for prey, there would be little reason for the cougar to extend its stay in Quebec's far north.

Saskatchewan
Cougars were rare in Saskatchewan. Transients may have moved in from time to time from Alberta to the west or from North Dakota and Montana to the south, but the resident population cannot have been large. There is some attractive cougar habitat to the west and south, along heavily vegetated water courses, which would seem to provide excellent cover for a cougar hunting deer. Saskatchewan formerly was prime bison habitat, but it is not believed that bison were ever common prey for the cougar.

Other Provinces
Ronald M. Nowak in *The Cougar in the United States and Canada* indicated that there had been sightings in the Northwest Territories, Yukon, Manitoba, and Nova Scotia. These were not confirmed except for one cougar shot in 1973 near Winnipeg, Manitoba (1976, 24).

MEXICO

When the Spaniards seized control of Mexico from the Aztecs in 1521, they learned that the Aztec ruler Moctezuma, or Montezuma, maintained a live exhibit of wild beasts native to the surrounding country. Included in this exhibit was an animal the Spaniards referred to as a lion, which we now know was an American cougar.

The cougar is found all over Mexico, along the forested areas of the Sierra Madre Mountain chains, the Occidental, the Oriental, and the del Sur, as well as water courses and brushy areas. The jungle areas of the southern Yucatan Peninsula and Tehuantepec seem as popular as a cougar habitat as the woods of northern Chihuahua. Taxonomists identify six subspecies of cougar in Mexico. However, all are stated to have many characteristics similar to one or more of the other identified subspecies.

CENTRAL AMERICA

All seven sovereign nations of Central America still register some level of cougar population. Parts of Belize are low and fertile, and bananas, sugar cane, and fruits are its primary products. In forests of mahogany and logwood and along the swampy coast, cougars are often sighted. They are occasionally killed by livestock owners when too troublesome.

Guatemala, to the south and west of Belize, is the principal habitat of one of the smaller subspecies of cougar. The cougar population was growing, but with an increase in industry and civil strife it is possible that the Guatemalan environment is no longer as capable of supporting wildlife as previously. Logging and large-scale agricultural programs have changed much of Central America's wildest terrain, but there still are areas of jungle.

If there is a cougar presence in El Salvador—the smallest and most crowded of Central American countries—it may only be that of a drifter or wandering animal. In Honduras and Nicaragua, the cougar is reported to be holding its own at higher elevations, but land reforms and exploitative governmental efforts have reduced what were common sightings to just a few fleeting glimpses.

Both Costa Rica and Panama are said to shelter a small population of cougars, but economic reverses in these two countries suggest that if any cougars still remain, the outlook for them is not favorable.

SOUTH AMERICA

Like North America, the continent of South America experiences great variations in climate, but nearly three-quarters of it is in the tropics. Animal life, too, is varied and profuse. Few large wild mammals remain on the continent. The tapir is rare and the capybara is becoming somewhat less than common even in eastern South America. The threatened guanaco (fewer than 100,000) is basically the only large, wild South American herbivore, and that is now limited to a few isolated areas in the high Andes and Patagonia. South American deer do not form large herds and are few in number. Most do not achieve the size of deer in North America. Although a South American marsh deer can weigh more than two hundred pounds, the deer that are the most numerous are the brockets, a species that will weigh only up to forty-five pounds and be less than two feet high at the shoulders.

Although industrialization has begun to deplete South America's jungles and rain forests, the Amazon basin still represents the largest continuous jungle in the world. To the north the Amazon jungle includes those lands south of the Guiana Highlands and extends into the heart of Brazil, embracing the Amazon River and its major tributaries, the Xingu, Tapajoz, Madeira, Purus, and Negro. From Brazil the jungle reaches south to Bolivia, Paraguay, and even into Argentina. The cougar is said to inhabit most, if not all, countries of the South American continent. The Argentine area of Patagonia boasts the greatest concentration of cougars on the continent, but other areas also maintain healthy cougar populations, as they have for many years.

Hunting regulations are not well enforced in most South American countries. In addition, domestic herds of sheep and cattle are increasing to meet the needs of growing populations and for export. Threats to these herds from cougars are met with swiftly and firmly. Stanley Young was of the belief that in spite of these pressures "the puma [cougar] will continue to hold its own indefinitely in the vast unbroken tropical forests of the larger river valleys, and along the slopes of the Andes (1946, 45)." There are, however, fewer cougar today in South America than there were. Tomorrow there probably will be fewer still.

Reported Human Fatalities
from Cougar Attacks

		Victim			Cougar		
Date	Location	Name	Sex	Age	Sex	Age	Weight
May 1751	Betty's Patch, Pennsylvania	Tanner	M	58	unk.	unk.	unk.
Early 1800s	North of Vicksburg, Mississippi	Unk./Unk.	M/M	Adult/ Adult	unk.	unk.	unk.
Early 1800s	Northeastern Louisiana, in the vicinity of the Bayou Macon River in West Carroll Parish	Unknown	M	Adult	unk.	unk.	unk.
Early 1800s	Southeastern Georgia or extreme northern Florida	Unknown	M	Adult	unk.	unk.	unk.

Cited in Young and Goldman (1946, 100) and *Daily Local News*, West Chester, Penn., Oct. 8, 1956. Philip Tanner owned a mill on Pigeon Creek and lived in the area. He was reportedly killed by a cougar, the circumstances of which were not further detailed, and the image of a cougar was carved on his tombstone.

From a handwritten manuscript drafted by the noted and colorful hunter Benjamin Vernon Lilly, reproduced in the J. Frank Dobie book *The Ben Lilly Legend* (1950, 186–204), and also restated by Fergus (1996, 39). Lilly indicated that "a squad of Negro men were clearing swamp land north of Vicksburg. They noticed a panther [cougar] slipping around in the woods and warned two white men, brothers, who lived in a cabin nearby. Not long afterwards while one of them [brothers] was chopping wood about a hundred yards away from the cabin, he heard the other one scream. He had left him covered up in bed, shaking with a chill. He rushed to the cabin and as he went through the door [he] was leaped upon by a panther. He had his ax but could not use it effectively. The panther escaped; it had killed the sick brother and the second one was so badly wounded that he died."

Another of the cougar/human incidents reported in the Ben Lilly manuscript as reproduced in the Dobie book and noted by Fergus (1996, 39–40). Lilly indicates that the circumstances of this incident were mentioned to him by Judge Henegan of West Carroll Parish in 1882. Lilly stated that this occurred a "long time back" and involved a white man and an Indian setting out to hunt deer right after dinner. Unable to find any game sign, they separated and the white man eventually returned to their cabin. The Indian never returned. After a search the following morning, the Indian was found "dead on the ground. Tracks made it plain that a large panther had leaped from a lean-ing oak tree under which he [the Indian] was passing, knocked him face down, apparently killing him instantly, and then rolled him over and sucked blood from his throat."

Young and Goldman (1946, 101–2) cite this Theodore Roosevelt (1905/1990, 23) report of an incident that had occurred many years ago in the Florida swamps. Also mentioned by Claude Barnes. (1960, 125). Roosevelt stated that one of his ancestral relatives owned a plantation near the Georgia/Florida border, one of his black workers, a man of "colossal strength," had a girl friend on another plantation and after visiting her was returning home through the swamps. He was attacked by a cougar, and, armed with a long knife, he defended himself. A later search revealed his body "all gashed and torn," and nearby the searchers also found the body of a cougar "stabbed and cut in many places."

Date	Location	Victim			Cougar		
		Name	Sex	Age	Sex	Age	Weight
Early 1800s	Mississippi	Unknown	M	Adult	unk.	unk.	unk.
Prior to 1827	The Catskill Mountain area south of Albany, New York	Unknown	M	Adult	unk.	unk.	unk.
Jan. 1830	Pennsylvania	Unknown	F	Adult	unk.	unk.	unk.
1844	Lycoming County, Pennsylvania	Reinwald	M	Adult	unk.	unk.	unk.
1867–70	Near Camp Grant, Arizona	Unknown	M	Adult	unk.	unk.	unk.
1876	Near Indian Creek, vicinity of Bandera, Texas	Ramsey	M	Adult	unk.	unk.	unk.

Another of Theodore Roosevelt's "undoubted cases" where a black male was attacked by a cougar. Cited by Roosevelt in *The Wilderness Hunter* (1893, 345), *Hunting the Grisly and Other Sketches* (1904, 158), *Outdoor Pastimes of the American Hunter* (1905/1990, 23), also Claude Barnes (1960, 125). Roosevelt states that he was informed by a General Wade Hampton, who had the reputation of being a famous hunter in South Carolina and Mississippi, that near his Mississippi plantation many years ago, a black man "who was one of a gang engaged in building a railroad through low and wet ground was waylaid and killed by a cougar later one night as he was walking alone through the swamp."

Cuvier and Griffith (1827, 438–39), and Young and Goldman (1946, 101). Two men with dogs were hunting and one of the men was attacked by a cougar. When the other responded to the sound of his friend's gun, he discovered his friend's body on the limb of a tree being guarded by a cougar. Sensing that he was in grave danger, he fired at the cat and retired, returning later with others. They then recovered the body of his friend as well as the cougar. In the Cuvier article, it was stated that this incident was "related to Major Smith by Mr. Skudder, the proprietor of the Museum at New York where the animal was preserved after death."

Seton 1913, 119–21. Seton quotes from M'Murtrie (1831, 115) in Cuvier's *Animal Kingdom*, and Seton adds that the report appears to be factual. Also see Cuvier and Edward Griffin (vol. 2, 1827, 438), Barnes (1960, 124), and True (1889, 602). Comments are only that it was "an unprovoked attack upon an unfortunate woman in Pennsylvania. The ferocious brute seized upon her as she was passing along the road and killed her in an instant."

Parsons (1947, 4). Dr. Reinwald, who lived on a farm, was walking through snow to see a patient at English Center. His nephew's wife, Mrs. William Reinwald, reported that "the doctor's body was found lying in the snow with the back of his neck bitten through; medical instruments scattered about, large cougar tracks all around." Also reported by Barnes (1960, 124).

Captain John G. Bourke (*On the Border with Crook*, 1971, 39–40) related how an injured survivor of an Apache ambush was subsequently attacked, killed, and carried off by a cougar.

Reported in *Pioneer History of Bandera County*, J. Marvin Hunter, 1922 (110) and reprinted in 1970. Information provided courtesy of Dr. E. Lee Fitzhugh, UC Davis. Hunter indicated that "a negro named Henry Ramsey . . . heard a disturbance out in his front yard. When he opened the door to investigate the trouble a large panther sprang into the room and attacked him. The only weapon the negro could secure quickly was a large butcher knife and with this he killed the panther, but not before the furious beast had bitten and lacerated his arms and body and torn his clothes into shreds." Although medical attention was reportedly made immediately available, Mr. Ramsey is reported to have died from "hydrophobia."

		Victim			Cougar		
Date	Location	Name	Sex	Age	Sex	Age	Weight
Oct. 1880	Near Dutch Flat, Humbug Canyon, Nevada	Unknown	M	Adult	unk.	unk.	unk.
March 1882	Near Kalama, Washington	Graves	M	5	unk.	unk.	unk.
Sept. 1885	Near Bruneau, Idaho	Unknown	M	8	unk.	unk.	unk.
Prior to 1888	In the vicinity of Hickory Grove, Mississippi	Unk./Unk.	M/M	14/11	unk.	unk.	unk.
Late-1880s	Within the present Capitan Mountain Wilderness Area, and approx. 15 miles from Ft. Stanton, New Mexico	Unknown	F	2–3	unk.	unk.	unk.
June 1890	Quartz Valley, California	Dangle	M	7	unk.	unk.	unk.

As reported by the *Battle Mountain Messenger*, on Oct. 27, 1880, an unknown young man was killed some time during the past week by a "California lion." His body was "almost wholly devoured, only the flesh on his feet and head remaining." He had been out hunting. Information provided by Nevada Division of Wildlife.

March 30, 1882 issue of the *Clarke County Register* provides an accounting of this incident as researched by Tinsley (1987, 82). Young Gussie Graves was attacked by a cougar while near his home. His screams brought neighbors to the scene and they were able to retrieve the body from the cat. The boy's injuries were so severe that he died.

Reported by the *Idaho Democrat*, the *White Pine News*, Sept. 19, 1885, and the *Elko Independent*, Sept. 22, 1885. The young boy was cutting wood when a cougar pounced on him from brush surrounding the Bruneau River. The boy was killed before his father, who witnessed the attack, could retrieve his rifle and kill the cougar. It still held the boy in its mouth when it was shot. Information provided by the Nevada Division of Wildlife.

Ben Lilly indicated that he was told of this attack by a trapper friend of his, and that the trapper was personally aware of this attack ("It was no hearsay matter with him"). This incident is also mentioned in the Dobie book (1950, 200) and by Fergus (1996, 40). As Lilly relates the incident, the two boys were out chopping wood, the older boy chopping and the younger one carrying. As the younger boy bent over to pick up a stick he was attacked by a cougar. The older boy rushed to defend his young companion, but before he could use his ax, the cougar also attacked him. A young man in a nearby barn heard the disturbance and reportedly "picked up a billet of wood used to rive boards, and with it hit the panther in the head killing it. It was not a large one." Lilly went on to say that the trapper told him that both of the boys died from their wounds before the next morning and were buried in the same grave.

Barnes (1960, 127) reports this attack and also quotes a Sam H. Nickels (1946) as his source. A Mexican woman and her small daughter went to a spring for water. As the girl began to pick up some nearby acorns, a cougar pounced on her and carried her away. Searchers using dogs discovered one of her arms and bits of her dress, but they lost the trail near the present town of Capitan.

Howard (1915, 162–63), Beier (1991, 404). Arthur Dangle was playing within 100 yards of his house when he was attacked. Two cougars were on young Dangle's body when his father, who was looking for him, came upon the scene. He ran home to get a gun, but before he could shoot the cougars the boy's mother drove them off of what remained of her son's body. The following day, trackers with a dog killed both cougars. According to Howard's report there were two cougars. He referred to the larger animal as "him," but it more likely would have been a female. Beier (1991, 404) suggests that it was a female with a older cub.

Date	Location	Victim			Cougar		
		Name	Sex	Age	Sex	Age	Weight
Prior to 1906	Southeast Texas	Unknown	unk.	Child	unk.	unk.	unk.
July 1909	Glen Willis, on Coyote Creek near Morgan Hill, California	Wilson/ Kennedy	M/F	10/Adult	F	Adult	150

In this incident related by Ben Lilly, he stated that in 1906 he was at a small railroad station above Lake Charles, Louisiana, when he met an elderly man who had formerly been a tanner. Lilly stated that the man "was truthful and had a good memory." He told Lilly about "at least a half dozen instances of panthers killing early settlers around his old home in southeast Texas." The attack that Lilly then described is mentioned in detail in the Dobie book (1950, 200–202) and repeated by Fergus (1996, 40). The cougar attack involved a settler, his wife, and two small babies. The family had just moved into a cabin near some thickets and the husband was busy clearing land to farm. The wife, at the time of the incident, was outside burning some trash and clearing up the yard in the front of the cabin. Hearing one of the babies crying inside the cabin, she went in to comfort it and then brought the other baby outside, setting it on the ground near her. When the baby began to cry she then quieted it and went back to her work. Shortly after this she heard the baby "give a terrible squall. She looked in time to see a panther bound over the fence carrying the baby into the dense thicket beyond." The mother ran after the cougar but without success. She heard the other baby cry that was still in the cabin, so she ran into the cabin, grabbed the baby, and while carrying her child left the cabin to again search for her other baby. The baby she was carrying was still crying, and hearing the baby screaming, a cougar came toward her. She ran to the cabin and shut and barred the door, apparently right in the face of the cougar. Coming upon this situation, and not owning a gun, the husband ran to his neighbor's house to borrow one. When he returned to the cabin he saw the cougar "reared up with his front paws on the door." He was, however, unable to shoot the cougar for fear of killing his wife on the other side of the door. The cat then ran into the thickets. The following day, and for two weeks after this attack, all the men in the settlement hunted with their dogs. They killed in total eleven cougars, but they "never found even a scrap of the dress worn by the baby that the panther carried off."

Reported by Howard (1915, 162), Tracy I. Storer (April 1923), Seton (1929, 122–24), and Barnes (1960, 125). Miss Isola Kennedy took three young boys with her on an outing to the nearby creek. While the boys were wading, a cougar leaped on the back of one of the boys, Earl Wilson, and then attacked Miss Kennedy, who came to help the boy. Armed only with a hatpin, she fought with the cougar until help summoned by the other two boys arrived. The cougar was then shot. Earl Wilson did not suffer serious injuries but he soon died, reportedly from tetanus. The cougar was claimed to be rabid, and, despite medical attention, Miss Kennedy died approximately two months later.

		Victim			Cougar		
Date	Location	Name	Sex	Age	Sex	Age	Weight
Dec. 1924	Near Olema and Lake Chelan, Chelan County, Washington	Fehlhaber	M	13	F	Adult	unk.
June 1949	Walter's Bay, near Kyuquot, Vancouver Island, B.C., Canada	Taylor	M	7	unk.	unk.	unk.
Jan. 1971	Near Lytton, B.C., Canada	Wells	M	12	unk.	unk.	unk.

Attack was noted by Haley (1953, 55, 125–27), Tinsley (1987, 82), Beier (1991, 404), Young and Goldman (1946, 100), Hilderbrand (1963, 22). Jimmy Fehlhaber was taking a shortcut to the home of a neighbor to pick up a team of horses. Wearing snowshoes, he maintained a steady pace until he was suddenly attacked by a cougar. Not surrendering his life easily, young Jimmy fought the cat with everything he had—a small knife and a lot of determination. When he failed to return home, search parties found the remains of his body and the dew-claw from the left front foot of the cougar that had attacked him. A considerable number of cougars were killed in anticipation of the reward offered for the killer cougar, but none really seemed to be "quite right." After several more weeks had passed, an old female cougar, missing a dew-claw on her left front foot, was killed as she crept toward some children on their way home from school. Sex and age of the cougar is subject to some question. Beier indicated that it was a thirteen-year-old male, Young and Goldman reported that it was a three-year-old female. Haley, who had been on the scene and inspected the bodies of suspected cougars, stated that it was an old and gaunt female. *The Journal of Mammalogy* (vol. 6, 1925, 197–99) reported that two cougars were responsible, an old female and a three-year-old male. The male's stomach contents contained material that was purportedly taken from the victim. The *Daily Colonist*, Jan. 8, 1961, in reviewing the incident, suggests that the attacking cougar was a three-year-old female.

Tinsley (1987, 82–83), Beier (1991, 404). Young Norman Taylor was on a picnic with his family and neighbors when he was attacked by a cougar. As the cougar attempted to drag the boy's body away, several men ran to Taylor's rescue. The cougar dropped the boy and ran. The cougar responsible for the attack was killed the next day. Press reports do not indicate sex, age, or weight of the cougar other than to say it was about of average size. An article in the *Daily Colonist* suggests that the boy was wandering by when the cougar was feeding on a deer and thus the cougar was "defending what was his own." The *Vancouver Sun*, Jan. 3, 1971, also reports that the boy "ventured too close to the animal's kill of two raccoons and a dog." The *Sun* also stated that the cougar weighed eighty pounds.

The *Vancouver Sun*, Jan. 3 and April 6, 1971, Beier (1991, 404), Tinsley (1987, 83). Lawrence Wells and his two sisters were playing by some railroad tracks near their home when a cougar seized the boy. The two girls ran for help, but by the time the boy's father arrived with a gun the cougar had already killed young Lawrence. The father shot the cougar as it was dragging his son's body away. Beier suggests that the cougar was an old male, approximately twelve years old, but newspaper reports and Tinsley, who quotes from the *Merritt Herald*, provide no information with respect to the cougar except to say that it was shot several times. The *Sun*, April 6, 1971, quoting young Wells's father, John Wells: "When it killed my son it couldn't have weighed more than 90 pounds. It was starved."

			Victim			Cougar		
Date	Location	Name	Sex	Age	Sex	Age	Weight	
Jan. 1974	Arroyo Seco, New Mexico	Nolan	M	8	F	1–2	50	
July 1976	Near Gold River, Vancouver Island, B.C., Canada	Samuel	F	14	M	2–3	unk.	
May 1988	Near Tofino, Vancouver Island, B.C., Canada	Bergman	M	9	M	4	150	
Nov. 1988	Foothills of the Sierras, Butte County, California	Gomez Dunton	F	51	unk.	unk.	unk.	
Sept. 1989	Evaro, Montana	Gardipe	M	5	F/F	Adult/ 1 yr.	unk./52	

Rocky Mountain News, Nov. 7, 1974, Tinsley (1987, 83), Beier (1991, 404). Kenneth Nolan and his half-brother, David Cordry, age 11, were just lying down under a tree along a rocky ridge when Kenneth was attacked. David tried to help his brother but could not dissuade the cougar from its assault on Kenneth. When David returned with his father the cougar was still abusing the Nolan boy. David's father emptied his revolver at the cat, driving it away. David's injuries were mostly scratches that he suffered in trying to pull the cougar off of young Kenneth. The cougar was soon tracked down and killed. The *Rocky Mountain News* stated that the cougar was sixteen months old and weighed between forty and fifty pounds. Tinsley (1987, 83) said that the cougar was young, a somewhat emaciated female cat weighing about fifty pounds. Beier (1991, 404) suggested that the cougar was a female, three years old, and underweight.

The *Vancouver Sun*, July 15 and 20, 1976, and Beier (1991, 404), Tinsley (1987, 83). Matilda Samuel was picking berries when a cougar jumped out of the bushes and seized her. Two older boys witnessed the attack and saw the girl being dragged off into the shrubbery. They ran from the scene and flagged down a passing vehicle, relaying what had occurred. An RCMP patrol later located the body. The cougar was treed and killed only a short distance from the scene of the attack. Beier indicated that the Samuel girl was seven. The B.C. Ministry of Environment reports that she was fourteen, and that a wildlife control officer killed the cougar responsible for the attack.

Vancouver Sun, May 19, 1988. Beier (1991, 404), Worth (1991, 81) reported that the boy was ten, and that he had wandered off the trail and that his remains were found the following day "guarded by a cougar." B.C. Ministry of Environment indicated that young Bergman "was hiking with family and friends near their cabin at Catface and he then went missing." His body was found a day later, and a family friend then shot the cougar.

Butte County Sheriff's Department, May 17, 1994. *Los Angeles Times*, April 3, 1995, in a listing of attacks put together by Trevor Johnson and Helene Webb. It was reported that "Lucy Gomez was found dead in the Sierra foothills of Butte County. Game wardens suspected that she had been killed by a mountain lion but could not prove it." No cougar search was undertaken by California Fish and Game officials. The informational release issued by the Butte County Sheriff's Department said that the deceased Lucy Gomez Dunton was not consumed by a bear, but more likely a cat.

Rocky Mountain News, Jan. 13, 1990, Beier (1991, 404), the *Spokesman-Review*, Sept. 14, 1989, Lewis (1995, 187). Jake Gardipe was last seen riding his tricycle in his back yard. His body was recovered about five hours later only thirty yards from his home. Searchers believed that young Gardipe was killed and/or assaulted by at least two cougars. A yearling cougar was killed near the body, but it was believed that an adult cougar, probably the mother of the younger cat, did the actual killing. It is understood that other cougars in the area were to be tracked, trapped, and killed. Beier (1991, 404) suggests that the responsible cougar was a female aged one and one-half years, of normal size.

		Victim			Cougar		
Date	Location	Name	Sex	Age	Sex	Age	Weight
Jan. 1991	Near Idaho Springs, Colorado	Lancaster	M	18	M	3	110
March 1991	Pinyon Pines, California	Zweig	M	3	unk.	unk.	unk.
May 1992	Kyuquot, Vancouver Island, B.C., Canada	Unknown	M	8	F	1–1/2	65
April 1994	Auburn State Recreation Area near Rancho Cordova, California	Schoener	F	40	F	2–3	82
Dec. 1994	Cuyamaca Rancho State Park, approximately 50 miles east of San Diego, California	Kenna	F	58	M	2–3	149
Aug. 1996	Near Princeton, B.C., Canada	Parolin	F	36	M	2	59

Rocky Mountain News, Jan. 17 and 18, 1991, *Clear Creek Courant,* Jan. 16, 1991, and Case Report 91–0097 Clear Creek County Sheriff. Scott Lancaster had set out on a cross-country jog in back of Clear Creek Secondary School. As he climbed the pathway up into the foothills he was ambushed by a cougar, killed, his body partially eaten. After searchers found his body, it was still being guarded by the attacking cougar. The cougar was shot by law-enforcement personnel.

Phoenix Gazette, Arizona Republic, March 13, 1991, and Palm Desert Sheriff's office. Little Travis Zweig wandered away from their cabin and his footprints ended at a slide area where there were obvious drag marks. The body of Zweig was never found. The local sheriff's office believes he was killed by a cougar.

B.C. Ministry of Environment, Feb. 25, 1996. The ministry reported "an eight-year-old boy was killed by a 27 kg. 1 1/2-year-old female cougar at Kyuquot at 7:00 p.m. Boy was sitting on log at edge of school yard watching kids play. Boy died shortly after cougar bites to neck area. School maintenance worker shot and killed cougar when attack took place."

Phoenix Gazette, April 29, 1994, and May 2, 1994, *Denver Post,* Dec. 13, 1994. Barbara Schoener was jogging along a popular trail within the recreation area when she was attacked from the rear by a cougar. The assault drove her down the slope and although she made a valiant effort to fight off the animal, it eventually was able to reach her neck, and then it bit through her skull. Searchers found her partially eaten body the following day. The cougar responsible was tracked down and killed a week later.

Denver Post, Dec. 13, 1994, *San Diego Union Tribune,* Dec. 19, 1994, *Newsweek* (Peyser, Jan. 8, 1996, 58). Iris Kenna was jogging in the recreation area when she was attacked by a cougar. The cougar quickly killed Kenna, ripping out her throat. It had just begun feeding from her body when it was disturbed by some hikers. The cougar was killed about ten hours after the attack. *Newsweek* (January 8, 1996, 58) reported that the cougar weighed 140 pounds, but the park superintendent, Greg Piccard, March 1, 1996, stated that it weighed 149 pounds.

Rocky Mountain News, Aug. 23 and 27, 1996. *Phoenix Gazette,* Aug. 21, 1996. Cindy Parolin, the mother of Steven Parolin, age six, was killed by a cougar when she attempted to save her son who was being attacked. According to Gary Gerhardt *(RMN),* the *Montreal Gazette* reported that Mrs. Parolin and her three children were on horseback when the cougar attacked, spooking Steven's horse and tumbling the boy, at which time the cougar attacked him. Grabbing a branch, Mrs. Parolin struck the cougar, who then attacked the mother. The children ran for help and reached a camper who then killed the cougar.

Date	Location	Victim Name	Victim Sex	Victim Age	Cougar Sex	Cougar Age	Cougar Weight
July 1997	Summerland Park area, along the North Inlet Trail, West Side Rocky Mountain National Park, Colorado	Miedema	M	10	F	2-1/2	88

Reference and Comments

Denver Post and *Rocky Mountain News*, July 18 and 19, 1997, and RMNP Public
Information Officer, July 21, 1997. Mark David Miedema, his parents, Dave and Kathy,
and his six-year-old sister, Rachel, were on a three-day camping trip to Rocky
Mountain National Park. After hiking the East Inlet Trail on the west side of the park,
they were walking back down the trail when young Mark got ahead of his parents and
was attacked. When his parents and sister reached the scene of the attack, all they saw
was his feet and legs on the trail, as they got closer, they saw the cougar pick him up
and start dragging him off the trail. The cat fled upon the arrival of the parents. People
skilled in CPR attempted to resuscitate Mark but they were unsuccessful. A ranger
who was guarding the attack scene was later threatened by the cougar and fired three
rounds at it, wounding the animal. Park rangers, and a tracker with dogs, later treed
the injured cougar and shot it. The coroner determined that Mark Miedema actually
died from asphyxiation, choking on his own vomit, rather than from wounds or from
trauma.

Reported Cougar Attacks on Humans
Not Leading to Human Fatality

			Victim		Cougar		
Date	Location	Name	Sex	Age	Sex	Age	Weight
Early 1830s	In the vicinity of Jasper, Arkansas, near Hudson Creek	Hudson	M	Adult	M	unk.	unk.
1834	Tippah County, northern Mississippi, near the Tennessee border	Forrest	F	Adult	unk.	unk.	unk.
1854	Nevada	Solon	M	Adult	unk.	unk.	unk.

Incident cited in *A Reminiscent History of the Ozark Region* (1894 and 1976, 290). Samuel Hudson and his young son left to cut down a bee tree. Hudson had just began to work on the tree when he saw a cougar approaching from a nearby ravine. He threw some rocks at the cat but was unable to hit it. When the cougar finally spotted the man and boy it poised, as if ready to spring. The father held fast to his axe when the cougar slowly advanced "its long tail waving from side to side." The cougar crouched for a moment then attacked. After a futile blow with his axe, which completely missed the animal, his son gave him a large knife which he plunged "time after time into the animal." Samuel Hudson suffered severe lacerations and significant loss of blood, but survived. It was reported that the "panther was one of the largest of its kind ever killed in the section, measuring nine feet from nose to end of tail."

Cited by Wyeth (1899, 8–10), Fergus (1996, 34). Mrs. Miriam Forrest, mother of the then thirteen-year-old Nathan Bedford Forrest (who would later become the acclaimed general of Confederate cavalry), was on horseback, accompanied by her sister Fannie Beck (also on horseback), and was precariously carrying a basket of newly hatched chickens when she and her sister were chased by a cougar. It was reported that the sound of the peeping chicks could be heard throughout the woods. Catching up to them at a creek bed, the cougar leaped upon Mariam Beck, clawing her neck and shoulder and raking the back of the horse she was riding. The horse bucked, freeing the cougar from the woman as well as the horse, inflicting more wounds in the process on Miriam Beck. The screams of the women brought help, and as soon as his mother was made comfortable, young Nathan called his dogs and took after the cat. After the dogs had treed the cougar in the early morning hours of the next day, Nathan shot the cougar through its heart and cut off the cat's scalp and ears.

James Capen (Grizzly) Adams related this cougar attack on his partner Solon (Hittell 1926, 207–8). Solon was attacked from behind, the cougar leaping on his back. Protecting his neck, he shouted out to Adams for help. Adams shot at the cougar, apparently missing it, and it fled.

		Victim				Cougar	
Date	Location	Name	Sex	Age	Sex	Age	Weight
1858	Along Oak Creek, on the prairie east of Sarasota, Florida	Unk./Unk.	M/F	Child/12	unk.	unk.	unk.
1878	Near Mount Shasta, California	Unknown	M	3	unk.	unk.	unk.
1880s	Sumas, Washington	Jorgenson	M	Adult	unk.	unk.	unk.
1880s	Northwest Whatcom County, vicinity of Lynden, Washington	Unknown	M	Child	unk.	unk.	unk.
1880s	Northwest Watcom County, vicinity of Ferndale, Washington	Drunal	F	Adult	unk.	unk.	unk.
1880s	Logging camp near Mt. Vernon, Skagit County, Washington	Harmon	M	Adult	unk.	unk.	unk.

Cited in the Charles Fergus book *Swamp Screamer* (1966, 42–43), which indicates that information on this attack had been taken from DeVanes *Early Florida History*. A settler was using an adz to cut and square some logs by his cabin site while his two children were otherwise occupied outside near the cabin. A cougar reportedly came from the woods and seized the young boy by his foot. His sister grabbed the boy away from the cougar, who then turned on her. The sounds of the struggle brought the father, mother, and their two dogs to the fray. The cougar let go of the girl and crawled under the uncompleted cabin floor, where it was then promptly killed by the father using the adz.

Goode (1943, 35) quotes from a letter addressed to a Dr. Merriam by Professor W. H. Brewer of Yale. The boy was playing in the yard when a cougar entered the yard and seized the boy by his throat. The mother, hearing the boy's cry of alarm, struck at the cougar with a broom. A man who was in the house at the time shot the cougar. Professor Brewer said that the cougar was "young, bold, stupid, and very hungry." Also in *Outdoor Pastimes of an American Hunter* (Roosevelt, 1905, 1990, 22–23).

W. A. Perry, *The Big Game of North America* (1890, 414–15), Roger A. Caras (1964, 25), Claude T. Barnes (1960, 118–19). While clearing some land, a new immigrant, Joseph Jorgenson, had his arm seized by a cougar. After battling the cougar with his bare hands and heavy boots, he finally killed it with his spade only after suffering some severe wounds. Jeffcott (1949, 340–41), indicates that the victim's name was Joe Christensen, but the circumstances of the attack were basically the same.

Jeffcott (1949, 342–43). George Goodwin, a long-time resident of Whatcom County, related an attack that occurred at Ten Mile where a girl and her younger brother were on their way to school and a cougar seized the boy by the arm. His older sister struck the cougar on the head with a bottle of milk that they were to have for lunch. The cougar promptly released the boy's arm and fled into the timber.

Jeffcott (1949, 343). While walking near the Glen Echo mill on the Nooksack, Mrs. Jim Drunal was confronted by a large cougar. Carrying an umbrella, she opened it in the cougar's face, and it leaped off the road but then quickly returned to threaten her. They continued this activity until she reached the home of one of her neighbors, Gus Westergrin. It was then reported that the cougar "killed a sheep in Gus' barnyard. Later the cougar was poisoned by Hanin Frost."

W. A. Perry (1890, 418–19). While looking for some oxen that had strayed from his logging camp, Charles Harmon was approached by a cougar. Not frightened off by Harmon's yelling, it followed Harmon back to his camp, occasionally licking his hands and intently staring at him. Before reaching the logging camp, the cougar tore off most of Charles Harmon's clothes. Upon reaching the camp, Harmon took shelter in a cabin, the cougar crouching near the door until it was shot.

		Victim			Cougar		
Date	Location	Name	Sex	Age	Sex	Age	Weight
Feb., early 1880s	Near York, B.C., Canada	Campbell	F	Adult	F	adult	unk.
Spring 1883	Near Pillsbury, Minnesota	Locke	M	Adult	unk.	unk.	unk.
Spring 1884	Northern Idaho	Unknown	M	Adult	M&F	unk.	unk.
1885	Snohomish, Washington	Cathcart	M	Adult	unk.	unk.	unk.
mid-1880s	Central Idaho, vicinity of Mount Idaho, Elk City, Idaho	Moody	M	Adult	unk.	unk.	unk.
late-1880s	Salmon National Forest, central Idaho, along a tributary of the Salmon	Carpenter	M	Adult	unk.	unk.	unk.
Spring 1886	Southwestern Mississippi	Unknown	M	Adult	F	unk.	unk.

W. A. Perry, *The Big Game of North America* (1890, 415–418). Perry detailed the attack in Mary Campbell's own words. While travelling by horseback, a cougar startled her horse and she was thrown. The cougar followed her as she retreated toward her own home. It became more intent, and even tore her dress. Believing that she would soon be killed, she was delighted to see her father and their two dogs arrive and slay the cougar.

Monroe Goode, in *Field and Stream*, Aug. 1944, vol. 49, p. 71, mentions that Frank J. Locke reported being attacked by a cougar in 1883 *(Forest and Stream)*. Mr. Locke's comments *(Forest and Stream*, 1883, 226) only mentions that he "recently had an encounter with a huge panther, the only one seen in this locality for years."

Seton (1929, 119) provides this incident as told to him by a James Fullerton. The attack involved kittens/cubs, and two adult cougars who may have been protecting their young were killed. The railroad section hand involved in the attack only had a knife, and he received near fatal injuries.

W. A. Perry, *The Big Game of North America* (1890, 419), Claude T. Barnes (1960, 119). Cougar presumedly sprang at Cathcart, who defended himself with a cane. His dog also came to assist and the cougar was treed. Cathcart was reported to have shot the cat later.

Cited in Charles S. Moody's "The Mountain Lion at Home," *Outing* 59 (Feb. 1912): 635–36, and in *The Cougar or Mountain Lion*, Claude Barnes, 1960, 113. Author Moody's father went in search of camp horses. He was later followed and attacked by a cougar. Moody senior escaped by swimming to the other side of a stream and staying in the water as the cougar prowled along the opposite shore looking for him.

Cited in "The Mountain Lion at Home," *Outing* 59 (Feb.1912): 635, and in *The Cougar or Mountain Lion*, Claude Barnes, 1960, 113. Author Moody indicated that a miner (George Carpenter) saw a cougar on an opposite bank, threw a rock at it, and the cougar leaped over the small stream and attacked him. Carpenter is supposed to have struck a match in the cougar's face, an act that sent the cougar snarling up a tree. Carpenter later shot the cat. He suffered minor injuries.

Another incident mentioned by Ben Lilly in his handwritten manuscript and included in the Dobie book (1950, 203–4). Lilly was in his camp along the Mississippi River bottoms when a Major Hamberling brought him his mail and indicated that he saw a dead "six-foot pantha on that gravel train that just passed." The cougar had apparently "sprang off the bank out of cane and caught at a Negro shoveling gravel onto a flat car." Warned in time by another worker, the gravel shoveler was able to dodge the attack with only the cougar's claws raking his jumper. All of the men nearby ran to the cat and beat it with their shovels and the train conductor then shot it in the head with a pistol. It was reported to be a young female.

		Victim			Cougar		
Date	Location	Name	Sex	Age	Sex	Age	Weight
Spring 1886	Near Olympia, Washington	Farnham/ Farnham	M/M	6/12	unk.	unk.	unk.
1908	Near Silver City, New Mexico	Unknown	F	Adult	F	unk.	unk.
Oct. 1909	Near Flagstaff, Arizona	Fairway/ Fairway	F/M	9/7	unk.	unk.	unk.
1912	East Fork, Bryce Canyon,	Neilson	M	Adult	unk.	unk.	unk.
1915	Near Bella Coola, B.C., Canada	Unknown	M	10	unk.	unk.	unk.
1916	Curry County, near Marial, Oregon	Jones	F	8	unk.	adult	unk.

W. A. Perry, *The Big Game of North America* (1890, 413–14), Roger Caras (1964, 25). The three Farnham boys were returning from school when a cougar seized the youngest and smallest boy and took him into the bushes. The oldest boy, Walter, went after his brother and began to beat the cat with a bottle. The bottle broke and he tried to jab out the cougar's eyes. The third brother went for help, and two nearby wood-choppers responded. One of the woodchoppers had a revolver and shot the cougar, who had earlier fled up a tree to escape from young Walter. Both boys were scratched and bruised.

Dobie (1943, 57) reported that he heard of this incident from Dr. L. S. Peters of Albuquerque, who treated a woman who had been attacked by a cougar that leaped over her husband to assault her in their one-room cabin.

Hibben (1948, 216–17). Hibben indicated it was believed that an old emaciated cougar killed in the vicinity was responsible for the attack upon the two Fairway children who had been on their way to school. Both children were bitten and clawed and the girl lost most of one of her ears.

Barnes (1960, 117), describes the incident as told to him by noted guide Utah and hunter Jim De Long. Cub Neilson of Panguitch, Utah, left his sheep to look for his horses when a young mountain lion sprang on him. He was able to throw the cat off and then clubbed it to death with a pine stock.

J. R. Lowther (1915, 132). Lowther reported that "this was the first instance of a human being attacked in this province." The boy was standing near his father's home at the time of the attack.

Oregon Sportsman 4(1961): 61 and Young and Goldman (1946, 102). This attack was related to the *Gold Beach Globe* by Hathaway Jones who owned a ranch at that time near Marial. Jones was working in the field when his daughter Myrtle was returning with some horses he had sent her to get. A large cougar met her midway in the field, sprang at her but missed. The girl screamed for help, and her brother Bill, who saw the cougar make the jump, called for his father. Grabbing an axe, the father ran to help, meeting the girl as she fled the scene. Meanwhile, the son ran to the house for a gun and his mother accompanied him on his return. Myrtle showed them where the cougar sprang at her, and while looking through the brush, the father, now carrying the rifle, indicated that the cougar "made a spring at my wife," and he shot it. The cougar landed "only about eight feet" from his wife. It still tried to spring at her a second time before it succumbed.

		Victim			Cougar		
Date	Location	Name	Sex	Age	Sex	Age	Weight
Sept. 1916	Cowichan Lake, Vancouver, B.C., Canada	Ashburnham/ Farrar	F/M	11/8	unk.	unk.	unk.
June 1931	Espinosa Inlet, near Tofino, Vancouver Island, B.C., Canada	Wishart	unk.	Infant	unk.	unk.	unk.
July 1931	Cowlitz Hills, Upper Toutle River, Washington Region,	Mattern	M	Adult	F	2	unk.
May 1934	Holberg, Vancouver Island, B.C., Canada	Jensen	M	Adult	unk.	unk.	unk.
May 1935	Quatsino, Vancouver Island, B.C., Canada	Johnson	M	Adult	unk.	unk.	unk.
Oct. 1942	Between Horsefly Lake and Quesnel, B.C., Canada	Carson	M	Adult	F	adult	unk.
June 1948	York County, New Brunswick, Canada	Saulnier	M	Adult	unk.	adult	unk.

Vancouver Daily Colonist, June 21, 1950, Tinsley (1987, 80), Beier (1991,404). Seton (1929, 124) quotes *New York Herald*. Both children left their homes together carrying bridles, intending to catch their saddle ponies. A cougar leaped on the girl, Doreen, first, and the boy, Tony, jumped on the cougar's back, after which the cougar began to attack him, tearing Tony's scalp. Then Doreen took the offensive and struck at the cougar with her bridle, eventually driving the cougar off. The cougar was later killed and both children received the Albert Medal for their bravery. Seton and the *Daily Colonist* stated that the cougar was old, blind, and starving. Beier claims that the cougar was two and one-half years old. Hornaday (1925, 294) stated that the cougar weighed about seventy-five pounds, and had cataracts.

Vancouver Sun, June 19, 1931. Mrs. David Wishart was about to place her three-month-old infant on the outside, and sunny, porch to nap on a cot as she had been doing for the past month. Her husband looked out the kitchen window only to see a cougar on the roof of an attached lean-to about to spring on the infant and its mother. Mr. Wishart went for his rifle, and his wife then also saw the cougar and screamed. The cougar was apparently frightened by the noise and fled the area.

Reported in the *Literary Digest* 111, Oct. 24, 1931. Mattern was attacked along the railway that served a logging camp. The cougar was later shot. Also reported by H. L. Dillaway in the *Philadelphia Public Ledger Magazine* (August 1931).

Beier (1991, 404) and DuFresne (1955, 86). DuFresne adds that the victim was attacked on a village street while riding his bicycle.

Beier (1991, 404) and DuFresne (1955, 86). DuFresne indicated that the man's name was Johnsen, and that he was a logger who was at work when he was attacked. Two other loggers came to his assistance with axes and were able to free him. The cougar was killed by a policeman the following day.

John Lesowski (1967, 106–7), Ellis (1971, 67), Ben East (1970, 180–81). Carson was returning to his cabin when the cougar tore out of the brush and leaped at him, but instead struck a small tree that was in her way. Attempting to spring again, Carson then shot her. Carson indicated that the cougar was large, healthy, and it was apparent (udders full of milk) that she had young nearby.

Robert Froman (1961, 71–72), Clarke (1969, 159). Saulnier, a woodsman working alone, went to a brook for a drink, and while he was lying down, the cougar jumped on his back, fastening its teeth in the muscles of his right shoulder. After receiving some additional injuries he was able to escape and make his way back to his camp. He said that the cougar was about "six feet overall."

		Victim			Cougar		
Date	Location	Name	Sex	Age	Sex	Age	Weight
Aug. 1950	Naimo, Vancouver Island, B.C., Canada	Churchhill/ Churchhill	M/F	6/5	unk.	unk.	unk.
Jan. 1951	Kelsey Bay-Sayward area, near Campbell River, Vancouver Island, B.C., Canada	McLean	M	63	F	1–1/2	unk.
May 1951	Boston Bar, B.C., Canada	Unknown	M	Adult	unk.	unk.	unk.
July 1951	Northern Idaho	Peterson	F	2	unk.	unk.	unk.
July 1951	Squamish, B.C., Canada	Wyssen	M	29	F	unk.	unk.
Dec. 1951	West Side of Alberni Inlet, Vancouver Island, B.C., Canada	Littleton	M	Adult	unk (3)	unk. (3)	unk.(3)
March 1952	Holberg Inlet near the northern tip of Vancouver Island, B.C., Canada	Hansen	F	Adult	unk.	unk.	unk.

Vancouver Sun, August 4, 1950. Jimmy and Sandra were playing near their home when their mother observed a cougar about to spring on them from behind a fence. She scared the large cat away and the cougar was later shot by a provincial policeman while it was still by their home.

Vancouver Daily Colonist and the *Vancouver Sun*, Jan. 27, 1951, Froman (1961, 82–83), DuFresne (1955, 47, 86), Bonnie Brown (1957, 90), Beier (1991, 404). McLean, a trapper, reported that the cougar leaped through a window to attack him. He grabbed a butcher knife off of his kitchen table and stabbed the cat repeatedly. He made his escape and left the wounded cat locked in the cabin. The cougar, reportedly of medium size, was later shot while still in the cabin. McLean received lacerations and bite marks on arms and body.

DuFresne (1955, 86), Froman (1961, 83). DuFresne states that the victim stepped out of his door only to see that a cougar was on his porch. DuFresne said that the cougar immediately attacked the man, knocking him down and mauling him. His dog came on the run, barking, and the cougar turned his attention to the dog, permitting the man to reach the safety of his home. After killing the dog, the cougar left.

Froman (1961, 84–85). A cougar reportedly picked up two-year-old Jane Peterson, trotted into the woods with her, then dropped her unharmed when pursued by Jane's mother and two young brothers.

Beier (1991, 404). Beier indicates that the attack was by an adult female cougar with her cub.

Daily Colonist, Dec. 8, 1951. William Littleton was at work near the Grumback Logging Co. operations when he was confronted by three cougars that he claimed were "hungry looking." He only had a small hatchet with him, but he lit fire to some of his notes and threw them and rocks at the cougars. He called for help and when someone then arrived two of the cougars left. The other cougar stayed until more crew members arrived. Littleton indicated that the "the skin on their bellies was flapping."

Vancouver Sun and *Daily Colonist*, May 13, 1952. Through a wireless report to the RCMP, Mrs. Carl Hansen stated that she was confronted by a cougar that had first gone for her and then her small dog. A contract hunter was unable to locate the cougar. Mrs. Hansen was not injured.

			Victim			Cougar	
Date	Location	Name	Sex	Age	Sex	Age	Weight
March 1953	Victoria Lake, Vancouver Island, B.C., Canada	Walters/ Richmond	M/M	43/Adult	F	2	110
April 1953	Along Lost Mine Trail, Big Bend National Park, Texas	Unknown	M	Adult	unk.	unk.	unk.
June 1953	Near Campbell River, Vancouver Island, B.C., Canada	Coon	F	26	F	unk.	70
July 1957	Near Squamish, Vancouver, B.C., Canada	Wyssen	M	26	unk. (5)	unk. (5)	unk. (5)
July 1958	Kelsey Bay-Sayward area near Campbell River, Vancouver Island, B.C., Canada	Despins	F	3	unk (3)	unk. (3)	unk. (3)
March 1962	Hinton, Alberta, Canada	Kilbreath	M	6	unk.	unk.	30

Vancouver Sun, Mar. 2, 1953, Lesowski (1967, 107), Ellis (1971, 67), Ben East (1970, 181–83), Beier (1991, 404), DuFresne (1955, 88), and Nicol (1958, 16–17). Walters and Richmond were on a fishing trip with Richmond's children when Walters was attacked while gathering bark for a campfire. While struggling with the cat, Walters called for help, and Richmond responded. Armed with a Boy Scout hatchet, Richmond killed the cougar. Walters suffered severe injuries, but Richmond only received a minor scratch. East indicated that the cougar was an adult, but thin. The *Vancouver Sun* stated that the cougar measured sixty-eight inches in length.

R. Skiles, BBNP, July 21, 1997, Packard (1991, 3), Beier (1991, 404). An unnamed man was walking along the Lost Mine Trail when a cougar approached and grabbed him by his pant leg. His shouts and aggressive actions drove the cat away. The cougar was shot the following day by park ranger G. Sholly.

Vancouver Sun, June 12, 1953, DuFresne (1955, 86), Beier (1991, 404). DuFresne stated that the cougar was prowling through the town and attacked Mrs. Coon, crushing her hand in its jaws, clawed her right shoulder, and peeled the flesh from her ribs. Mrs. Coon's husband, Peter, ran for help and brought Lawrence Landsdowne who pulled the cat off of Mrs. Coon. The cougar was later killed by a hunter with dogs.

Vancouver Sun, July 3, 1957. Chris Wyssen was operating a bulldozer in a logging operation about eight miles north of Squamish when he was attacked by five gaunt cougars. One of the cougars managed to tear off his pants and scratch his legs before he could make his escape on his dozer. Two of the cougars were shot immediately by a hunting party. The others were killed later. The owner of the logging operation said he believed that "the cougars had not eaten for a month." The two that were immediately shot were stated to be about five feet long and weighed not more than thirty pounds each.

Vancouver Daily Colonist, July 25, 1958. On July 24, Paul Despins went out in his yard, where his young daughter was playing, and saw three cougars circling the little girl. He picked her up, rushed her into the house, and returned with a gun, killing the largest of the three cats. The other two cougars fled.

Beier (1991, 405), Caras (1964, 25–26), Assoc. Press, March 1962. Brian Kilbreath was playing two hundred yards from his home when a young cougar jumped him. A neighbor woman pulled the cat off, but not before Kilbreath had received claw marks on his face and a scratch to one eye. The young cougar was later killed. Caras indicates that Bruce Wright informed him that "it was a half-grown cub, in very poor condition, weighing little more than thirty pounds." Beier reported that it was one and a half years old but body mass was below normal.

		Victim			Cougar		
Date	Location	Name	Sex	Age	Sex	Age	Weight
July 1962	Mahood District, northern Vancouver Island, B.C., Canada	Uhrig	F/F	Child/Child	unk.	unk.	unk.
Aug. 1962	Deception Point, Mahood District, northern Vancouver Island, B.C., Canada	Naismith	F	Adult	unk.	unk.	unk.
June 1963	Near Prince George, B.C., Canada	Moore	M	6	M	1+	unk.
March 1965	Clinton, B.C., Canada	Simpkins	M	15	F	3	70
June 1966	Near Armstrong, B.C., Canada	Nash	M	16	unk.	unk.	unk.
Oct. 1966	Chilcotin, B.C., Canada	Unknown	M	Adult	M	adult	unk.
Sept. 1969	Port Alberni, Vancouver Island B.C., Canada	Zimmerman	M	13	unk.	unk.	unk.

Vancouver Sun, Aug. 2, 1962. While her two young girls played in their yard, Mrs. Robert Uhrig reported seeing a cougar snarling at them, holding its face pressed against their picket fence. She snatched up the two little girls and ran into the house with them. Her brother, who was in the home, grabbed a gun and shot the cougar. The animal was reported to be quite thin.

Vancouver Sun, Aug. 2, 1962. Mrs. Grace Naismith was in her yard with her dog, when a reportedly scrawny cougar attacked. Mrs. Naismith kicked the cat and knocked it sprawling, after which it retreated to the brush. The dog was mauled, but Mrs. Naismith received no injuries. The cougar was later tracked down and killed.

Vancouver Sun, June 18, 1963, Beier (1991, 405). Millworker Robert Moore and his three children were returning to their home from a fishing trip when a cougar attacked from the bushes, sinking its fangs into the back of Bobbie Moore. Bobbie's two siblings, Michael, eight, and Diana, six, charged the cougar, Michael wielding a shovel and Diana throwing their fish at it. The children's shouts were heard by their mother, who then called her husband for help. By the time he arrived at the scene of the attack the cougar had fled. The father indicated that from the children's description, the animal must have been about one year old. Beier indicated that the cougar was also considered underweight.

Lesowski (1967, 107-8), Ben East (1970, 183–85), Beier (1991, 405), Ellis (1971, 67). John Simpkins was helping Jim Baker build a fence on his ranch when a cougar, in a single leap of fifteen feet, landed on his back. Baker stabbed the cat with a pocket knife and pulled the cat off, but not before young Simpkins received lacerations to his face, head, and arm. The cougar believed to be responsible for the attack was later killed. Lesowski and Ellis both stated that the cougar was starving—skin and bones.

Vancouver Sun, June 18, 1966. Ken Nash went to get his father's cows when he was chased by a cougar. He lost his rubber boot and when the cougar stopped to chew it he was able to make it back to the Nash farmhome. Ken's father shot the cougar and pieces of the boot was found in its stomach along with the remains of a small animal. A conservation officer who performed an autopsy on the cougar said that it was "abnormally lean."

Beier (1991, 405). Beier reported that the cougar was underweight.

Beier (1991, 405).

Date	Location	Name	Victim Sex	Age	Cougar Sex	Age	Weight
June 1970	Lewis, Colorado	Imel	M	2	M	adult	unk.
June 1970	Kootenay National Park, B.C., Canada	Smith	F	50	unk.	unk.	unk.
Dec. 1970	Harrison Lake, B.C., Canada	Collie	M	29	F	2	unk.
Feb. 1971	Near Banff and Banff National Park, Alberta, Canada	Udall	M	Adult	unk.	adult	unk.
July 1971	Eureka County, Nevada	Bird/Sieh	M/M	Adult/ Adult	F	adult	70
June 1972	Ralph River campsite, Strathcona Park, Vancouver Island, B.C., Canada	Unknown	unk.	Infant	unk.	unk.	unk.
June 1972	Strathcona Park, Vancouver Island, B.C., Canada	Hurford	M	25	unk.	unk.	unk.

Beier (1991, 405). Tel. interview with Ms. M. Imel, June 12, 1997. Travis Imel was playing in a car in his grandparents' garage. He got out of the car and saw an animal that he thought was a large yellow dog. He reached out to touch the animal when it swatted at him several times and then bit him in the leg. His cries were heard by his grandmother, who stared the cougar down, locked the garage doors, and called for help. A neighbor, who was a game warden, responded and tranquilized the cougar and took it away. In attempting to move it again, the cat received too large a drug dose and died. The cougar was otherwise in good health and of normal body weight.

Vancouver Sun, Jan. 3, 1971, Ellis (1971, 110), Beier (1991, 405). The Smith woman, a member of a climbing-and-hiking club, was attacked while walking a trail. She used a backpack as a buffer, and received only gashes above her elbow. Upon the approach of other members of the hiking party the cougar ran away.

Vancouver Sun, Jan. 3, 1971, Beier (1991, 405). Dennis Collie was returning to his bunkhouse at a logging camp near Ten Mile Camp when he was attacked. The cougar bit him on the chin and clawed him rather severely before the animal was shot. Beier states that the cougar's body weight was estimated to be normal for its age.

Udall (1971, 65, 116, 121–22). Udall referred to the cougar as "he" and also suggested that it was a large cat, weighing perhaps 180 pounds. But later in his article he said the cougar was "lean and hungry looking." Turbak (1986, 29) also provided a report about a "young man" who was snowshoeing alone near Banff and was seriously threatened by a cougar.

Beier (1991, 405). Tel. report June 12, 1997, Div. of Wildlife memorandum June 14, 1997, from Game Warden Dale Elliott. Dennis Bird and Kerry Sieh were geology students who were exploring the north side of Roberts Mountain. As they walked through Dry Canyon, Mr. Bird was attacked and knocked over a ledge. The cougar pawed him and then attacked Sieh, who was able to scare the cat away by throwing rocks at it. Bird received scratches to the top of his head and his shoulders. Representatives from Animal Damage Control, with dogs, later killed the female cougar and transported her three kittens to the Hogle Zoo in Salt Lake City. Beier states that the cougar's body weight was estimated to be normal for its age.

Dan Dwyer, B.C. Fish and Game, July 31, 1997, Beier (1991, 405). Dwyer reports that a "baby survived a mauling at a Ralph River campsite, cougar was not located." Dwyer suggests that this incident occurred in 1970 rather than 1972 as claimed by Beier.

Dan Dwyer, B.C. Fish and Game, July 31, 1997, Beier (1991, 405). Dwyer stated that Hurford was mauled by a cougar while he was still in his sleeping bag. This attack occurred one week after the Ralph River incident above. Cougar was not located. This was also recorded by Fish and Game as a 1970 incident rather than in 1972 as claimed by Beier.

Date	Location	Name	Victim Sex	Age	Cougar Sex	Age	Weight
July 1972	Campbell Lake, Vancouver Island, B.C., Canada	Kelly	M	8	unk.	unk.	unk.
April 1973	Spanish Peaks Wilderness Area, west of Trinidad, Colorado	Paintin	M	31	M	2	unk.
Sept. 1973	Campsite in the Oak Creek area, about five miles from Cano City, Colorado	Hodges	M	Adult	M/M/ unk.	unk./ unk./ unk.	unk./ unk./ unk.
Oct. 1973	Trujillo Creek drainage west of Aguilar, Colorado	Keller	M	Adult	M/M	adult/ adult	135/120

Daily Colonist, July 27, 1972, Beier (1991, 405). Young Robert and his brother Charles were returning to their campsite from a swim when a cougar attacked Robert. Charles ran for help, and when his mother heard his shouts she ran to help Robert. Her screams startled the animal as it was dragging Robert toward the woods and it fled. The cougar was estimated to weigh at least one hundred pounds. Robert was critically mauled and had to undergo plastic surgery for his extensive head injuries.

Denver Post, Nov. 4, 1973, Lewis (1976, 16). Bob Paintin, a Colorado Division of Wildlife conservation aide, was testing the range of his new two-way radio when his progress through heavy snow was stopped by mechanical problems in the drive train of his truck. Paintin called in for assistance and while he was waiting he elected to take some "target practice" with his service revolver on a nearby tree limb. He then thought he should look under the truck to see if he could see what the problem was. As he got down on his hands and knees he heard a growl. Thinking it was a bear, he straightened up only to look into the eyes of a cougar standing only twenty feet from him. Since it appeared that the cougar was planning to attack, Paintin shot at it with his service pistol. He shot a second time, then went into his truck and retrieved a .22 rifle and shot it in the head. An autopsy revealed the cougar's esophagus was full of porcupine quills.

Denver Post, Nov. 4, 1973. Richard Hodges of Sedalia, Colo., his wife, and their three children were in their sleeping bags at 1 A.M. when movement near his camp awakened him. He aimed a flashlight over the camp and discovered a crouching cougar. He reached for a shotgun and fired when the cougar started for him. Hearing a second cougar prowling about, Hodges and his wife built up their campfire. The cat stayed around the camp and circled toward some horses that the Hodges had with them. Going to protect the horses, Hodges spied the second cougar ready to spring and killed it with the shotgun. A third cougar was also near the camp but soon left. Wildlife conservation officers speculated that the cougars were attracted by an injury earlier suffered by one of the horses, but were unable to explain why the three cougars were traveling together nor why they would be willing to surround the camp.

Denver Post, Nov. 4, 1973. Carl Keller, a Colorado State conservation officer, was hunting deer when he heard a "scraping noise" behind him. Turning, he saw the head and neck of a cougar staring down at him from a rock a short distance away. It appeared that the cougar was about to pounce on him. Keller rolled to one side and fired at the cat, striking it in the side. He followed up with another shot, killing a large male cougar he estimated to weigh 135 pounds. An inspecting officer indicated that the cougar was already in the air when the first shot hit the cat. When Keller walked down to inspect the dead cougar he was confronted by another cougar that was coiled and ready to pounce. He was able to get a shot off before the cougar leaped at him, striking it in the face and killing it instantly. It was reported to be another male, weighing approximately 120 pounds. Colorado state wildlife investigating officers agreed that both cougars were in the attack mode and that Keller acted in self-defense.

			Victim			Cougar	
Date	Location	Name	Sex	Age	Sex	Age	Weight
Nov. 1974	Near Terrero, New Mexico	Mendoza	M	Adult	F	2–3	unk.
June 1975	Near the Polder Landing on the Pitt River, adjacent to Coquitlam, B.C., Canada	Jones	M	8	M	Adult	130
Dec. 1976	Near Rye, Colorado	Morgan	M	14	F	1–1/2	66
June 1977	Near Enumclaw, Washington	O'Neal/ O'Neal	F/F	28/3	M	1–1/3	69
Nov. 1978	Along the Lost Mine Trail Big Bend National Park, Texas	Rives/Rives	M/M	Adult/3	unk.	adult	unk.

Rocky Mountain News, Nov. 7, 1974. Mendoza was a bowhunter who was after deer when he saw the cougar crouched to spring at him. Not having time to fit an arrow in his bow, he merely stabbed the cat with an arrow. Agents with dogs from Fish and Game later shot the animal. Reports indicated that the cougar was healthy but had an empty stomach.

Vancouver Sun, June 2, 1975, Beier (1991, 405). Wiliam Atsma, his wife, and her four children had been camped on the beach, and were planning to hike up a nearby mountain. Eight-year-old Kevin Jones and his thirteen-year-old sister Marilyn went on ahead. Marilyn came running back screaming about a cougar and it attacking Kevin. Atsma grabbed an oar and went to Kevin's aid, striking at the cat and hollering. The cougar circled around Atsma, but instead of attacking Atsma or going for the boy's body, it left. The boy was seriously injured. Animal-control officer Jack Lay later tracked the cougar with dogs, and, after it was treed, he killed it.

Rocky Mountain News, Dec. 24, 1976, *Denver Post*, Dec. 23 and 24, 1976, Beier (1991, 405), Saile (1977, 66–67). Thane Morgan was snowshoeing in the foothills west of Pueblo, Colo., when he was attacked by a cougar. Young Morgan had a hunting knife in his backpack and used it to defend himself. Although he seriously wounded the cat, causing it to retreat, Thane received bites to his face, scalp, and hand, receiving over a thousand stitches. A nearby resident shot the animal. Later reports indicated that the cougar that attacked Thane was a yearling female, in good shape, but lean at sixty-six pounds and blind in one eye.

Enumclaw Courier-Herald, June 30, 1977, Beier (1991, 405). Mrs. Cheri Lee O'Neal was sunbathing on a log near the Green Water River while her young daughter was wading nearby. The cougar apparently stalked the mother, pouncing on her and pulling her from the log onto the ground. Mrs. O'Neal fought with the cat, and then it turned its attention to young Keri. Their screams brought Mrs. O'Neal's husband Don to the scene, and upon his approach, the cougar fled. The cougar was later killed. It was reported that the cougar "seemed to be quite thin. Its teeth were in good shape, but its stomach was empty." Mrs. O'Neal suffered bites and scratches to her back, thigh, and arm, as well as a mutilated left thumb. Keri's injuries were less severe.

R. Skiles, BBNP, July 21, 1997, BBNP Case Incident Record 000556, dated Nov. 11, 1978. Mr. T. Rives and his family were walking along the Lost Mine Trail early in the afternoon, and after leaving the upper end of the trail, Rives said, a "large, purring, tail-waving lion" ran toward his three-year-old son. The father ran toward the cougar and thrust his son in back of him and "stood with the lion inches from him, face-to-face." After a few moments it walked off the trail and remained in the bushes.

			Victim			Cougar	
Date	Location	Name	Sex	Age	Sex	Age	Weight
Nov. 1978	Along the Lost Mine Trail, Big Bend National Park, Texas	Latch/ Latch	M(5) Unk.(3)	Adult/ Child(4)	unk.	adult	unk.
Nov. 1978	Laguna Meadows Trail, Big Bend National Park, Texas	Glenn	M	7	unk.	adult	unk.
Feb. 1979	Boston Bar, B.C., Canada	Fife	F	9	F	5	unk.
Aug. 1979	Port Hardy, Vancouver Island, B.C., Canada	Walkus	F	4	F	unk.	unk.
May 1981	Near Canyon Church Camp, Waterton Lakes National Park, Alberta, Canada	Orchard	M	12	F	1+	unk.

R. Skiles, BBNP, July 21, 1997, Packard (1991, 3), BBNP Case Incident Record 00556, dated Nov. 11, 1978, Beier (1991, 405). Four boys, accompanied by their four fathers, were hiking along the Lost Mine Trail. The boys, who ranged from six to nine years of age, had strolled ahead, temporarily out of sight. Suddenly two of the boys reappeared, running down the trail toward the four men, with a cougar chasing them. The elder Latch ran up the trail, placing himself between the two boys and the cougar. As the cougar continued to approach, Latch began swinging a red parka at the cougar. When it continued its advance, Latch struck it in the face with the parka. It then walked off the trail and "hunkered-down" in the brush. The four boys indicated that the cougar jumped down off a cliff into their midst, thus scattering the boys.

R. Skiles, BBNP, July 21, 1997, BBNP Case Incident Record 000556, dated 11/22/78. Mr. Bennie Glenn and his family were walking back from Laguna Meadow, and approximately two and a half miles above the basin, Mrs. Glenn saw a "yellow streak" come up the trail toward her two young sons, Phillip and Bennie Jr. The cougar apparently had its eye on seven-year-old Phillip. When Phillip began screaming, both parents ran toward the boy only to see a large cougar "crouching and snarling" a short distance from Phillip. Glenn tried to frighten the cat away by waving a stick, and then he threw a rock at it, hitting the cat in the foot, which seemed only to irritate it further. The cougar followed the family for more than a quarter of a mile, assuming attack positions and snarling at them with teeth bared. The family felt that the cougar's attention was primarily directed toward young Phillip. A later search by park rangers for the cat was unsuccessful.

Beier (1991, 405). Beier adds that the cougar had a body mass that was less than normal.

Beier (1991, 405). B.C. Ministry of Environment, Feb. 26, 1996. The young Walkus girl was on a swing at home when she was attacked. Taken to the hospital, she remained there for four days before she could return home. A B.C. wildlife-control officer killed the cougar responsible. Beier adds that the cougar may have had a body mass less than normal.

R. A. Watt, *Parks Canada*, June 26, 1997, Beier (1991, 405). On May 27, a church group was on a short hike and Warren Orchard was lagging somewhat behind. He heard something moving in the bush and stopped to see what it was. A cougar approached him from the rear, rolled over on its back, and when Warren yelled at it, it clawed at him and then left. It was thought that the sounds of others approaching from the church group may have frightened the cat off. Five stitches were required to close scratches to Orchard's lower leg. Park rangers searched the area and frightened out of the area a female yearling cougar. Beier indicated that the attack was by an adult female with a cub.

Date	Location	Name	Victim Sex	Age	Cougar Sex	Age	Weight
July 1981	Near Lone Mountain, Big Bend National Park, Texas	Atkins	M	Adult	unk.	unk.	unk.
1981	Oyster River, Vancouver Island, B.C., Canada	Unknown	M	Adult	F	1–1/2	unk.
Aug. 1982	Near junction of Bertha Bay and Bertha Lake Trail, Waterton Lakes National Park, Canada	Bisby	M	9	unk.	unk.	unk.
1983	Esperanza, Vancouver Island, B.C., Canada	Unknown	M	Adult	unk.	unk.	unk.
April 1983	Port McNeill, Vancouver Island B.C., Canada	Unknown/ Unknown	M/M	10/11	unk.	unk.	unk.
1983	Holberg, Vancouver Island, B.C., Canada	Unknown	M	16	M	3	unk.
Aug. 1983	Near mile 6, along the Basin Road, adjacent to a park campground, Big Bend National Park, Texas	Unknown/ Unknown	M/M	Child/ Child	unk.	unk.	unk.
April 1984	Junction of South Rim and Park Blue Creek Trails, Big Bend National Park, Texas	Roe	F	Adult	M	1	unk.

R. Skiles, BBNP, July 21, 1997, Packard (1991, 3–4), C. Fleming BBNP, May 25, 1988 and Jan. 5, 1990. On July 25, a female park ranger was receiving riding instructions when her mount bolted. While another ranger gave chase on horseback, ranger D. Atkins ran after them on foot. Atkins noticed a cougar coming out of the brush and it approached him, taking a swipe at his leg. Atkins got a shrub between himself and the cougar and finally hit it with a large rock before it departed.

Beier (1991, 405). B.C. Ministry of Environment indicated that "A man on horse was jumped but not hurt by a spotted adult [?] cougar." A wildlife-control officer later killed the cougar that was presumed responsible for the attack.

R. A. Watt, *Parks Canada*, June 26, 1997, Beier (1991, 405). Adam Bisby was walking ahead of his parents when he was attacked by a cougar. He received minor puncture wounds and scratches. His parents indicated that Adam was stalked and then "mildly" attacked. The cougar was not located even though dogs were used. Beier reports that the cougar was of average bodymass for its age. According to Waterton Lakes Occ. Rept. # 82/265, the cougar was described as small, "about the size of a labrador dog."

Beier (1991, 405). B.C. Ministry of Environment indicates that a "man on bridge [was] jumped by cougar but not seriously injured." A wildlife officer killed the cougar.

B.C. Ministry of Environment, Feb. 26, 1996, Beier (1991, 405). Beier indicated that the attack occurred at Port Alice. B.C. Ministry states, "Three boys chased by a cougar in second growth on hill above town site. One boy was mauled on arm and another mauled on leg. Wildlife Control killed cougar."

Beier (1991, 405). B.C. Ministry of Environment indicates that the boy was attacked on a bike on a C.A.F. Base entrance road. "Oncoming vehicle scared cougar away. Boy not seriously hurt. Wildlife Control Officer killed cougar."

R. Skiles, BBNP, July 21, 1997, Packard (1991, 3–4). On August 8, two young boys were pushing their bicycles up the road when a cougar came out of the bushes after them. It followed them for a short distance, gradually getting closer as the boys picked up the pace. Oncoming road traffic caused the cougar to leave before it could close.

R. Skiles, BBNP, July 21, 1997, Packard (1991, 3–4), Beier (1991, 405). Ranger Susan Roe was walking along the South Rim Trail and looked up in time to see a cougar about to spring. He leaped and hit her with his shoulder, knocking her to the ground and in the process of falling Roe twisted her ankle. Roe claimed that the cat was a male, and still a juvenile because she said that there were still detectable spots on his body. She also claimed that the cat weighed about sixty-five pounds, which would seem to be unusually large for a cougar still showing spots.

Date	Location	Name	Victim Sex	Age	Cougar Sex	Age	Weight
Aug. 1984	Along the Basin Loop Trail, Big Bend National Park, Texas	Vaught/ Brown	M/M	9/Adult	M	1–3/4	85
May 1985	Pacific Rim Natl. Park, Vancouver Island, B.C., Canada	Wilson	M	12	unk.	unk.	unk.
Aug. 1985	Camp Thunderbird, Glinz Lake Area, Sooke, Vancouver Island, B.C., Canada	Parker	F	10	M	1–1/2	77
March 1986	Ronald W. Caspers Wilderness Park, Orange County, California	Small	F	5	M	2	unk.
Aug. 1986	Vicinity of Siskiyou National Forest, near Port Orford, southwest Oregon	Bess	M	Adult	M	4–5	150
Oct. 1986	Ronald W. Caspers Wilderness Park, Orange County, California	Mellon	M	6	unk.	unk.	unk.

Mueller (1985, 50–51, 108–11), Packard (1991, 3–4), Beier (1991, 405). David Vaught, accompanied by his mother, Kim Brown, and his stepfather, Chris Brown, just arrived in the park and were walking a trail when a cougar attacked David. With the cougar astride David, Chris Brown, with considerable effort, was able to pull the cougar off and seek medical attention for David. The cougar was tracked and killed by park rangers and a state predator hunter and trapper with dogs. Beier commented that the cougar had a bodymass less than normal for its age.

Vancouver Sun, Aug. 6, 1985, Beier, 1991, 405). Johnny Wilson was with his mother and aunt on the West Coast Trail when he was attacked. The cougar tried to drag young Wilson away but it was beaten back by the boy's mother and aunt. B.C. Ministry of Environment indicates that the boy "suffered scalp lacerations and puncture wounds to the neck." The cougar was not located.

Vancouver Sun, Aug. 6, 1985, Worth (1991, 81), Beier (1991, 405). Worth and Beier indicate that the cougar was of average size for its age. The *Sun* stated that it weighed thirty-five kilograms (seventy-seven pounds). Alyson Parker and some of her young campmates were walking a trail near the YM/YWCA camp, when the cougar attacked Alyson. The screams of the children brought the girl's camp counselor, nineteen-year-old Lila Lifely, to the scene of the attack. As the cougar was trying to drag Alyson away, Lila and one of the other counselors were able to drive the cat away and provide first aid to the stricken girl. The cougar was killed after three days of hunting. B.C. Ministry of Environment indicated that the girl "suffered skull punctures, scalp lacerations and 15 punctures to the neck."

Los Angeles Times, Feb. 8, 1989, Beier (1991, 406). Laura Small was wading in a stream and searching for tadpoles when she was attacked. Saved by a hiker with a stick, Laura was severely injured, including loss of sight in one eye.

Range (1987, 34–37). Ken Bess was bowhunting for elk when he was attacked by a very large cougar. The cougar was warned by Bess several times, and Bess used his bow to ward off the initial assault of the cat. After several attacks Bess had no choice but to kill the cougar. The Oregon Department of Fish and Wildlife could find no reason for the attack.

Laycock (1988, 94–95), Beier (1991, 405), *Los Angeles Times*, Feb. 2, 1989; Aug. 8, 15, and 24, 1991; and Feb. 6, 1992 (mainly Small). Timothy Mellon was on an outing with his family when he stopped to tie his shoe. As soon as he bent down, a cougar leaped upon him and seized the boy's head in its mouth. Timothy's father, armed with a knife, responded to his son's screams and the cougar then released its grip on the boy's head and fled. The cougar was not located.

			Victim			Cougar	
Date	Location	Name	Sex	Age	Sex	Age	Weight
April 1987	Along the Basin Loop Trail, Big Bend National Park, Texas	Burt	F	31	M	1–1/4	unk.
May 1988	Near Payson, Arizona	Fuller	F	6	F	1–1/2	50
May 1988	Mount Wrightson, Santa Rita Mountains, Arizona	Dorsey	M	27	M	7–8 mo.	30
Sept. 1988	Aquarius Plateau area, Dixie National Forest, Southern Utah	Treadwell	M	Adult	M	2	125
Jan. 1989	Hot Springs Cove, Tofino, Vancouver Island, B.C., Canada	Lucas	M	28	F	2	unk.
April 1989	Canyon Lake, near the Palo Verde boat ramp, Arizona	Walsh	M	5	unk.	unk.	unk.

Beier (1991, 406), Bolgiano (1995, 114). A cougar approached a family of three walking the trails. The father picked up their small child and stared at the cat. The mother, however, elected to run and was subsequently attacked. Her wounds were minor. The cougar was later tracked and killed. Beier indicates that the cougar's body mass was below average for its age. Bolgiano (1995, 114) indicated that the attack occurred in 1986. An abstract report by Carl M. Fleming (BBNP) dated May 25, 1988, and updated Jan. 5, 1990, indicated that the cougar had been radio-collared in January 1987, when it was eleven to twelve months old; its weight was seventy-five pounds.

Arizona Republic, June 1, 1988. Worth (1991, 56, 79), Beier (1991, 406). Sarah Fuller was playing with her older sister outside their cabin near Whispering Pines when she was attacked by a cougar. Her stepfather rushed to help, knocked the cougar off the girl, and later was able to shoot it. Sarah suffered puncture wounds on her right shoulder, arm, and left ear. Beier indicates that the cougar's body mass was below average for its age. Worth suggested that the cougar responsible for the attack was a female one to two years old and between thirty and forty pounds in weight.

Arizona Republic, May 26 and June 4, 1988. After attempting to kill a dog belonging to campers, a cougar approached Dan Dorsey and when it was within twenty feet it crouched to spring, at which time Dorsey threw rocks and yelled at the cougar. The cat backed off slightly but trailed Dorsey as he made his escape. A seven-to-eight-month-old cougar later killed (June 4, 1988) by a N.M.Game and Fish hunter, with dogs, was presumed to be the animal responsible.

Treadwell (1990, 24, 84–87). Joseph Treadwell was bowhunting deer when he discovered that he was being stalked by a cougar. When the cat crouched, Treadwell sent an arrow toward it. The arrow skimmed off the cougar, and Treadwell released another arrow, which penetrated the cougar's shoulder. After contacting Utah wildlife authorities they indicated that the cougar, a healthy two-year-old male, was apparently frustrated by a recent unsuccessful attempt at a deer.

Beier (1991, 406). Beier indicates that the cougar's body mass was below average for its age. B.C. Ministry of Environment indicated that an adult male was attacked outside his cabin while gathering firewood. Another resident scared off the cougar, which was later killed.

Arizona Republic, May 1, 1989. Joshua Walsh was hiking up a little hill with his six-year-old brother when a cougar rushed them and seized Joshua by the head, shook him, and started to drag him off. Joshua's father hit the animal with a rock and the cougar dropped the boy. Joshua required more than a hundred stitches to close the wounds to his head and to reattach his ear. The cougar was reported to be "about four feet long, not including the tail."

| | | | Victim | | | Cougar | |
Date	Location	Name	Sex	Age	Sex	Age	Weight
March 1990	In the vicinity of Boulder Meadows, Camp # 4, Big Bend National Park, Texas	Stevens	M	Adult	unk.	unk.	unk.
March 1990	Along the Basin Loop Trail, Big Bend National Park, Texas	McNab	M	2	M	1+	unk.
June 1990	Four-Mile Canyon, west of Boulder, Colorado	Walters	F	28	F	unk.	unk.
July 1990	Near Kalispell, Montana	Quinn	M	Adult	unk.	adult	unk.
July 1990	Glacier National Park, Montana	O'Hare	M	9	M	1–1/4	40
March 1991	Nellis Air Force Range, Nevada Test Site, southwest Nevada	Sacthre	F	mid-20's	F	2–1/2	70

R. Skiles, BBNP July 21, 1997, Packard (1991, 3–4). On March 3, 1990, Shawn Stevens was near his campsite when he saw a cougar chasing a deer. Shortly thereafter he heard a chirping sound and then saw a cougar walking through the campground. He took to a tree, and about five minutes later two more cougars entered the campground and he could hear yet another cougar in the bushes. Not long after he saw a cougar on the ground under his tree, and shortly after the cat was in the tree, near his feet. He kicked the cougar in the head and screamed. The cougar then left the tree. He continually called for help and remained in the tree until the following morning.

R. Skiles, BBNP July 21, 1997, Packard (1991, 3–4). On March 19, Connie McNab was walking along the Basin Loop Trail with her husband, two-year-old son, and six-year-old daughter. She and her two children were somewhat ahead of her husband when she saw a cougar on the trail, crouched, with bared teeth, and ready to spring upon her young son. She quickly ran to the boy, picked him up, and held her ground. The daughter ran to get her father, and when the father and another hiker approached the cougar quickly left. Park rangers later captured the cat, placing a collar on it, and when it attacked a dog three months later it was relocated.

McGraw and Sanger, *Los Angeles Times*, March 1, 1992, report indicated that the attack involved two cougars. Turback (1991, 73–74), Beier (1991, 406). Beier adds that the attack was by an adult female and her cub. Lynda Walters was hiking along a trail when she came upon a cougar that was crouched down waiting for her. She shouted and threw rocks at the animal but it continued to stalk her. She then saw another cougar moving toward her and she retreated up the side of the canyon, throwing rocks and branches at the cats. She was able to climb a tree, and one of the climbing cats was able to reach her leg, inflicting two deep lacerations. By jabbing at them she was able to keep them off of her until the cougars decided to leave. The cougars were not caught.

The *Missoula, Montana, Missoulian* reported on July 13, 1990, in an article by Gregg Lakes, that "most recently, a game warden killed a lion near Kalispell on Wednesday as it was attacking him." *Rocky Mountain News*, Sept. 23, 1990, said that "he turned to see a large cougar stalking him. The warden fired two shots from his service revolver, but the lion didn't stop, so he used his shotgun to drop it right at his feet." Also, Worth (1991, 79).

Rocky Mountain News, Sept. 23, 1990. Beier (1991, 406). Worth (1991, 79). Worth reported that the cougar weighed forty pounds and was between twelve and eighteen months of age. The O'Hare boy was bitten on his face and the back of his neck. Beier indicated that the cougar's body mass was below average for its age.

Information provided by Tonapah office and confirmed by Mike Cox, Nevada Division of Wildlife, Las Vegas. Three biologists were involved in research work that placed them near a cougar den. The female cougar elected to attack the female biologist, Mary Sacthre. The cougar was driven off by one of the two male biologists. An ADC tracker with dogs, who was later called in, was threatened by the cougar and when it charged him he shot it in its midair leap.

		Victim			Cougar		
Date	Location	Name	Sex	Age	Sex	Age	Weight
June 1991	Near Arboles, close to New Mexico border, SW Colorado	Swanemyr	M	Adult	unk.	adult	unk.
July 1991	Lillooet, southern B.C., Canada	Allen/ O'Laney/ Leech	M/F/F	2/2/44	unk.	unk.	unk.
? 1992	Nellis Air Force Range, Nuclear Testing Site, south central Nevada	Unknown	unk.	unk.	unk.	unk.	unk.
March 1992	Gaviota State Park, Santa Barbara County, California	Arroyo	M	9	unk.	unk.	unk.
July 1992	West Cracroft Island, adjacent to Robsons Bight, Johnstone Strait, Vancouver Island, B.C., Canada	Unknown	F	29	unk.	unk.	unk.
Aug. 1992	Glacier National Park, Montana	Moore	M	12	M	unk.	98
Sept. 1992	Angeles National Forest, near Altedena, California	Massey/ Mueller	M/M	28/31	unk.	unk.	unk.

Deborah Frazier, *Rocky Mountain News*, July 20, 1991. Bob Swanemyr, a farmer, while walking with his dog, was jumped by a cougar. The only injury suffered by Swanemyr was a bruised shoulder. Swanemyr and his dog chased the cougar up a tree. Although a hunter with dogs was hired, no information was received as to whether or not the cougar was ever killed. Swanemyr reported that the cougar weighed about one hundred pounds.

Mary Murray (1993, 87–92), Schuyler (1992, 220, 222). Five children in a day-care center were confronted by a young cougar while they were on a picnic. Instead of immediately attacking, it began licking the face of two-year-old Mikey Allen, and when disturbed by the day-care center operator Larrance Leech, it clawed both Allen and Leech as well as a two-year-old girl, Lisa O'Laney. Because of Leech's bravery in defending her charges, no one was seriously hurt. The cougar was reportedly killed eight days later by a neighbor woman armed with a shotgun.

Information provided by Tonapah office and Las Vegas office of the Nevada Division of Wildlife indicated that an attack did occur but they were unable to provide other than the most limited of information regarding the cougar attack on two geologists.

Riverside, Calif., Press-Enterprise, March 4, 1996. A listing of attacks identified by Amie DeFrain and Becky Hageman. *Los Angeles Times*, April 3, 1995, a listing of attacks put together by Trevor Johnson and Helene Webb. Young Darron Arroyo received only minor injuries as a result of the cougar attack. The cougar was later killed.

B.C. Ministry of Environment Feb. 26, 1996. Victim sustained puncture wounds to her face and thighs. A nearby camper shot the cougar in the face. The cougar could not be located later, even though dogs were used in the search.

Arizona Republic, AP., Aug. 14, 1992. Nathaniel Moore and his father Romano Scaturro had just climbed an embankment off the roadway when the cougar attacked the boy. Scaturro, hearing his son yell, responded, kicking and hollering at the cat. The cougar left. Moore suffered facial cuts and puncture wounds to his chest, right arm, and wrist. The cougar was killed by rangers and trackers.

Phoenix Gazette, Sept. 14, 1992. While hiking along a rocky ridge, Massey and Mueller were charged and eventually cornered by a cougar. A rescuing helicopter scared off the animal. No information as to what may eventually have happened to the cougar.

			Victim			Cougar	
Date	Location	Name	Sex	Age	Sex	Age	Weight
Oct. 1992	On a logging road north of Columbia Falls, Montana	Wensel	M	Adult	M	adult	160
Aug. 1993	Near Wickenburg, Arizona	Irwin	F	53	F	1–1/2	60
Aug. 1993	Los Padres National Forest in Santa Barbara County, California	Foote	M	6	unk.	unk.	unk.
Sept. 1993	Paso Picacho Campground Cuyamaca State Park, California	Kowalski	F	10	F	adult	41
May 1994	Gold River, Vancouver Island, B.C., Canada	Unknown	M	7	M	2	80
May 1994	Along the Pine Creek Trailhead, Mt. Jefferson County, west central Nevada	Werfel	M	Adult	F	adult	unk.
July 1994	Near Apache Lake, Tonto National Forest, Arizona	Humphreys	M	2	unk.	unk.	unk.
Aug. 1994	Near Dos Rios, California	Winslow/ Winslow/ Strehl/ Strehl	F/M/ M/F	48/50/ Adult/48	F	2	60

Jerry A. Lewis (1995, 194) reports that Gene Wensel relayed to him a story of how his brother, Barry Wensel, a top bowhunter, was out after elk when he was attacked by a healthy male cougar. He talked to the cat and there was no doubt that the cougar knew he was a human. The cougar flattened and came for him and he killed it with an arrow at thirty-eight feet. Also in *Bowhunter Magazine* 22 (April/May, 1993): 28–29. A Montana Fish and Game warden reported the confrontation as an attack.

Arizona Republic, Phoenix Gazette, Aug. 21, 1993. While working on her ranch, Merlue Irwin had just finished repairing a cedar fence when she saw a cougar running right at her. When it was about five feet away, it crouched and sprang. Irwin hit it in midair with a cedar post. While Irwin was backing away, the cougar continued to stalk her, but did eventually leave. A friend of Irwin, who was a tracker, used a dog to tree the cat and then shot it.

Los Angeles Times, April 3, 1995. Devon Foote was attacked by a cougar but injuries were minor. Witnesses described what the cougar looked like, but since no paw prints were found California Game and Fish reported it as an unverified attack.

Arizona Republic, Sept. 19, 1993, *Los Angeles Times,* Sept. 19, 1993, Calif. Fish and Game news release, Dec. 24, 1994. The underweight female cougar approached Lisa Kowalski and her dad as they were playing catch within the campground. The cougar then attacked Lisa, biting her once on the buttocks. The cougar was later located and killed by park rangers.

B.C. Ministry of Environment, Feb. 26, 1996. The boy was walking to school with two other children when he was attacked. The other two children could not chase the cougar away and they ran to a nearby home for help. The cougar was later killed by an RCMP officer.

Nevada Division of Wildlife reports that a Mr. Werfel notified them of an attack on him by a cougar on May 27, 1994. Using a stick, Werfel was able to drive off the cougar, although the cougar had managed to take the stick in its mouth at one point and bite the end of the stick off. Also Frank Mullen, *Reno Gazette-Journal,* Jan. 16, 1996.

Phoenix Gazette, July 20, 1994, *Tucson Citizen,* July 20, 1994. While on a camping outing with his family, Jesse Humphreys was sleeping on a mat when a cougar pawed at the boy and seized the mat and attempted to drag young Jesse away. Hearing the boy's cries, his father ran and grabbed the boy away from the cougar. The Humphreys boy needed ten stitches to close a wound to his ear after the attack. Arizona Game and Fish officers decided not to attempt to track the cougar down.

San Jose Mercury News, Aug. 17, 1994, *Phoenix Gazette, Gazette News Service,* Aug., 17, 1994, *Santa Rosa Pr. Democrat,* Aug. 18, 1994. While camping in a remote area of Mendocino County, four campers and their dog were attacked by a cougar that was reportedly rabid. All campers, except for Chuck Strehl, received some injuries. Troy Winslow's thumb was bitten off in the struggle. Mrs. Robin Winslow stabbed the cougar to death with a serrated kitchen knife.

Date	Location	Victim			Cougar		
		Name	Sex	Age	Sex	Age	Weight
Oct. 1994	Gold River, Vancouver, B.C., Canada	McKerracher	M	Adult	unk.	unk.	unk.
Nov. 1994	East Elk Creek, near New Castle, Colorado	Champagne	M	Adult	unk.	unk.	unk.
Dec. 1994	Ute Mountain Ute Indian Reservation, Colorado	Groves	F	25	F	adult	63
Mar. 1995	Mt. Lowe, San Gabriel Mtns., Los Angeles County, above Altadena, Angeles N. Forest, California	Fike	M	27	F	unk.	96
Sept. 1995	Big Meadows, Tonahuto Trail, Rocky Mountain National Park, Colorado	Street	M	47	unk.	adult	unk.
Feb. 1996	Near Little Espinosa Inlet, Zeballos, Vancouver Island, B.C., Canada	Annand	M	36	unk.	unk.	unk.
June 1996	East Shore Trail, Grand Lake, West Side, Rocky Mountain National Park, Colorado	Austin	F	Adult	unk.	unk.	unk.

B.C. Ministry of Environment, Feb. 26, 1996. Off-duty RCMP officer was riding his horse when the cougar jumped out of the bushes at him and his horse. Constable McKerracher kicked at the cougar and was scratched just above the boot of his right leg. Cougar was not located.

Rocky Mountain News, Nov. 16, 1994. Fred Champagne was hunting elk when attacked by a cougar. He shot the cougar, and when a second cougar approached him shot it, too. The shootings were determined by a judge to be appropriate acts of self-defense.

Rocky Mountain News, Dec. 14 and 15, 1994. Ms. Groves was attacked while taking water samples. Her struggle with the cougar began in a stream and ended on the bank. ADC trackers with dogs later killed the cougar.

Riverside, Calif., Press-Enterprise, March 4, 1996. A listing of attacks identified by Amie DeFrain and Becky Hageman, *Los Angeles Times*, April 3, 1995, a listing of attacks put together by Trevor Johnson and Helene Webb. Bolgiano (1995, 131). Scott Fike, an athletic six-foot four bicyclist, was attacked by a cougar. Fike was clawed and bitten on the head before he was able to drive the cougar off by throwing rocks at it. Federal trackers later killed the cougar. The animal was in good health and not starving.

RMNP case incident no. 951759, *Estes Park Trail Gazette*, Oct. 4, 1995, *National Geographic*, Nov. 1996. Photographer Street was jogging on Sept. 13, 1995, when he was surprised by a cougar. Armed with a sharpened stick he took to a tree. After five hours the cougar began to climb after him. He jabbed the cougar with a stick and the cat then fled. RMNP rangers found Street still in the tree at 2:10 A.M.

B.C. Ministry of Environment, Feb. 26, 1996. Logger "was attacked [by] a cougar while falling a tree. The cougar jumped on his back as the logger started to move away from the cut snag." The protective clothing the logger was wearing plus the punches and kicks delivered by the logger, and the appearance of another logger drove the cougar away. A later search for the cougar with dogs was unsuccessful.

Rocky Mountain News and *Denver Post*, July 19, 1997, and D. Caldwell, RMNP, July 23, 1997. Linda Austin, a seasonal park ranger at RMNP, was jogging on a trail when out of the corner of her eye she caught sight of a large tawny form approaching from cover rapidly. She dodged the charge, but received scratches to her right elbow and forearm. When she saw that it was a cougar, she curbed her impulse to run, and yelled. She also picked up a stick. The cougar then left the trail and went back into the underbrush.

		Victim			Cougar		
Date	Location	Name	Sex	Age	Sex	Age	Weight
July 1997	Mesa Verde National Park, Colorado	DeGrave	M	4	M	1+	60
July 1997	Summerland Park area, along the North Inlet Trail, West Side Rocky Mountain National Park, Colorado	Philippi	M	Adult	F	2–1/2	88
Oct. 1997	Walker Ranch Trail, west of Boulder, Colorado	Dunbar	M	25	M	unk.	unk.
Oct. 1997	On Sweetwater Ranch, Cliffs area, near Book Maeser, Utah	Massey	M	64	F	unk.	unk.

Denver Post, July 15, 1997, and *Rocky Mountain News*, July 16, 1997. Rafael DeGrave was with his family hiking a trail within the park when they were alerted by park rangers that a cougar had been seen in the area. The young DeGrave boy and his family were being evacuated to a parking lot when the cougar came out of some underbrush near the footpath and frightened Rafael, who screamed and ran. The cougar immediately gave chase and grabbed the boy by the head and began to drag him off into the brush. The boy's brothers and parents were able to scare the cougar away. The animal was later shot by park rangers. The boy received numerous scratches to his face and his shoulder, a puncture wound to his nose, and a ripped ear. Wildlife officials stated that the young male cougar appeared to be in good health. Mesa Verde information officer Jane Anderson indicated that the cougar was approximately one year old, and weighed about sixty pounds.

Rocky Mountain News and *Denver Post*, July 19, 1997. Seasonal Park Ranger Chris Philippi, who was awaiting the arrival of the coroner in response to the fatal cougar attack on Mark David Miedema, was suddenly confronted by the returning cougar. Philippi stated that the cougar approached to fifteen feet and then crouched to attack. Ranger Philippi fired three shots at the cat with his revolver, hitting it twice. The cougar was later treed and killed by park rangers and a tracker with dogs.

Denver Post, Oct. 23, 1997, *Rocky Mountain News*, Oct. 23 and 24, 1997. Todd Dunbar was riding his trail bike on Oct. 22 when he was confronted by a cougar. Both Dunbar and the cougar were startled, but instead of leaving, the cougar "hunkered down . . . twitched his tail and laid his ears back." Dunbar placed his bike between him and the cat, shouted, and tried to make himself look bigger, but these tactics did not impress the cougar. The cat tried to work its way around the bike, and Dunbar struck out with the bike, hitting the cat on the nose with the rear tire. The cougar jumped back six or seven feet and also hissed at him. Dunbar retreated, throwing sticks and rocks, but the cougar followed. Eventually Dunbar was able to get to a clear place on the trail, mount his bike, and move away. A Colorado Division of Wildlife employee stated that the "lion was probably young and didn't know how to catch prey yet." Dunbar suggested that the cougar may have weighed about ninety pounds.

Denver Post, Nov. 7, 1997. Don Massey was herding cattle on the Sweetwater Ranch, accompanied by his young Labrador dog, when he was confronted by a cougar. His horse bolted after it was clawed. Massey was thrown from the horse and, after a short chase after the horse, the cougar turned its attention to the young dog and to Massey. Grabbing a large cedar branch, Massey attacked the cougar, striking it four times and then making sure it was dead by picking up a large rock and crushing its skull. Massey was clawed on his right thumb when the cougar charged the horse. Massey claimed that the female cougar was a young animal and he estimated its weight at one hundred pounds. A Utah Division of Wildlife Resources employee claimed the cougar and reportedly shipped the head of the animal to the Utah State Health Laboratory to determine if it was rabid. The dog was seriously injured.

| | | | Victim | | Cougar | | |
| | | | | | Cougar | | |
Date	Location	Name	Sex	Age	Sex	Age	Weight
Dec. 1997	Pinhead area, Ronald W. Wilderness Park, Orange County, California	Unknown with children	F	Adult	F	unk.	unk.
May 1998	Carpenter Peak Trail, Roxborough State Park, Jefferson County, Colorado	Peterson	M	24	unk.	unk.	unk.
July 1998	In the vicinity of Marshall Mountain, near Missoula, Montana	Swallow	M	6	M	2-3	unk.

Orange County Register, Jan. 1, 1998, *Denver Post,* Jan. 6, 1998. A group of women and children were approached by a cougar less than a hundred yards from the park's day use area in the early afternoon of December 28. The park had been closed to minors for more than eleven years because of cougar problems, and had only reopened for minors again on December 16. The cougar emerged from the brush and began circling in a crouched position. The women in the group yelled at it but it then merely switched its tail, hissed, began crawling on its belly, and charged within three feet of the children, ages five, six, seven, and eight. The cougar retreated only after one of the women threw a child's hiking boot at it. The cougar was later seen in the old corral area of the park, where it seemed unconcerned by all the people watching it. Since several prior cougar encounters had been reported the preceding week, the cougar was tracked and shot. Dogs were not used because its behavior was so blatant. The cougar was a female, in good health, and was not with kittens. Orange County supervisor Charles Smith indicated that he would propose closing the park again to minors, stating: "We have to decide if this is going to be a park for children to play in or a park for mountain lions—the two are not compatible."

Denver Post, May 1, 2, and 6, 1998, *Rocky Mountain News,* May 1 and 2. Andy Peterson of Littleton, Colo., was hiking in the Carpenter Peak area of Roxborough State Park in the early afternoon of April 30, 1998, when he encountered a young cougar that was apparently just chewing on a stick. Peterson tried all of the usual preventive measures, but when he tried to back down the trail the cougar attacked. In the attack, the cougar "clamped its jaws on Peterson's head, and left claw scratches all over the man's body." Peterson was able to dissuade the cougar from further attacks by stabbing it with a small knife and jabbing his thumb in its eye. According to Roxborough park officials, Peterson was slight of build and approximately five feet six to five feet eight in height. Wildlike officials used a baited deer carcass and dogs in an attempt to locate the cougar, presumed to be a young one, but were unsuccessful.

Missoulian, Aug. 1, 1998, Missoula, Montana; *Rocky Mountain News,* Aug. 1, 1998. Dante Swallow was hiking July 31, 1998, on a Marshall Mountain trail with other campers and counselors when he was attacked by a young adult male cougar. One of the counselors, Aaron Hall, age 16, rushed to Swallow's side, waving his hands and kicking at the animal. The cougar released the boy. Game wardens, deputies, and trackers with dogs were able to locate and kill the cat shortly after the attack. Swallow received puncture wounds on his neck and scratches on his back and abdomen. Fish and Game officials indicated that the cougar appeared to be in good health. No weight was available.

BIBLIOGRAPHY

Acosta, Gilbert. "Lions Beat Them All." *Outdoor Life* 131 (May 1963): 64–67, 165–68, 170.

Aldis, James. *Animals as Friends.* Taplinger Publishing, New York, 1973.

Allen, Durward, L. *Our Wildlife Legacy.* Funk & Wagnalls, New York, 1962.

Alvarez, Ken. *Twilight of the Panther.* Myakka River Publishing, Sarasota, FL, 1993.

Anderson, Allen E. *A Critical Review of Literature on Puma (Felis concolor).* Special report no. 54, Colorado Division of Wildlife, February 1983.

———, David C. Bowden, and Donald Kattner. *The Puma on Uncompahgre Plateau, Colorado.* Technical publication no. 40, Colorado Division of Wildlife, August 1992.

Arizona Game and Fish Department. *Wildlife Views, Annual Report—50 Years,* vol. 23, no. 1, January 1980.

Arnold, Oren. *Wildlife of the Southwest.* Banks Upshaw, Dallas, 1935.

Atwood, Cap. "The Harder They Come." *Outdoor Life* 138 (October 1966): 64–67, 156–59.

Audubon, John J., and John Bachman. *The Viviparous Quadrupeds of North America.* 3 vols. Robert Havell, London; reprint, ed. with new text by Victor H. Cahalane, Hammond, Maplewood, NJ, 1968.

Bacon, Francis. *The Essays or Counsels, Civil and Moral, of Francis Ld. Verulam.* Peter Pauper Press, Mount Vernon, New York, 1974.

Bamford, Larry R. "One for the Books." *Field and Stream* 73 (September 1968): 42, 90, 92, 94.

———. "Lion of a Lifetime." *Field and Stream* 76 (August 1971): 64, 108, 110, 112.

Barker, Elliott S. *Western Life and Adventures in the Great Southwest.* Lowell Press, Kansas City, 1974.

Barnes, Claude T. *Mammals of Utah.* Bulletin of the University of Utah 12, no. 15. Inland Printing, Kaysville, UT, 1922.

———. *The Cougar or Mountain Lion.* Ralton, Salt Lake City, UT, 1960.

Bartlett, John Russell. *Personal Narrative of Explorations and Incidents in Texas, New Mexico, California, Sonora, and Chihuahua 1850–1853.* Rio Grande Press, Chicago, 1965.

Bashline, James L., and Dan Saults, eds. *America's Great Outdoors.* J. L. Ferguson, Chicago, 1976.

Bauer, Erwin A. *Predators of North America*. Grolier, New York, 1988.

Beier, Paul. "Cougar Attacks on Humans in the United States and Canada." *Wildlife Society Bulletin* 19: 403–12, 1991.

Betzinez, Jason. *I Fought with Geronimo*. University of Nebraska Press, Lincoln, 1959.

Block, Eugene B. "Lion Hunting for a Living." *Sunset Magazine* 58 (April 1927): 15, 65–66.

Bolgiano, Chris. "Concepts of Cougar." *Wilderness* 54 (summer 1991): 26, 28–33.

———. *Mountain Lion—An Unnatural History of Pumas and People*. Stackpole, Mechanicsburg, PA, 1995.

Botero, Giovanni. "The Greatness of Cities." In *The Reasons of State*, 1588, 1606, trans. R. Peterson, p. 227, London, 1956 (cited in Spiro Kostof, *The City Assembled*, Thames & Hudson, London, 1992).

Bourke, John G. *On the Border with Crook*. Reprint of the 1891 Scribner's edn., University of Nebraska Press, Lincoln, 1971.

Boyle, Robert H. "The Cat Came Back." *Outdoor Life* 798, no. 6 (December 1996): 41–50.

Bradley, Hugh. *Such Was Saratoga*. Doubleday, Doran, New York, 1940.

Brakefield, Tom. *Big Cats—Kingdom of Might*. Voyageur Press, Stillwater, MN, 1993.

Brandt, Anthony. "Lions on the Haunt." *Outdoor Life* 197 (January 1996): 14–18.

Brent, Jeff A. "Bowhunting Big Cats." *Bowhunter* 17 (January 1988): 68–72.

Brentano, Francis, ed. *Big Cats—An Anthology*. Ernest Benn, London, 1949.

Brown, Bonnie. "Lady and the Cougar." *Outdoor Life* 120 (July 1957): 48–49, 87–90.

Brown, Frank E. "A Cougar Hunt in Idaho." *Outdoor Life* 30 (1912): 226–31.

Browning, Meshach. *Forty-Four Years of the Life of a Hunter*. Winston Printing, Winston-Salem, NC, 1942. Unabridged republication of the first (1859) edn.

Bruce, Jay. "Lioness Tracked to Lair." *California Fish and Game* 4 (July 1918): 152–53.

———. "The Problem of Mountain Lion Control in California." *California Fish and Game* 11 (January 1925): 1–17.

———. "The Why and How of Mountain Lion Hunting in California." *California Fish and Game* 8 (April 1922): 108–14.

Bryant, Harold C. "Mountain Lion Hunting in California." *California Fish and Game* 3 (1917): 160–66.

Burbridge, Ben. "Bear and Lion Hunting in Mexico." *Outdoor Life* 23 (January 1909): 17–26.

Burt, Jesse, and Robert B. Ferguson. *Indians of the Southeast: Then and Now*. Abingdon Press, Nashville, TN, 1973.

Caesar, Gene. *The Wild Hunters*. G. P. Putnam's Sons, New York, 1957.

Cahalane, Victor H. "King of Cats and His Court." *National Geographic* 83, no. 2 (February 1943): 217–59.

———. *Mammals of North America*. Macmillan, New York, 1961.

————. *A Preliminary Study of Distribution and Numbers of Cougar, Grizzly and Wolf in North America*. New York Zoological Society, 1964.

————, ed. *Audubon Game Animals*. Original text by John James Audubon and John Bachman. Hammond, Maplewood, NJ, 1968.

Calder, William A. "Man and the Mountain Lion in the Early 1900s: Perspectives from a Wildcat Dump." *Journal of the Southwest* 32, no. 1 (spring 1990).

Camp, Raymond R., ed. *The Hunter's Encyclopedia*. Stackpole, Harrisburg, PA, 1948.

Cansdale, G. S. *Animals and Man*. Frederick A. Praeger, New York, 1953.

Capstick, Peter Hathaway. *Maneaters*. Peterson Publishing, Los Angeles, 1981.

————. *Death in the Silent Places*. St. Martin's, New York, 1981.

Caras, Roger A. *Dangerous to Man*. Chilton, New York, 1964.

————. *Panther*. University of Nebraska Press, Lincoln, 1969.

Carmony, Neil B., ed. *Afield With J. Frank Dobie*. High-Lonesome Books, Silver City, NM, 1992.

Carson, Rachel. *Silent Spring*. Houghton Mifflin, Boston, 1962.

Catlin, George. *Letters and Notes on the Manners, Customs, and Conditions of the North American Indians*, vols. 1 and 2. Unabridged republication of the first edn. (London, 1844), Dover, New York, 1973.

Chadwick, Douglas H. *A Beast the Color of Winter*. Sierra Club Books, San Francisco, 1983.

Chaudhuri, Joy, ed. *Indians and 1776*. Amerind Club, University of Arizona, Tucson, 1973.

Chittenden, Hiram Martin. *A History of the American Fur Trade of the Far West*. Press of the Pioneers, New York, 1935. Academic Reprints, Stanford, CA, 1954.

Clarke, James. *Man Is the Prey*. Stein & Day, New York, 1969.

Colinvaux, Paul. *Why Big Fierce Animals Are Rare*. Princeton University Press, Princeton, NJ, 1978.

Collier, H. R. "A Lion That Wouldn't Stay Caught." *Outdoor Life* 29 (1912): 45–48.

Collinson, Frank. *Life in the Saddle*. University of Oklahoma Press, Norman, 1963.

Cook, James H. *Fifty Years on the Old Frontier*. 3rd printing, Yale University Press, 1923. Reprint, University of Oklahoma Press, Norman, OK, 1980.

Cook, John R. *The Border and the Buffalo*. Citadel, New York, 1967.

Cooney, Judd. "Once in a Lifetime Cougar." *Bow & Arrow Hunting* 26–27 (February 1990): 48–51, 78–80.

Cooper, James Fenimore. *The Deerslayer*. Lea & Blanchard, Philadelphia, 1841. Reprint, Charles Scribner's Sons, New York, 1925.

Corbett, Jim. *Man-Eaters of Kumaon*. Oxford University Press, New York, 1946.

Coues, Elliot. "The Quadrupeds of Arizona." *The American Naturalist* 1 (1867): 281–91, 351–63, 393–400, 531–41.

Cowan, Farck C. "The Scream of the Cougar." *Outdoor Life* 43 (April 1919): 229.

Cremony, John C. *Life among the Apaches*. A. Roman, San Francisco, 1868. Reprint, Arizona Silhouettes, Tucson, 1951.

Crockett, David. *A Narrative of the Life of David Crockett of the State of Tennessee*. E. L. Carey and A. Hart, Philadelphia, 1834. Reprint, University of Nebraska Press, Lincoln, 1987.

Cronemiller, F. P. "Mountain Lion Preys on Bighorn." *Journal of Mammalogy* 29, no. 1 (February 1948): 68.

Cuvier, Georges (Baron) and Edward Griffin. *The Animal Kingdom*, vol. 2, G. B. Whittaker, London, 1827.

———. *The Animal Kingdom Arranged in Conformity with its Organization*. Trans. H. M'Murtrie, vol. 1, Carvill, New York, 1831.

Dallas, W. C. "Still-Hunting Mountain Lions." *Outdoor Life* 30 (1912): 117–21.

Darwin, Charles. *The Voyage of the Beagle*. Ed. Leonard Engel. Originally published as *Journal of Researches into the Natural History and Geology of the countries visited during the Voyage of the H.M.S. Beagle round the world under the Command of Capt. Fitz Roy, R.N.* (Revised version of *The Voyage of the Beagle*). John Murray, London, 1845; The Natural History Library, Doubleday & Co., Garden City, New York, 1962.

———. *The Origin of Species by Means of Natural Selection*. Reprint of 1859 edn., Watts, London, 1929.

Davis, Goode P. Jr. *Man and Wildlife in Arizona*. Arizona Fish and Game Department, Phoenix, 1982.

Davis, J. C. "Killing a Lion in Sight of Denver." *Outdoor Life* 41 (March 1918): 198.

Davis, Walter Lee. "I Heard a Cougar Scream." *Outdoor Life* 75, no. 4 (April 1935): 39, 63, 73.

Day, Donald, ed. *The Hunting and Exploring Adventures of Theodore Roosevelt*. Dial Press, New York, 1955.

Dean, David M. "Meshach Browning: Bear Hunter of Allegany County, 1781–1859." *Maryland Historical Magazine* 91, no. 1 (spring 1996): 73–83.

Denevan, William M., ed. *The Native Population of the Americas in 1492*. 2nd edn. University of Wisconsin Press, Madison, 1992.

Derby, Pat. *The Lady and Her Tiger*. Dutton, New York, 1976.

De Smet, P. J. *Letters and Sketches among the Indian Tribes of the Rocky Mountains*. Philadelphia, 1843. Reprinted in *Early Western Travels, 1748–1846*, ed. Reuben Gold Thwaites, vol. 27, *De Smet's Letters and Sketches (1841–1842)*. AMS Press, New York, 1966.

———. *Oregon Missions in 1845–46*. Edward Dunigan, New York, 1847. Reprinted in *Early Western Travels, 1748–1846*, ed. Reuben Gold Thwaites, vol. 29, *De Smet's Oregon Missions (1845–1846)*. AMS Press, New York, 1966.

Despain, Don, et al. *Wildlife in Transition*. Roberts Rinehart, Boulder, CO, 1986.

Dixon, Joseph K. *The Vanishing Race*. Doubleday, Garden City, NJ, 1913.

Dmitriyev, Yuri. *Man and Animals*. Raduga Publishers, Moscow, 1984.

Dobie, J. Frank. *The Ben Lilly Legend*. Little, Brown, Boston, 1950.

———. "Tales of the Panther." *Saturday Evening Post* 216 (December 11, 1943): 22, 57, 60–61.

———. *The Voice of the Coyote*. University of Nebraska Press, Lincoln, 1949.

Dodge, Natt N. "Wildlife of the American West." In *The Book of the American West*, ed. Jay Monaghan, 427–500. Simon & Schuster, New York, 1963.

Dodge, Colonel Richard Irving. *The Plains of the Great West and Their Inhabitants*. Archer House, New York, 1959.

Dougherty, Jim. "Cougar: The Big-Game Prince." *Bow & Arrow Hunting* 30–31 (December 1992): 24–29, 53.

DuFresne, Frank. "Crazy Cougars." *Field and Stream* 60 (December 1955): 46–47, 86–88.

East, Ben. *Bears*. Outdoor Life, Crown Publishers, New York, 1977.

———. "Cougar Comeback in the East." *American Forests* (November 1979): 21, 54–59.

———. *Danger!* Outdoor Life, Dutton, New York, 1970.

———. *Narrow Escapes and Wilderness Adventures*. Outdoor Life, Dutton, New York, 1960.

Easton, Robert, and MacKenzie Brown. *Lord of the Beasts—The Saga of Buffalo Jones*. University of Arizona Press, Tucson, 1961.

Eaton, Evelyn. *Snowy Earth Comes Gliding*. Draco Foundation, Independence, CA, 1974.

Eckert, Roger. *Animal Physiology*. 2nd edn. W. H. Freeman, New York, 1983.

Ekins, Steve. "A Lion Roping Record." *Outdoor Life* 41 (July 1918): 47.

Ellis, Don D. "Hound Man's Dream." *Outdoor Life* 140 (November 1967): 51–53, 100–103.

———. "The Cougar Does Attack." *Outdoor Life* 148 (September 1971): 64–67, 110, 112, 114.

Evans, Will F. "The Super-Strength of the Mountain Lion." *Outdoor Life* 49 (May 1922): 344–45.

Farnham, Thomas J. *Travels in the Great Western Prairies*. Richard Bentley, London, 1843. Reprinted in *Early Western Travels, 1748–1846*, ed. Reuben Gold Thwaites, vol. 28, *Farnham's Travels (1839)*. AMS Press, New York, 1966.

Fergus, Charles. *Swamp Screamer*. North Point, New York, 1996.

Finley, William L. "Cougar Kills a Boy." *Journal of Mammalogy* 6, no.3 (August 1925): 197–99.

Fischer, Hank. *Wolf Wars*. Falcon, Helena, MT, 1995.

Fitz, Grancel. *North American Head Hunting*. Oxford University Press, New York, 1957.

Flint, Timothy, ed. *The Personal Narrative of James O. Pattie of Kentucky*. John H. Wood, Cincinnati, OH, 1831. Reprinted in *Early Western Travels, 1748–1846*, ed. Reuben Gold Thwaites, vol. 18, *Pattie's Personal Narrative (1824–1830)*. AMS Press, New York, 1966.

Franchere, Gabriel. *Narrative of a Voyage to the Northwest Coast of America.* Redfield, New York, 1854. Reprinted in *Early Western Travels, 1748–1846,* ed. Reuben Gold Thwaites, vol. 6, *Franchere's Narrative (1811–1814).* AMS Press, New York, 1966.

Franklin, William L. "The Lord of Land's End." *National Geographic* 179, no. 1 (January 1991): 102–12.

Frazier, Deborah. "Two cougars attack pets in southwest part of state." *Rocky Mountain News,* July 20, 1991, p. 11.

Froman, Robert. *The Nerve of Some Animals.* J. B. Lippincott, Philadelphia, 1961.

Frome, Michael. *Battle for the Wilderness.* Praeger, New York, 1974.

———. "Panthers wanted—alive, back East where they belong." *Smithsonian* 10, no. 3 (June 1979): 82–88.

Froncek, Thomas, ed. *Voices from the Wilderness.* McGraw Hill, New York, 1974.

Frost, N. W. "The Cry of the Mountain Lion." *Outdoor Life* 29 (1912): 143–44.

Goldman, Edward A. "The Predatory Mammal Problem and the Balance of Nature." *Journal of Mammalogy* 6, no. 1 (February 1925): 28–33.

Goode, Monroe H. "Killers of the Rimrock" (two articles). *Field and Stream* 48 (June 1943): 32–34, 75–76, (July 1943): 35, 60–61.Goodman, Jeffrey. *American Genesis.* Summit, New York, 1981.

———. "The Real Cougar." *Field and Stream* 49 (August 1944): 26–27, 70–72.

———. "The Scourge of the Livestock Country." *Cattleman* (December 1941): 59–72.

Goodman, Jeffrey. *American Genesis.* Summit, New York, 1981.

Goodrich, L. L., Capt. "Midnight Encounter with a Panther." *Outdoor Life* 10, no. 2 (October 1902): n.p.

Goodspeed Brothers, comp. *A Reminiscent History of the Ozark Region.* Chicago, 1894. Reprint, Ramfre Press, Cape Girardeau, MO, 1976.

Graham, Stanley R. "The Lion of the Rockies" (two articles). *Outdoor Life* 41 (February 1918): 91–95; (March 1918): 171–75.

Gray, Robert. *Cougar.* Grosset & Dunlap, New York, 1972.

———. "The Ghost Cat." Zoological Society of San Diego *Zoo Nooz* 52, no. 10 (October 1979): 7–10.

Gregg, Josiah. *Commerce of the Prairies.* 2 vols. New York and London, 1844. Reprint of the 1857 edition in *Early Western Travels, 1748–1846,* ed. Reuben Gold Thwaites, vol. 19, *Gregg's Commerce of the Prairies (1831–1839).* AMS Press, New York, 1966.

Gregory, Tappan. *Eves in the Night.* Thomas Y. Crowell, New York, 1939.

Grey, Zane. *Roping Lions in the Grand Canyon.* Grosset & Dunlap, New York, 1922; reprint 1924.

———. *The Young Lion Hunter.* Harper & Brothers, New York, 1910. Reprinted by Grosset & Dunlap, New York, 1939.

Grinnell, Joseph, and Tracy Irwin Storer. *Animal Life in the Yosemite*. University of California Press, Berkeley, 1924.

Grzimek, Bernard. *Grzimek's Animal Life Encyclopedia*. Vol. 12, *Mammals 3*. Van Nostrand Reinhold, New York, 1975.

Guggisberg, C. A. W. *Wild Cats of the World*. Taplinger, New York, 1975.

Haines, Aubrey L. *The Yellowstone Story*. Colorado Associated University Press, Yellowstone Library and Museum Association, vols. 1 and 2, Yellowstone Park, WY, 1977.

Haley, Charles. "Killer Cougar." *Field and Stream* 57, pt. 2 (March 1953): 55, 125–27.

Haley, J. Evetts. *Charles Goodnight—Cowman and Plainsman*. University of Oklahoma Press, Norman, 1949.

Hall, E. Raymond, and Keith R. Kelson. *The Mammals of North America*, vol. 2. Ronald Press, New York, 1959.

Hancock, Lyn. *Love Affair with a Cougar*. Doubleday Canada, Toronto, 1978.

Hansen, Kevin. *Cougar—The American Lion*. Mountain Lion Foundation, Northland Publishing, Flagstaff, AZ, 1992.

Harlin, J. E. "A Cougar-Trailing Incident." *Outdoor Life* 43 (June 1919): 356–57.

Harrison, Dean, and Bobbi Harrison. *Back to Eden*. Three-pamphlet set, "In the Beginning," "The Big Move," and "In Search of Motivation," Out of Africa Wildlife Park, Fountain Hills, AZ, n.d.

Haynes, Bessie Doak, and Edgar Haynes, eds. *The Grizzly Bear*. University of Oklahoma Press, Norman, 1966.

Herrero, Stephen. *Bear Attacks*. Winchester Press, Piscataway, NJ, 1985.

Hert, Carl. *Tracking the Big Cats*. Caxton Printers, Caldwell, ID, 1955.

Hibben, Frank C. *Hunting American Lions*. Thomas Y. Crowell, New York, 1948.

———. "The Killer of Tonto Rim." *Field and Stream* 53, pt. 1 (September 1948): 51, 124–27.

———. *A Preliminary Study of the Mountain Lion*. University of New Mexico Press, bulletin no. 318, Biological Series vol. 5, no. 3, Albuquerque, 1937.

Hilderbrand, E. Boyd. "Cougar Nightmare." *Outdoor Life* 132 (July 1963): 21–23, 119–22.

Hill, H. R. "The Trail of the Mountain." *Popular Mechanics* 51 (June 1929): 946–99.

Hittell, Theodore H. *The Adventures of James Capen Adams*. 4th edn. Charles Scribner's Sons, New York, 1926.

Hoffmeister, Donald F., and Woodrow W. Goodpaster. *The Mammals of the Huachuca Mountains, Southeastern Arizona*. Illinois Biological Monographs 24, no. 1. University of Illinois Press, Urbana, 1954.

Hornaday, William T. *The American Natural History*. 16th edn. Charles Scribner's Sons, New York, 1935.

———. *A Wild Animal Roundup*. Charles Scribner's Sons, New York, 1925.

Hornocker, Maurice G. "Learning to Live with Mountain Lions." *National Geographic* 182, no. 1 (July 1992): 52–65.

———. "Stalking the Mountain Lion—to Save Him." *National Geographic* 136, no. 5 (November 1969): 638–54.

Houston, Douglas B. *Cougar and Wolverine in Yellowstone National Park.* U.S. Department of the Interior, National Park Service, Yellowstone. Research note no. 5, Yellowstone Park, WY, 1973.

Howard, Charles B. "An Instance of a Mountain Lion's Attack upon a Boy." *Outdoor Life* 36, (August 1915): 162–63.

Hudson, W. H. *The Naturalist in La Plata.* Aldine House, London, 1892. Reprint, J. M. Dent & Sons, London, 1929.

Humphrey, W. E. "Notes on the Cougar." *Outdoor Life* 61 (April 1928): 102.

Hunter, John Dunn. *Memoirs of a Captivity among the Indians of North America (1824).* Ed. Richard Drinnon. Schocken Books, New York, 1973.

Hunter, J. Marvin. *Pioneer History of Bandera County.* Hunter's Printing House, Bandera, Texas, 1922.

Huntington, Dwight W. *Our Big Game.* Charles Scribner's Sons, New York, 1904.

Hyatt, C. D. "A Deer and Lion Hunt in Colorado." *Outdoor Life* 43 (June 1919): 341–42.

Jackson, Hartley H. T. *Mammals of Wisconsin.* University of Wisconsin Press, Madison, 1961.

James, Edwin. *Account of an Expedition from Pittsburgh to the Rocky Mountains.* 2 vols. Reprint of the 1823 publication in *Early Western Travels, 1748–1846,* ed. Reuben Gold Thwaites, vols. 14–17, *S. H. Long's Expedition (1819–1820).* AMS Press, New York, 1966.

James, M. R. "The Cat in Pace Canyon." *Outdoor Life* 147 (January 1971): 56–57, 136–37, 142–43.

Jeffcott, P. R. *Nooksak Tales and Trails.* Sedro-Woolley Courier-Times, Ferndale, WA, 1949.

Jenkinson, Michael. *Beasts beyond the Fire.* E. P. Dutton, New York, 1980.

Johnson, Neil R. *The Chickasaw Rancher.* Redlands Press, Stillwater, OK, 1961.

Jones, J. Knox Jr. "The Occurrence of the Mountain Lion in Nebraska." *Journal of Mammalogy* 30, no. 3 (August 1949): 313.

Jorgensen, S. E., and L. David Mech. *Proceedings of a Symposium on the Native Cats of North America, Their Status and Management.* United States Department of the Interior, Fish and Wildlife Services, Twin Cities, MN, 1971.

Josephy, Alvin M. Jr. *The Indian Heritage of America.* Bantam American History Books, 10th printing, New York, 1981.

Keith, Elmer. *Big Game Hunting.* Little, Brown, Boston, 1948.

Kelsey-Wood, Dennis. *The Atlas of Cats of the World.* T.F.H. Publications, Neptune City, NJ, 1989.

Kent, William L. "The Trail of the Big Cat—Lion Hunting: Ace of Sports." *Colorado Outdoors* (January/February 1957): 6–11.

Kirchshofer, Rosl, ed. *The World of Zoos*. Viking, New York, 1968.

Kirk, Don. "The Challenge of Mountain Lions." *Bow & Arrow Hunting* 26–27 (April 1989): 18–21.

Kitchener, Andrew. *The Natural History of the Wild Cats*. Comstock Publishing, Ithaca, NY, 1991.

Knottnerus-Meyer, Th. *Birds and Beasts of the Roman Zoo*. Century, New York, 1928.

Koebner, Linda. *Zoo Book—The Evolution of Wildlife Conservation Centers*. Tom Doherty, New York, 1994.

Koller, Larry. *The Treasury of Hunting*. Odyssey, New York, 1965.

Laing, Hamilton M. "The Man of Many Lions." *Sunset* 57 (September 1926): 46–47.

Lane, Stanford S. "Short Order Cougars." *Outdoor Life* 129 (May 1962): 68–71, 173–75.

Lawrence, R. D. *The Ghost Walker*. Holt, Rinehart & Winston, New York, 1983.

Laycock, George. "Cougars in Conflict." *Audubon* (March 1988): 87–95.

———. *The Hunters and the Hunted*. Outdoor Life Books, Meredith Press, New York, 1990.

Lecomte, Jacques. *Animals in Our World*. Holt, Rinehart & Winston, New York, 1962.

Lee Rue, Leonard III. *The Deer of North America*. Grolier Book Clubs, Danbury, CT, 1989.

Leopold, B. D., and P. R. Krausman. "Diets of Three Predators in Big Bend National Park, Texas." *Journal of Wildlife Management* 50:290–95.

Lesowski, John. "The Silent Hunter." *Outdoor Life* 140 (July 1967): 44–47, 104, 106–8.

———. "Two Observations of Cougar Cannibalism." *Journal of Mammalogy* 44, no. 4 (November 1963): 586.

Lewis, Jerry A. *The Longwalkers*. Wolfe Publishing, Prescott, AZ, 1995.

Lewis, Pete. "The Mountain Lion." *Colorado Outdoors* 25, no. 1 (January/February 1976): 14–18.

Line, Les, ed. *Audubon Nature Yearbook—1991*. Meredith, New York, 1991.

Linn, Amy. "Wild Cats Wild." *Audubon* 95 (July–August 1993): 22, 24–25.

Linnaeus, Carolus [Carl von Linné]. *Systema Naturae per regna tri naturae, secundum classes, ordines, genera, species, cum characteribus, differentiis, synonymis, locis.* 10th edn. Laurentii Salvii, Stockholm, 1758.

———. "Regni animalis." *Mantissa plantarum generum editionis VI et specierum editionis II.* Laurentii Salvii, Stockholm, 1771.

Literary Digest. "A Man Who Catches Mountain Lions in Trees." *Literary Digest* 84 (March 14, 1925): 46, 50.

———. "Mr. Cantankerous Cougar's Movie Career." *Literary Digest* 104 (February 15, 1930): 46, 48, 50, 52.

Lloyd, H. Evans. *Travels in the Interior of North America by Maximilian, Prince of Wied.* Ackermann, London, 1843. Reprinted in *Early Western Travels, 1748–1846*, ed. Reuben Gold Thwaites, vol. 22, *Maximilian's Travels (1832–1834)*. AMS Press, New York, 1966.

Long, John. *Voyages and Travels of an Indian Interpreter and Trader.* Robson, Bond, Street, et al., London, 1791. Reprinted in *Early Western Travels, 1748–1846*, ed. Reuben Gold Thwaites, vol. 2, *J. Long's Voyages and Travels (1768–1782)*. AMS Press, New York, 1966.

Long, William J. *The Spirit of the Wild.* Doubleday, 1956.

Lopez, Barry. "The Elusive Mountain Lion." *GEO* (June 1981): 98–116.

———. *Of Wolves and Men.* Charles Scribner's Sons, New York, 1978.

Lorenz, Konrad. *On Aggression.* Bantam, New York, 1969.

———, and Paul Leyhausen. *Motivation of Human and Animal Behavior.* Van Nostrand Reinhold, New York, 1973.

Lowther, J. R. "The Cougar in British Columbia." *Outdoor Life* 36 (August 1915): 131–32.

Lyon, T. J. (Shorty). "Lion in My Lap." *Outdoor Life* 120 (August 1957): 39, 72–74.

———. "Very Big Lion." *Outdoor Life* 119 (May 1957): 61, 122–26.

MacClintock, Dorcas. *A Natural History of Raccoons.* Charles Scribner's Sons, New York, 1981.

Macdonald, David. *The Velvet Claw.* BBC Books, London, 1992.

Mails, Thomas E. *The Mystic Warriors of the Plains.* Doubleday, Garden City, NY, 1972.

Mann, William M. *Wild Animals in and out of the Zoo.* Smithsonian Series, vol. 6, ed., Charles Greeley Abbot. Series Publishers, New York, 1949.

Mannix, Daniel P. *A Sporting Chance.* E. P. Dutton, New York, 1967.

Manville, Richard H. "Report of Deer Attacking Cougar." *Journal of Mammalogy* 36, no. 3 (August,1955): 476, 478.

Marksman [pseud.] *The Dead Shot; or, Sportsman's Complete Guide.* W. A. Townsend, New York, 1864.

Martin, Paul S., and Richard G. Klein. *Quaternary Extinctions.* University of Arizona Press, Tucson, 1984.

Maull, L. L. "Five Arrows—Four Lions." *Outdoor Life* 99, no. 1 (January 1947): 23, 71–72.

McCabe, Robert A. "The Scream of the Mountain Lion." *Journal of Mammalogy* 30, no. 3 (August 1949): 305–6.

McCafferty, Keith. "The Heart of the Pack." *Field and Stream* 87 (February 1983): 66–67, 125–26, 129–30.

McCall, Karen, and Jim Dutcher. *Cougar—Ghost of the Rockies.* Sierra Club Books, San Francisco, 1992.

McCoy, J. J. *Wild Enemies.* Hawthorn, New York, 1974.

McGlone, Pat. "The Cowardice of Wild Animals." *Outdoor Life* 41 (January 1918): 47.

McGraw, Carol, and S. L. Sanger. "Big Cats, Big Trouble." *Los Angeles Times*, Magazine section, March 1, 1992: 25–33.

McGuire, J. A. "A Western Lion Roper." *Outdoor Life* 29 (1912): 391–96.

McIntyre, Thomas. *The Way of the Hunter*. E. P. Dutton, New York, 1988.

McKee, Thomas H. "Uncle Jim Owen and His Dogs Have Killed 1500 Cougars." *American Magazine* (April 1927).

McLuhan, T. C. *Touch the Earth*. Promontory Press, New York, 1971.

McMullen, James P. *Cry of the Panther: Quest of a Species*. Pineapple Press, Englewood, FL, 1984.

McReynolds, Edwin C. *The Seminoles*. University of Oklahoma Press, Norman, 1957.

McTimmonds, J. V. "Oregon Bear and Lion Hunters." *Outdoor Life* 29 (1912): 336.

Mery, Fernand. *The Cat*. Madison Square Press, Grosset & Dunlap, New York, 1968.

Mile, Alfred H. *Five Hundred Fascinating Animal Stories*. Dodd, Mead, New York, 1895.

Mills, Enos A. *The Adventures of a Nature Guide*. Houghton Mifflin, New York, 1932.

———. *The Grizzly*. Houghton Mifflin, New York, 1919; reprint, Comstock, Sausalito, CA, 1973.

———. "The Mountain Lion." *Saturday Evening Post* 190, no. 38 (March 23, 1918): 125–27.

———. *The Rocky Mountain Wonderland*. University of Nebraska Press, Lincoln, 1991. Reprint of the Houghton Mifflin original edn. (New York, 1915).

———. *The Spell of the Rockies*. University of Nebraska Press, Lincoln, 1989. Reprint of the Houghton Mifflin original edn. (New York, 1911).

———. *Wildlife on the Rockies*. Houghton Mifflin, New York, 1909.

Milne, Lorus J., and Margery Milne. *The Cougar Doesn't Live Here Anymore*. Prentice-Hall, Englewood Cliffs, NJ, 1971.

Milner, Joe E. *California Joe*. Caxton Printers, Caldwell, ID, 1935.

Milstein, Michael. "The Hidden Lion." *National Parks* 64 (January/February 1990): 19–23, 44.

Mooney, James. *The Aboriginal Population of America, North of Mexico*, ed. J. R. Swanton. Smithsonian Miscellaneous Collections, 80, no. 7, 1928.

———. "Population." In *Handbook of American Indians North of Mexico*, ed. F. W. Hodge, vol. 2. Govt. Printing Office, Washington, 1910.

Moore, Ron D. "Cliffhanger Lion." *Bowhunting World* 38, no. 6 (October 1989): 29, 32–38.

Monson, Gale, and Lowell Sumner, eds. *The Desert Bighorn—Its Life History, Ecology & Management*. 3rd edn. University of Arizona Press, Tucson, 1985.

Montgomery, Rutherford G. *The Living Wilderness*. Caxton Printers, Caldwell, ID, 1969.

Morden, Irene. "Lions Almost Anytime." *Outdoor Life* 131 (January 1963): 47–49, 51, 56–58.

Morgan, Lewis H. *A Classic of Natural History and Ecology*. Dover, NY, 1986. Reprint of *The American Beaver and His Works*. J. B. Lippencott, Philadelphia, 1868.

Morison, Samuel Eliot. *The European Discovery of America*. Oxford University Press, New York, 1971.

———. *The Great Explorers*. Oxford University Press. New York, 1978.

Morris, Richard B. *Encyclopedia of American History*. Harper, New York, 1953.

Moseley, Edwin Lincoln. *Our Wild Animals*. D. Appleton, New York, 1927.

Mossman, Frank. "The Cougar and Lion of the Pacific Coast." *Outdoor Life* 8, no. 3 (September 1901): n.p.

Mueller, Larry. "Cougar Attack." *Outdoor Life* 175 (April 1985): 50–51, 108–11.

Murie, Adolph. *The Wolves of Mount McKinley*. U.S. Government Printing Office, Washington, D.C., 1944.

Murie, Olaus. *A Field Guide to Animal Tracks*. Peterson Field Guide Series, Houghton Mifflin, Boston, 1954.

Murray, Mary. "The Woman Who Wrestled a Cougar." *Canadian Reader's Digest* (May 1993): 87–92.

Neider, Charles, ed. *The Great West*. Bonanza, New York, 1958.

Nentvig, Juan. *Rudo Ensayo—A Description of Sonora and Arizona in 1764*. University of Arizona Press, Tucson, 1980.

Nequatewa, Edmund. *Truth of a Hopi*. Museum of Northern Arizona bulletin no. 8, Flagstaff, 1936.

Neuberger, Richard L. "They've Gone Wild—and Love It." *Saturday Evening Post* 220 (July 19, 1947): 15–17, 77–79.

Newell, David. "Panther!" *Saturday Evening Post* 208 (July 13, 1935): 10–11, 70–72.

Nicol, James Y. "He Wrestled a Cougar." *True West* 5, no. 3 (January/February 1958): 16–17, 33–34.

Nowak, Ronald M. *The Cougar in the United States and Canada*. U.S. Department of the Interior, Fish and Wildlife Service [FWS], Washington D.C.; and New York Zoological Society, New York, 1974. Amended by FWS 1976.

———, and John L. Paradiso. *Walker's Mammals of the World*, vol. 2, 4th edn. Johns Hopkins University Press, Baltimore, 1983.

Nuttall, Thomas. *Travels into the Arkansas Territory—1819*. Thomas J. Palmer, Philadelphia, 1821. Reprinted in *Early Western Travels, 1748–1846*, ed. Reuben Gold Thwaites, vol. 13, *Nuttall's Journal (1818–1820)*. AMS Press, New York, 1966.

O'Connor, Jack. "The Mountain Lion." *Outdoor Life* 124 (November 1959): 48, 50–51, 88–91.

Orlando, Count. "Cougar Hunting in the Northwest." *Outdoor Life*, 23 January, 1909, 27–29.

Ormond, Clyde. *Complete Book of Outdoor Lore*. Harper & Row, Outdoor Life, New York, 1964.

———. *Hunting Our Medium Size Game*. Stackpole, Harrisburg, PA, 1958.

Outdoor Life, eds. *The Story of American Hunting and Firearms*. McGraw-Hill, New York, 1959.

Packard, Jane M. *Behavior of High Risk Mountain Lions In Big Bend National Park, Texas*. final report, Cooperative Agreement no. 702990004, prepared for the National Park Service, June 1991.

Palmer, Joel. *Journal of Travels over the Rocky Mountains to the Mouth of the Columbia River*. J. A. and U. P. James, Cincinnati, 1847. Reprinted in *Early Western Travels, 1748–1846*, ed. Reuben Gold Thwaites, vol. 30, *Palmer's Journal (1845–1846)*. AMS Press, New York, 1966.

Palmer, Rose A. *The North American Indians*. Smithsonian Scientific Series, ed. Charles Greeley Abbot, vol. 4. Smithsonian Institution Series, New York, 1944.

"Panther Falls to Pistol Shot." *Outdoor Life* 30 (1912): 179.

Parsons, P. A. "All over the Map." *Outdoor Life* 100, no. 2 (August 1947): 4.

Patterson, J. H. *The Man-eaters of Tsavo*. Macmillan, 1907.

Pennisi, Elizabeth. "Heavy Cougar Traffic at City Edges." *Science News* 143 (June 26, 1993): 410.

Perez de Villagra, Gaspar. *A History of New Mexico* (trans. from the Spanish by Gilberto Espanosa). Rio Grande Press, Chicago, 1962.

Perry, W. A. "The Cougar." In *The Big Game of North America*, ed. G. O. Shields, Rand, McNally, New York, 1890.

Petersen, P. C. "A Sidelight on the Habits of the Cougar." *Outdoor Life* 29 (1912): 335.

Peyser, Marc. "Predators on the Prowl." *Newsweek* (January 8, 1996): 58.

Phelps, McKinnie L. *The Indian Captivity of Mary Kinnan, 1791–1794*. Pruett Press, Boulder, CO, 1967 (reprint and compilation including the original publication, *True Narrative of the Sufferings of Mary Kinnan*, dictated to and printed by Shepard Kollock, Elizabethtown, NJ, 1795).

Pike, Zebulon Montgomery. *Sources of the Mississippi and the Western Louisiana Territory*. Reprint of the 1810 publication *An Account of the Expeditions To The Sources of the Mississippi, And Through The Western Parts of Louisiana, To The Sources of the Arkansaw, Kans, La Platte, and Pierre Jaun Rivers, and a Tour Through the Interior Parts of New Spain*. March of America Facsimile Series no. 57, University Microfilms, Ann Arbor, 1966. *The Journals of Zebulon Montgomery Pike—with letters and related documents*. Ed. and annotated Donald Jackson. University of Oklahoma Press, Norman, 1966.

Platt, Rutherford. *Wilderness*. Dodd, Mead, New York, 1961.

Polley, Jane, ed. *American Folklore and Legend*. The Readers Digest Association, Pleasantville, NY, 1978.

Porter, J. Hampden. *Wild Beasts*. Charles Scribner's Sons, New York, 1894.

Powell, Addison M. "The American Panther, or Puma." *Outdoor Life* 42 (October 1918): 243–45.

Quaife, M. M., ed. *Yellowstone Kelly—The Memoirs of Luther S. Kelly.* Yale University Press, New Haven, CT, 1926.

Rabinowitz, Alan. *Jaguar.* Arbor House, New York, 1986.

Radin, Paul. *The Story of the American Indian.* Liveright, New York, 1934.

Rae, William E., ed. *A Treasury of Outdoor Life.* Outdoor Life Books and Harper & Row, New York, 1975; 2nd updated edn., Stackpole Books, 1982.

Range, Lester A. "Stalked by a Cougar." *Bowhunter* (September 1987): 34–37.

Ray, Brandon. "Going after North America's Biggest Cat." *Bowhunting World* (February 1998): 46–50.

Reed, Howard S. "Danged Varmints." *Collier's* 92 (August 5, 1933): 29, 34, 36, 39.

Reneau, Jack, and Susan C. Reneau, eds. *Records of North American Big Game.* 10th edn. Boone & Crockett Club, Missoula, MT, 1993.

Ricciuti, Edward R. *Killer Animals.* Walker, New York, 1976.

Robinette, W. Leslie, Jay S. Gashwiler, and Owen W. Morris. "Notes on Cougar Productivity and Life History." *Journal of Mammalogy* 42, no. 2 (1961): 204–17.

Roosevelt, Theodore. "A Cougar Hunt on the Rim of the Grand Canyon." *Outlook* 105 (October 4, 1913): 259–66.

———. *Hunting the Grisly and Other Sketches.* G. P. Putnam's Sons, 1889; reprint, Charles Scribner's Sons, New York, 1904.

———. *Outdoor Pastimes of an American Hunter.* Charles Scribner's Sons, New York, 1905; reprint, Stackpole, Harrisburg, PA, 1990.

———. *Ranch Life and the Hunting Trail.* Pemberton Press, Austin, TX, 1888; reprint, Gramercy Books, Avenel, NJ, 1995.

———. *The Wilderness Hunter.* G. P. Putnam's Sons, Alleghany edn., New York, 1893.

Roze, Uldis. *The North American Porcupine.* Smithsonian Institution Press, Washington D.C., 1989.

Ruark, Robert. *Use Enough Gun.* New American Library, New York, 1966.

Rue, Leonard Lee III. *The Deer of North America.* Grolier Book Clubs, Danbury, CT, 1989.

Rush, William Marshall. *Wild Animals of the Rockies.* Harper, New York, 1939.

Russ, Wayne Paul. *The Rare and Endangered Terrestrial Vertebrates of Virginia.* M.S. thesis, Virginia Polytech Institute, Blacksburg, VA, 1973.

Russell, Andy. *Andy Russell's Adventures with Wild Animals.* Knopf, New York, 1978.

Russell, Osborne. *Journal of a Trapper.* Syms-York, Boise, ID, 1914; reprint, University of Nebraska Press, Lincoln, 1965.

Russo, John P. *The Kaibab North Deer Herd—Its History, Problems and Management.* 2nd edn. Arizona Game and Fish Department, Wildlife Bulletin no. 7, Phoenix, 1970.

Ruxton, George Frederick. *Life in the Far West.* University of Oklahoma Press, Norman, 1951.

Saile, Bob. "Cougar Attacks: New Crisis for the Big Cats." *Outdoor Life* 160 (August 1977): 66–68, 126–28.

Sass, Herbert Ravenel. "The Cougar Prowls the East Again!" *Saturday Evening Post* 226 (March 13, 1954): 31, 133–34, 136.

Scheffer, Victor B. *A Voice for Wildlife.* Charles Scribner's Sons, New York, 1974.

Schueler, Donald G. *Incident at Eagle Ranch.* Sierra Club Books, San Francisco, 1980.

Schueren, Arnold C. "Utah Lion Hunt." *Field and Stream* 50, pt. 1 (September 1945): 21–23.

Schulyer, Lynne. "Help! Cougar!" *Good Housekeeping* (Canadian edn.) (April 1992): 220, 222.

Scott, William Berryman. *A History of Land Mammals in the Western Hemisphere.* Rev. edn., Hafner Publishing, New York, 1962.

Sealander, John A. "Mountain Lion in Arkansas." *Journal of Mammalogy* 32, no. 3, (August 1951): 364.

Seidensticker, John C. IV, et al. *Mountain Lion Social Organization in the Idaho Primitive Area.* Wildlife Monograph no. 35: 1–61, Wildlife Society, 1973.

Seton, Ernest Thompson. *Lives of Game Animals,* vol. 1, pt. 1, "Cats, Wolves, and Foxes." Doubleday, Doran, Garden City, NY, 1929.

———. *Wild Animals at Home.* Grosset & Dunlap, New York, 1913.

Shaw, Harley G. *Ecology of the Mountain Lion in Arizona.* Arizona Game and Fish Department, project W-78-R, work plan 2, job 13, final report, 1980.

———. *Mountain Lion Field Guide.* Arizona Game and Fish Department special report no. 9, 1987: 1–47.

———. *Soul among Lions.* Johnson Books, Boulder, CO, 1989.

Shaw, Marjorie Betts. "The Ghost Cat." Zoological Society of San Diego *Zoo Nooz* 52, no. 10 (October 1979): 7–10.

Sheldon, Charles. "Absence of the Cat Family in the Far North." *Outdoor Life* 29 (1912): 257.

Shillingsburg, Miriam Jones. "An Edition of William Gilmore Simms's *The Cub of the Panther.*" Ph.D. dissertation, University of South Carolina, 1969.

Shoemaker, Henry W. *Extinct Pennsylvania Animals.* Pt. 1 (1917): *The Panther and the Wolf.* Pt. 2 (1919): *Black Moose, Elk, Bison, Beaver, Pine Marten, Fisher, Glutton, Canada Lynx.* Altoona Tribune, Altoona, PA.

———. "The Panther in Pennsylvania." *Pennsylvania Game News.* Pennsylvania Game Commission, Harrisburg, February 1943: 7, 28, 32.

Sletholt, Erik. *Wild and Tame.* Charles Scribner's Sons, New York, 1975.

Smith, Herndon. *Centralia: The First Fifty Years, 1845–1900. Daily Chronicle* and F. H. Cole, Centralia, WA, 1942.

Smith, J. Cecil. "A Famous Cougar Dog's Last Fight." *Outdoor Life* 29 (1912): 51–52.

Springer, Kim, ed. *Biologue.* "Looking at the American Lion" 2, no. 1 (fall 1987) Teton Science School, Kelly, WY, 1987.

Stafford, Jean. *The Mountain Lion.* Random House, New York, 1947.

Stevenson, Robert Louis. "Requiem" (*Underwoods* XXI). In *The Works of Robert Louis Stevenson.* Black's Readers Service Company, New York [n.d.].

Stimson, Thomas E. "Lion Hunt." *Popular Mechanics* 89 (June 1948): 161–65, 232.

Stone, William L. *Reminiscences of Saratoga and Ballston.* Virtue & Yorston, New York, 1875.

Storer, Tracy I. "Rabies in a Mountain Lion." *California Fish and Game* 9, no. 2 (April 1923): 45–48.

Swadesh, Morris. "Linguistic Relations across Bering Strait." *American Anthropologist* 64, no. 6 (1962): 1262–91.

Swanton, John R. *The Indian Tribes of North America.* Smithsonian Institution Press, Washington, D.C., 1952.

Thomas, Elizabeth Marshall. *The Tribe of Tiger.* Simon & Schuster, New York, 1994.

Thoreau, Henry David. *Walden.* Running Press, Philadelphia, 1987. Reprint of *Walden: or, Life in the Woods.* Ticknor & Fields, Boston, 1854.

Thwaites, Reuben Gold., ed. *Early Western Travels, 1748–1846.* 30 vols. AMS Press, New York, 1966.

Time. "Cougar!" (February 21, 1944): 46.

Tinsley, Jim Bob. *The Puma—Legendary Lion of the Americas.* Texas Western Press, University of Texas at El Paso, 1987.

Toops, Connie. "Cats of One Color." *National Parks* (July/August 1995): 30–35.

Townsend, John K. *Journey across the Rocky Mountains to the Columbia River.* Henry Perkins, Philadelphia, 1839. Reprinted in *Early Western Travels, 1748–1846,* ed. Reuben Gold Thwaites, vol. 21, *Townsend's Narrative (1833–1834).* AMS Press, New York, 1966.

Treadwell, Joseph. "Cougar Encounter." *Bowhunting World* 39, no. 1 (February 1990): 24, 84–87.

Trenton, Patricia, and Patrick T. Houlihan. *Native Americans.* Harry N. Abrams, New York, 1989.

True, Frederick William. "The Puma, or American Lion: Felis Concolor of Linnaeus." National Museum report 591–608, miscellaneous document 224, Washington, D.C., 1889.

Turbak, Gary. *America's Great Cats.* Northland Press, Flagstaff, AZ, 1986.

———. "The Cougar Makes a Comeback." *Field and Stream* 95 (January 1991): 34–35, 73–74.

———. *Survivors in the Shadows.* Northland Publishing, Flagstaff, AZ, 1993.

Turgenev, Ivan S. *Fathers and Sons.* Modern Library, New York, 1950.

Tyrrell, J. B., ed. *David Thompson's Narrative of his Explorations in Western America, 1784–1812.* Champlain Society, Toronto, 1916.

Udall, Scott. "Encounter with a Cougar." *Field and Stream* 76, no. 7 (November 1971): 65, 116, 121–22.

Udall, Stewart L. *The Quiet Crisis.* Holt, Rinehart & Winston, New York, 1963.

U.S. Department of the Interior, National Park Service, Yellowstone. *Cougar and Wolverine in Yellowstone National Park*, by Douglas B. Houston. Research note no. 5, Yellowstone Park, WY, 1973.

Verrill, A. Hyatt. *Strange Animals and Their Stories.* Grosset & Dunlap, New York, 1939.

Volkhardt, Davey Gnann. "When Florida was Panther Country." *Guide to North Florida Living* (March–April 1982): 44–45.

Wagner, Frederick H., et al. *Wildlife Policies in the National Parks.* Island Press, Washington, D.C., 1995.

Walker, Lloyd. "Seven Cougars." *Outdoor Life* 128 (September 1961): 61, 91–95.

Wallace, A. F. "Trapping the Mountain Lion." *Outdoor Life* 30 (1912): 460–62.

Waterman, Charles F. *Hunting in America.* Holt, Rinehart & Winston, New York, 1973.

Wayne, Robert K., et al. "Molecular and Biochemical Evolution of the Carnivora." In *Carnivore Behavior, Ecology, and Evolution*, ed. John L. Gittleman. Cornell University Press, Ithaca, New York, 1989.

Wells, Hunter. *They Call Me Hunter.* Ralph Tanner, Prescott, AZ, 1984.

Wells, William. "Cougar!" *Field and Stream* (March 1932): 16–18, 80.

Whittlesey, Lee H. *Death in Yellowstone—Accidents and Foolhardiness in the First National Park.* Roberts Rinehart, Boulder, CO, 1995.

Williams, Samuel Cole, ed. *Adair's History of the American Indians.* Watuga Press, Johnson City, TN, 1930.

Williams, Ted. "The Lion's Silent Return." *Audubon* 96 (November–December 1994): 28–32, 34–35.

Wilson, Bruce A. *Late Frontier—A History of Okanogan County, Washington.* Okanogan County Historical Society, WA, 1990.

Wilson, Don E., and DeeAnn M Reeder. *Mammal Species of the World.* 2nd edn. Smithsonian Institution Press, Washington, D.C., 1993.

Winsett, Marvin. "The Truth about Cougars." *Field and Stream* 49 (June 1944): 28–29, 68.

Wirth, Conrad L. *Parks, Politics, and the People.* University of Oklahoma Press, Norman, 1980.

Wissler, Clark. *Indians of the United States.* Doubleday, Doran, New York, 1940.

Woods, John. *Two Years Residence in the Settlement of the English Prairie in the Illinois Country.* Longman, Hurst, Rees, Orme & Brown, London, 1822. Reprinted in *Early Western Travels, 1748–1846*, ed. Reuben Gold Thwaites, vol. 10, *Wood's English Prairie (1820–1821).* AMS Press, New York, 1966.

Worth, Nick. "When Cats Go Bad." *Outdoor Life* 187 (January 1991): 56, 79–81.

Wright, Bruce S. *The Eastern Panther.* Clark, Irwin, Toronto, 1972.

———. "The Fundy Lions." *Field and Stream* 53, pt. 1 (September 1948): 54, 118–19.

———. *The Ghost of North America*. Vantage, New York, 1959.

Wyeth, John Allan. *Life of Lieutenant-General Nathan Bedford Forrest*. Harper, New York, 1899.

Yanez, J. L., et al. "Food Habits of the Southernmost Mountain Lions *(Felis concolor)* in South America: Natural versus Livestocked Ranges." *Journal of Mammalogy* 67 no. 3 (August, 1986): 604–6.

Young, Stanley P. *The Bobcat of North America*. University of Nebraska Press, Lincoln, 1958.

———, and Edward A. Goldman. *The Puma: Mysterious American Cat*. American Wildlife Institute, Washington D.C., 1946.

———, and Hartley H. T. Jackson. *The Clever Coyote*. University of Nebraska Press, Lincoln, 1951.

Zumbo, Jim. "The Great Cougar Comeback." *Outdoor Life* 171 (February 1983): 61–63, 95–97.

INDEX

Krausman, P. R., 80

Labrador, 148
Lancaster, Scott Dale, 159–61, 238–39
Latch (cougar attack victims), 264–65
Lawrence, R. D., 28
Lee, Clell, 139–40
Lee, Dale, 139–40
Lee, Ernest, 139–40
Lee, Vince, 139–40
Leech, Larrance, 274–75
Leon, Ponce de, 144
Leopold, B. D., 80
Lesowski, John, 67–68, 142
Lewis, Jerry A., 53, 126
Lewis, Meriwether, 149
Lifely, Lila, 174
Lilly, Benjamin Vernon, 29, 45, 53, 60, 85, 87, 97, 130–33, 136 Linnaeus, Carl (von Linne), 11, 16, 43, 92
lion. *See* cougar
Littleton, William, 252–53
Locke, Frank J., 246–47
London Zoo, 41
Long, John, 19
Lopez, Barry, 151, 162
Lorenz, Konrad, 179
Louisiana, 155, 214
Louisiana Department of Game and Fish, 214
Lucas (cougar attack victim), 270–71
Lutz, John and Linda, 215
lynx *(Lynx canadensis)*, 17, 93, 94, 121
Lyon, T. J. ("Shorty"), 142

McBride, Roy, 142
McCabe, Robert A., 53
McCall, Karen, 42–43, 84
McGaa, Ed, 111
McGraw, Carol, 191
McKee, Thomas H., 136
McKerracher, 278–79
McLean, Ed, 252–53
McLuhan, T. C., 187
McMullen, James P., 16
McNab, Connie and children, 272–73
McReynolds, Edwin, 107
McTimmonds, J. V., 142
Mails, Thomas E., 102
Maine, 147, 150, 192, 215
Manitoba, 71, 156, 223
Mannix, Daniel, 141
Manville, Richard H., 71
margay *(Leopardus wiedi)*, 93

marten *(Martes americana)*, 97
Maryland, 149, 192, 215
Massachusetts, 215
Massey, Don, 280–81
Massey, Naveed, 274–75
Mattern, Charles E., 250–51
Maull, L. L., 127
Mecham, Hal, 142
Mellon, Timothy, 268–69
Mendoza, Sam, 262–63
Mesa Verde National Park, 171
Mexico: bighorn sheep, 77; cougar attack data, lack of, 177, 181; cougar range and population, 146, 224; fox, 90; and Indians, 106, 144; jaguar, 93; pronghorn antelope, 75; ringtail, 96
Michigan, 71, 91, 156, 215
Miedema, Mark David, 240–41
Mifflin, Thomas, 187
Miller, Cleve, 142
Mills, Enos A., 7, 49, 58–59, 79, 83, 85, 88
Milne, Lorus J. and Margery, 26
Minnesota, 72, 91, 156, 215–16
Minnesota Division of Wildlife, 215–16
Mississippi, 155, 216
Missouri, 155, 216
Monson, Gale, 78
Montana: cougar depredations, 190; cougar population and range, 146, 216; grizzly bear, 201; moose, 72; wolf, 91
Montana Department of Fish, Wildlife and Parks, 216
Moody, Charles, 246–47
Mooney, James, 102
Moore, Bobbie, 256–57
Moore, Nathaniel, 274–75
Moore, Ron D., 127
moose *(Alces palces)*, 71–72, 73, 215
Morgan, Thane, 173, 262–63
Mossman, Frank, 23
mountain goat *(Oreamnos americanus)*, 74, 75–77, 81, 134
mountain lion. *See* cougar
Mountain Lion Foundation, 205, 207
Mueller, Larry, 173
Mueller, Michael, 274–75
Murie, Adolph, 91
Murray, Roy, 58, 71

Naismith, Grace, 256–57
Nash, Ken, 256–57
National Elk Refuge, 183
National Museum (US), 92